THEY CAME
AND
THEY SAW

Western Christian Experiences
of the Holy Land

edited by

Michael Prior C.M.

D0988445

M E L I S E N D E
LONDON
2000

They came and they saw
First published 2000 by
Melisende
An imprint of Fox Communications and Publications
39 Chelmsford Road London E18 2PW England
tel. +44 (0)20 8 498 9768
fax +44 (0)20 8 504 2558
e-mail: melisende@cwcom.net

ISBN 1 901764 40 0

The publishers gratefully acknowledge permission from HarperCollinsPublishers to reproduce material from William Dalrymple's *From the Holy Mountain: A Journey in the Shadow of Byzantium* (London, 1998).

Cover: procession inside the Damascus Gate, Jerusalem (photo: Michael Prior).

Editor: Leonard Harrow
Assistant editor: Alan Ball

Printed and bound in England at the St Edmundsbury Press

CONTENTS

3

INTRODUCTION
Michael Prior, C.M.

A ll the chapters in this volume have been written for this publication. Each contributor has a knowledge of Israel-Palestine which was gained by frequent visits to or residence in the Holy Land. They are all Christians, from a variety of denominations: English, Irish and US Roman Catholics; English, US and Australian Anglicans/ Episcopalians; Scottish and US Presbyterians; a US United Methodist; and a Canadian Mennonite of Russian background. Some are ordained ministers, some are scholars by profession, and some are active in advocacy for justice and peace. While various factors drew them to Israel-Palestine, their perceptions have been strongly influenced by seeing things for themselves.

The contributions record how they considered the Israel-Palestine question before seeing it, describe the influences which brought their changes of attitude, and indicate what they have done about it since. The intended readership is the general reading public. The autobiographical style makes for attractive reading. Analysis is kept to a minimum. I invite those who, like myself, are generally distrustful of the elevation of personal experience into universal assertions, to consider Patrick Kavanagh's aphorism, 'the self serves only as an example.' Nevertheless, while the contributors' personal journeys or pilgrimages have something of the character of the universal they do involve particular experiences, the most significant of which they describe. The reader will draw her/his own conclusions, and register her/his own emotions.

*   *   *

Early pilgrims

In chronicling their experiences these modern pilgrims continue a long-standing tradition. From virtually the earliest days of Christianity, individual Christians visited the Holy Land to provide a physical anchorage for the Sacred Scriptures. Melito of Sardis, the earliest known Christian pilgrim, visited the Holy Land in *c.* 160 AD, so as to establish accurately the books of the Old Testament, and to examine the Holy Places. Similarly with Alexander, a future bishop of Jerusalem, in the reign of Caracalla. Origen, too, sought out the location of events recorded in the Scriptures. Firmilianus, a Cappadocian bishop, wished to trace the footsteps of Jesus.

Such interest intensified when Emperor Constantine ordered the restoration of the Church's property in the eastern part of the empire (324). A number of the accounts of these early pilgrims are preserved. That of the Bordeaux Pilgrim (333) lists the places to which he attaches an incident from the Bible; there is no mention of praying, or liturgies, or of any contact with the people. Egeria's pilgrimage (381-384) was punctuated by worship, with the central place given to the reading of the appropriate biblical text. St Jerome records the piety of two Roman noblewomen, Paula and her daughter, as they venerated the sacred sites in Jerusalem (*c.* 385). Veneration of the Holy Places is prominent also in Peter the Iberian's pilgrimage as recorded by John Rufus (*c.* 500), while the Pilgrim from Piacenza conveys better than any other writer of the period the variety of his experiences (*c.* 570).

A major concern was to visit the biblical sites, especially those associated with the ministry of Jesus in Jerusalem. According to Bishop Paulinus of Nola (403), 'No other sentiment draws people to Jerusalem than the desire to see and touch the places where Christ was physically present, and to be able to say from their own experience, "We have gone into his tabernacle, and have worshipped in the places where his feet stood." ' As if by way of some kind of osmosis, the pilgrim absorbed some of the holiness of the place.

19th-century explorers and pilgrims

Nevertheless, however important as a pilgrimage site, the Holy Land never attracted more than a handful of mainly affluent pilgrims from abroad. By the end of the 18th century, the real Palestine was virtually unknown, *terra incognita*. The perceptions of most Western Christians were influenced by the imagined world of the biblical text, with its shepherds, olive trees, donkeys, etc. But even this picture of the Holy Land was Westernised in the religious imagination, a process aided by European paintings and literary depictions of biblical scenes, with their European-like landscapes in no way reflecting Levantine realities.

In the early decades of the 19th century the general hostility in Palestine towards foreigners ensured that the practice of pilgrimage was virtually moribund, although that period was marked by a new appetite for purely antiquarian exploration among Europeans. Europe's search for the origins of its own civilisation was reflected in the establishment of permanent national societies for the exploration of Palestine: in Britain, the US, Germany, and France. In line with the spirit of the age, Western scholarship was in search of the origins of Europe's civilisation in the biblical lands. Inevitably that engagement influenced Europe's estimation of ancient Palestine. Rather than being a region with its own intrinsic wider value, it was esteemed primarily as the location of the biblical and associated events. Moreover, the Western scholars' investigation of the Holy Land from the perspective of its biblical origins coincided with the wider European territorial ambitions. There was, then, an integral relationship between scientific investigation and its imperial supporters.

With Muhammad 'Ali's rise to power in Syria-Palestine in the first part of the 19th century Christian activity in the region proceeded with greater freedom, and a wave of religious exploration followed. The importance of the land lay in its sacred sites whose locations were fixed by traditional pieties. The people and modern locations were little more than a distraction to visiting the Holy Places. This is reflected in the early photography of the region which projected a Palestine of stones and relics of religious antiquity. It resembled an empty shell, a deserted landscape, witnessing to some romanticised past, with no sense of a place where people lived, worked, or worshipped. Scientific scholarship, too, would play its own part in intensifying the disjuncture between its contemporary inhabitants and the land's witness to earlier civilisations. Concentration on the archaeological past was marked by a decided detachment from the contemporary lives of the people of the cities and villages. The lifeless mounds witnessing to earlier civilisations were much more significant than the throbbing Arab villages scattered throughout the country.

At a political level also, several of the European nations were flexing their colonial muscles around the globe. At a time when the Ottoman empire was showing signs of disintegration the Middle East was an attractive target for Western economic, cultural, and political penetration. The 'scramble for Palestine' invariably included the establishment of Christian institutions, thereby uniting Christian missionary endeavour with national influence. By the end of the 19th century England, Russia, Germany, France, Austria, etc. had consuls in Jerusalem, and their respective Churches had established a great number of foundations. An Anglican bishop was in place in Jerusalem since 1841, and the Latin patriarchate, which had fallen into desuetude since the Crusades, was revived in 1847. Some thirty Catholic religious orders had established convents, hospices, schools, orphanages, and hospitals throughout Palestine. It seemed that the West would dominate the region by a 'peaceful crusade' of Western Christian culture, bringing with it not only Bibles, but medical and educational innovations, and in some instances, ploughs and fertilisers. Such was the extent of Western influence that the Turks feared that it might be a prelude to attempting to recover Palestine as a Christian state. While many of the European religious institutions were established in the service of the indigenous population they mirrored to some extent the colonialist spirit of the age.

Interest in the investigation of ancient sites was fuelled also by the challenge to the authority of the Bible which discoveries in science and the higher criticism of the Bible offered. The assault could be withstood by providing scientific evidence of the accuracy of the biblical narrative, and no location could be more suitable for the task than the biblical land itself. The process gave birth to 'biblical geography' and an avalanche of books on the Holy Land. These reflected typical Western attitudes to the exotic East: suspicion of the traditional pilgrimage sites, and disdain for the 'superstitious practices' and 'medieval legends' of the East.

The numbers of Western pilgrims, Catholic, Orthodox and Protestant, increased substantially due to improved political circumstances, and not least to the advent of the steamship in the 1850s. Typically, Protestant pilgrims were in search of a mixture of the biblically familiar and the exotic East. While visits to the Holy Sites in Jerusalem and elsewhere were *de rigueur*, their preferences lay in the landscape sites of the Mount of Olives and the Garden of Gethsemane, and particularly of Galilee which was free of 'encrusted icons and flickering, oily, smelly lamps'. Protestant pilgrims were determined to avoid contamination by 'superstitious' practices, especially at the Holy Sepulchre, which, like the Second Temple, ought to be cleansed of its defilement. In general, Western pilgrims avoided contact with 'the natives', were disdainful of their customs and pious practices, and were unchanged by the encounter with the region. It was enough that the Holy Land had brought the Bible 'alive' in their imagination, and confirmed them in the assurance of the religious, social, and moral superiority of their Western Christianity. The land was the Fifth Gospel, or a Second Bible, confirming the first.

20th-century pilgrims

Visiting the Holy Land was facilitated further by air travel in the 20th century. The most significant factor influencing 'Western' visitors in the 20th century was the establishment of a state for Jews in 1948, as partial fulfilment of the goal of political Zionism which was born in Europe in 1897. The most distinctive feature of the Zionist enterprise was the transformation of the demography of Palestine. In the course of the century the Jewish population rose dramatically, from some 15,000 in 1800 to some four million today. Paradoxically, the Palestinian Arab population also has increased, from some 435,000 in 1800 to some 3 million today. This is the case in Israel/Palestine, despite the fact that 75 percent (some 750,000 people) of the Arab population of that part of Palestine which became the State of Israel was expelled in 1948, and some 418 Arab villages were destroyed to ensure they could not return. A further 300,000 Palestinian Arabs were expelled from the Occupied Territories in the wake of the Israeli conquest of June 1967. The human cost of that tragedy is marked by a widespread Palestinian diaspora, with the result that today an estimated 5.4 million Palestinians, out of a total world-wide Palestinian population of some 8.4 million live in camps within the Occupied Territories and in the surrounding Arab states.

Although it began as an altogether secular, and indeed frequently anti-religious, movement which was repudiated by virtually all religious Jews from the beginning, over the next hundred years political Zionism was metamorphosed. By the 1940s both Orthodox and Reform Jews had replaced their theological and moral opposition to the establishment of a Jewish state with a zeal to support it. Indeed by the end of the 20th century the link between Judaism and Eretz Yisrael was considered to be a constitutive element of the Jewish faith. Meanwhile, by the 1940s, the leadership of the Jewish community in Palestine had established itself as a government-in-waiting, and had, since the mid 1930s determined to expel the majority Arab population, putting in place 'Population Transfer Committees' to effect the integral requirement of Zionist ideology from the beginning to cleanse the land of Arabs. Encounter with Palestinians, whether expelled from their homes and villages, or living as second-, or third-class citizens within the State of Israel, or under Israeli occupation, has been a transforming experience for many Westerners.

In visiting the Holy Land the contributors to this volume brought with them some of the dispositions which marked their predecessors from the West. They wished to walk in the footsteps of Jesus, to confirm their biblical pieties, or to make the Bible come alive. They were much more interested in searching out their religious roots than in investigating the conditions of those who live in the land. Invariably they shared a sympathy for Jews, particularly in the wake of the *Shoah*, and were in admiration of their achievement in establishing a state. What has disturbed many of them is the discovery that the establishment of a homeland for Jews resulted in making another people homeless, and for those who searched deeper, that the displacement of the indigenous population was a Zionist aspiration from the beginning. The problem was exacerbated by learning that the Arab victims of expulsion included fellow-Christians, the 'living stones', who confidently and proudly traced their Christian identity to Pentecost.

Questions flooded to the surface. If the establishment of the State of Israel, and its behaviour since 1948, were in conformity with the prophetic hopes for Jewish restoration, where did this leave one's biblical faith? While one might be able to skip over the biblical narrative detailing Yahweh's demand in days of old that the original inhabitants of the Land of Canaan be exterminated, encountering contemporary victims of 'ethnic cleansing' could not so easily be pushed to the side. Compassion for the victims of 'ethnic cleansing', especially by those with a record of engagement in moral discourse and human rights activity, was to be expected. But one would have to go beyond a shallow sentimentality.

Inevitably the experience of encountering the Holy Land in our generation poses the most profound soul-searching on the part of religious and moral visitors. One's discoveries interrogate one's earlier perceptions and, in some cases, this profound questioning leads to a life-changing conversion. The contributions to this volume witness to their authors' personal journeys of encounter with the Holy Land. They do not simply have their prejudices refined. These modern Christian pilgrims are deeply moved by their encounters with the people of the land, and are particularly impressed by the vigour with which the 'living stones' witness to their faith in trying circumstances. Encountering such people in the place of their tragedy is, for many, a sacred experience. Religious dispositions, such as the admiration of virtue, moral outrage in the face of systemic sin, a determination to work for justice, and a sense of being in the company of the suffering Christ rise spontaneously to the surface of one's consciousness. One begins to appreciate that theophanies occur in the midst of the *quotidian trivialities* of the *Suq*, as they do also in the formal liturgies of the churches and shrines, and on the heights of numinous mountains. Such pilgrims encounter something altogether Other, and in the process are changed profoundly.

> Sometimes, the seeker
> becomes the sought.
>
> Thereafter, the burden's
> to bear the benediction—
> as the priest his symbols,
> the poet his vision,
> woman love, the mother
> her child and mortal man
> immortality.
>
> (from Desmond O'Grady's *Initiates*)

25 January 2000, Feast of the Conversion of St Paul

CONTRIBUTORS

Elizabeth (Betsy) Barlow grew up in Kalamazoo, Michigan. While she was educated at Carleton College, MN and St Anne's College Oxford she had little understanding of the Middle East prior to teaching in Lebanon. Subsequently, she received an MA in Middle Eastern Studies from the University of Michigan. Since 1982 she has served as Outreach Co-ordinator at the University of Michigan's Center for Middle Eastern and North African Studies, where she organises workshops and summer institutes for teachers, evaluates textbooks, designs supplementary material and offers study tours overseas and media briefings. She is an Episcopalian, and since 1996 has served as co-ordinator of Friends of *Sabeel*—North America, a support group for *Sabeel*, the Ecumenical Liberation Theology Centre in Jerusalem.

The Revd Dr Ray Barraclough is an Anglican priest and is Academic Dean of St Francis' Anglican Theological College in Brisbane, Australia. He also is a lecturer in New Testament in the Brisbane College of Theology, an ecumenical institution of which St Francis' College, Pius XII Provincial Seminary, and Trinity Uniting Church Theological College are constituent members. His doctorate entailed study of the New Testament writers' political ideas and their attitude to Roman rule. Ray and his wife Dorothy served at St George's College, Jerusalem, from 1989 to 1993. Ray was Senior Lecturer at St George's College. His writings from that time were published as *Reflections from the Holy Land—Place of Conflict, Place of Hope* (1992) and he has recently written *Equal and More—Equality and Authority amongst Christian Disciples with John's Gospel as the Resource Text* (1999).

Kathy Bergen is the National Co-ordinator of the Middle East Peace Education Program of the American Friends Service Committee (AFSC) based in Philadelphia, Pennsylvania. Prior to coming to AFSC, she worked in Geneva, Switzerland as the Executive Director of the International Coordinating Committee for NGOs on the Question of Palestine (ICCP). She lived and worked in Jerusalem from 1982-1991.

The Revd Dr David Burrell, CSC, is Theodore Hesburgh Professor in Philosophy and Theology at the University of Notre Dame, and has been working since 1982 in comparative issues in philosophical theology in Judaism, Christianity, and Islam, as evidenced in *Knowing the Unknowable God: Ibn-Sina, Maimonides, Aquinas* (1986), *Freedom and Creation in Three Traditions* (1993), and two translations of al-Ghazali: *Al-Ghazali on the Ninety-Nine Beautiful Names of God* (1993) and *Al-Ghazali on Faith in Divine Unity and Trust in Divine Providence* (2000). With Elena Malits he co-authored *Original Peace* (1998). He served as Luce Professor of Abrahamic Faiths at Hartford Seminary and University of Hartford in the fall of 1998, and will direct the University's Jerusalem programme, in the Tantur Ecumenical Institute each spring until 2004.

The Revd Dr Kenneth Cragg was Assistant Bishop in Jerusalem (1970-85), and since 1982 has been Honorary Assistant Bishop in the Diocese of Oxford. He was Warden of St Augustine's College, Canterbury (1961-67). A D.Phil. (Oxon.), he has an Honorary D.D. from the University of Leeds. He is an Honorary Fellow of Jesus College, Oxford, and a Bye-Fellow of Gonville and Caius College, Cambridge. He has written extensively on the Middle East, Islam and on the relations between Judaism, Christianity and Islam. His recent books include *The Arab Christian. A History of the Middle East* (1992) and *Palestine. The Prize and Price of Zion* (1997).

William Dalrymple is a writer and broadcaster, and the author of four award-winning travel books, *In Xanadu: A Quest* (1989), *City of Djinns: A Year in Delhi* (1992), and *The Age of Kali* (1998). His *From the Holy Mountain* (1998)—'The best and most unexpected book I have read since I forget when' (Peter Levi)—records his journey in the Levant in the footsteps of John Moschos, the sixth century monk-author of *The Spiritual Meadow*. It chronicles how the fourteen million Christians in the Middle East struggle to keep afloat amid 180 million non-Christians, with their numbers shrinking annually.

Janet Davies is the Co-ordinator for Friends of *Sabeel*, U.K. She was previously Area Co-ordinator for Christian Aid, Merseyside (1969-

86), has been Area Secretary for United Society for the Propagation of the Gospel North West (1986-92), and National Co-ordinator for the United Reformed Church's 'Commitment to Life' Programme (1992-95). She studied at the Centre for Black and White Christian Partnership, Selly Oak Colleges, and holds a Diploma in Theology from Birmingham University. She has travelled widely in the developing world, and has visited the Holy Land on ten occasions.

The Revd Garth Hewitt is Guild Vicar of All Hallows on the Wall in the City of London. He is Leader of the London and South East Team of Christian Aid, and Director of the Amos Trust. He is the author of *Nero's Watching Video* (1986), *Pilgrims and Peacemakers* (1996), and *A Candle of Hope* (1999). As singer and songwriter he has recorded over thirty albums, most recently 'Gospel Singer', which includes a song about the assassination of Yitzhak Rabin, 'In the Name of God', and another about the Open House reconciliation project in Ramle, 'Three Trees and an Open House'. He has written a musical for Christian Aid for the start of the millennium, 'The Feast of Life', and has produced a boxed set of albums, 'Journeys', comprising '1. The Holy Land', '2. Africa', '3. Asia' and '4. Latin America'. Other recent albums are 'Stronger than the Storm', 'Lonesome Troubadour' and 'Walk the Talk'.

Dr Ruth Victor Hummel teaches history at Holton-Arms School in Bethesda, Maryland. She was educated at Yale and Oxford universities. She has written a number of articles on the history of photography in the Ottoman Empire, the most recent of which will be published in the major work, *Ottoman Jerusalem* (2000). She co-authored *Patterns of the Sacred* (1995), and lectures frequently at conferences in Jerusalem. Currently she is working on a study of World War I in Palestine with George Hintlian.

The Revd Dr Thomas C Hummel is the Chair of the Department of Theology of Episcopal High School, and Adjunct Professor of Church History, both in Alexandria, Virginia. He is the co-author of *Patterns of the Sacred* (1995), and an editor of *Patterns of the Past Prospects for the Future: The Christian Heritage in the Holy Land* (1999). He has written and lectured extensively on the theology of pilgrimage, and is a Senior Fellow of the Christian Heritage Research Institute in Jerusalem.

Sr Elaine Kelley, SFCC, is a Development Officer at Bethlehem University and a regular contributor to the *Washington Report on Middle East Affairs* in Washington, DC. In Oregon she works in peace and justice projects through St Francis Catholic Church and the Inter-religious Committee for Peace in the Middle East, with an emphasis on Palestinian human rights.

The Revd Duncan Macpherson is a Principal Lecturer in Theology and Religious Studies at Saint Mary's College, Strawberry Hill (University of Surrey), England. He is Chair of *Friends of Bir Zeit University* and Director of *Living Stones*, an organisation that seeks to promote links between Christians in the Holy Land and Christians in Britain. He is a frequent visitor to the Holy Land. He has published books, and a range of articles on the Bible, Hinduism, Christian-Muslim Relations and Palestinian Rights. He is a Permanent Deacon in the Roman Catholic Church.

The Revd Peter J Miano is the Founder and Executive Director of The Society for Biblical Studies, a non profit organisation dedicated to contextual study of the Bible and Mission in the Holy Land. SBS. seeks to redeem pilgrimage from commercial sightseeing, reform biblical scholarship by introducing contextual study of the Bible to clergy and laity, by making biblical scholarship accessible to the broader Church, and activate participants in its programs in missions in the Holy Land. Educated at Harvard Divinity School (Th.M., New Testament Studies), Union Theological Seminary (M.Div., New Testament Studies) and Boston University (B.A.) he is currently a doctoral student in New Testament and Missiology at Boston University School of Theology. Professional experience includes ten years serving United Methodist churches in the Boston area, two years as Unite Methodist Liaison in Jerusalem and five years teaching Bible courses in the Holy Land.

Carol Morton has worked in the alternative trade movement for the last twenty years in Scotland and in Jerusalem where she was the director of a fair trade shop. Her degree in Religion from Mount Holyoke College was followed, after four children went to school, by an Edinburgh qualification and ten years' primary school teaching. She currently works as consultant in fair trade issues, and is secretary/treasurer of the Scottish Palestinian Forum.

The Revd Canon Colin Morton is now retired. He is an ordained minister of the Church of Scotland, having served in industrial parishes in Scotland, and from 1988-1997 as minister of St Andrew's Scots Memorial Church in Jerusalem. He was Field Secretary in Israel for the Church of Scotland from 1995, chairman of the board of the Jerusalem International YMCA for five years, and was made an honorary canon of St George's Episcopal Cathedral. He is now focal person of the Middle East Forum of Churches Together in Britain and Ireland.

The Revd Dr Michael Prior, CM, is a Principal Lecturer in the Department of Theology and Religious Studies in St Mary's College, Strawberry Hill (University of Surrey), England. He did postgraduate biblical studies in Dublin, Rome, Jerusalem and London, and was Visiting Professor in Bethlehem University, and Scholar-in-Residence in Tantur Ecumenical Institute, Jerusalem. He is Chairman of the *Catholic Biblical Association* of Great Britain, and of *Living Stones* (An Ecumenical Trust promoting contact between Christians in Britain and in the Holy Land). He has written widely on the Bible and on Middle East affairs, including *The Bible and Colonialism. A Moral Critique* (1997) and *Zionism and the State of Israel: A Moral Inquiry* (1999).

Dr Rosemary Radford Ruether is the Georgia Harkness Professor of Applied Theology at Garret Theological Seminary and North-western University in Evanston, Illinois, USA. She is author or editor of thirty-five books and numerous articles on feminist theology, peace and justice issues, particularly on the Middle East. She is author, with Herman J Ruether, of *The Wrath of Jonah: The Crisis of Religious Nationalism in the Israeli-Palestinian Conflict* (1989).

The Revd Dr Stephen R Sizer is the Anglican Vicar of Virginia Water, Surrey, England. He is an Associate Professor of International Management Centres and an Area Tutor for Westminster College, Oxford. He is active in several organisations in the UK (*Living Stones,* Friends of *Sabeel* UK, Amos Trust, and Highway Journeys). He has undertaken post-graduate research into the impact of Holy Land pilgrimages on the indigenous Church as well as into the ethical management of pilgrimages. He is currently doing further doctoral research into the history, theology and politics of Christian Zionism. He has written extensively on the ethics of pilgrimage, dispensationalism and Zionism, and the future of the Palestinian Church. His *Panorama of the Bible Lands,* a sequel to his *Panorama of the Holy Land* (1998) will be published in 2000.

The Revd Dr Donald E Wagner is an Associate Professor of Biblical and Theological Studies at North Park University in Chicago where he also serves as Director of the Center for Middle Eastern Studies. He is co-founder and National Director of Evangelicals for Middle East Understanding. He previously served Presbyterian churches in New Jersey and Evanston, Illinois, where he resides. Previous books include *All in the Name of the Bible* (editor, 1986), *Peace or Armageddon* (with Dan O'Neill, 1993); and *Anxious for Armageddon* (1995). His forthcoming *Dying in the Land of Promise* will be published by Melisende in early June 2000. He serves on the Friends of *Sabeel* North America board as well as boards for Holy Land Trust, Pilgrims of Ibillin, Holy Land Christian Ecumenical Foundation, and Youth Advocates.

SEEKING THE SPIRITUAL MEADOW
IN THE WILDERNESS
William Dalrymple

I left Scotland in the summer of 1994 on a journey through the Levant, which took me from Mount Athos, through Istanbul, Antioch, the Tur Abdin, Aleppo, Beirut, the West Bank, Jerusalem, Alexandria and the Egyptian desert. I completed my journey a few days before Christmas in the Kharga Oasis, once the southernmost point of the Byzantine empire.

My itinerary was inspired by *The Spiritual Meadow* written by the 6th-century monk, John Moschos. John and his companion Sophronius had gone before me, and left behind a guide to the monasteries and holy men of the eastern Roman Empire as they were in his day. I was determined to see wherever possible what Moschos and Sophronius had seen, to sleep in the same monasteries, to pray under the same frescoes and mosaics, to discover what was left, and to witness what was in effect the last ebbing twilight of Byzantium. Like Moschos, I made a record of my journey, and over the next couple of years worked it into book form, *From the Holy Mountain: A Journey in the Shadow of Byzantium* (London, HarperCollinsPublishers, 1998).

I am pleased to offer these extracts, kindly edited by Michael Prior—based on my original material which is substantially that published in the book—as a contribution to the current volume of personal reflections by Western Christians on their encounters in the Holy Land.

The Monastery of Mar Saba, Israeli Occupied West Bank (24 October 1994)

Again I inhabit a bare cell with white walls and a blue dado. Again, through the window, I hear the quiet rumour of hushed monkish talk, the occasional peal of bells, the purposeful rustle of habits. It could be Athos, but one glance at the bare rock wall of the cliff-face opposite my cell places this monastery firmly in the wilderness of Judaea, far from the cooling waters of the Aegean.

This is the desert where John Moschos took his vows and where he spent most of his monastic life; tales of the monks of these bare hills fill the pages of *The Spiritual Meadow.* Having read so much about these Judaean desert fathers it is strange finally to see the austere landscape that forms the background to their exploits. It is stranger still to find many of their superstitions, fears and prejudices alive in the conversation of the monks who still inhabit this, the last of the ancient monasteries of the Holy Land to survive as a functioning community. But the stories of devils and demons, visions and miracles which sometimes seemed ludicrously outlandish when I first read them under a grey London sky, sounded quite plausible last night, when told in the starlight looking out onto a cliff-face honeycombed with the cells of long-dead hermits and Holy Men.

I had arrived at the Great Lavra of Mar Saba earlier that afternoon. From Beirut the distance is less than three hundred miles, but this being the Middle East it took a six hundred mile detour via Damascus and Amman—three and half days non-stop travel—to get here. I finally crossed the Jordan into Palestine at noon yesterday afternoon.

The West Bank, and with it East Jerusalem, were seized by Israel from the Jordanians in the 1967 Six Day War. East Jerusalem was annexed, while the West Bank was put under Israeli military occupation. In defiance of International Law both areas have since been subject to a campaign of colonisation: around 150 exclusively Jewish settlements have been established in the conquered territory, between them containing some 280,000 Israeli settlers. The military authorities have also appropriated 80 percent of the West Bank's water, most of which is now piped south to Israel. Despite the stumbling peace process and the handing over of some fragments of land to Yasser Arafat's Palestinian Authority, the area, like Beirut or Rwanda, still seems inexorably linked to violence, refugee camps and army patrols. On the journey from the small Jericho oasis to Jerusalem, the modern West Bank is, at first sight, still much closer to David Roberts' prints of early 19th-century Palestine than to the harrowing television images of refugees and razor wire.

Yet beautiful as it is, the signs of conflict are still there. In some valley bottoms where there should be cornfields, there are UN camps, home to those Palestinians expelled from their ancestral homes at the birth of Israel in 1948: huge, shockingly dirty shanty towns surrounded by army watchtowers and floodlights. Above them squat newly-built Israeli settlements: modern suburban towns made up of ranks of detached and whitewashed houses, with long lines of solar panels glinting on their roofs. Two different peoples, separated by thick tangles of razor wire and a small matter of legal status: the settlers have guns, enjoy Israeli civil justice and can join the army; the Palestinians under Israeli occupation are forbidden to own weapons of any sort, and are subject to the arbitrary and dismissive verdicts of military courts. Torture—known in the statute books under the euphemism 'moderate physical pressure'—is more or less routine ...

The largest and most ugly of the settlements is Ma'ale Adumim, a vast ring of concrete blockhouses, cranes and half-completed apartment blocks, recently built over the site once occupied by the great Byzantine monastery of St Martyrius. Just beyond the settlement the road splits. The main branch heads on to Jerusalem. The smaller branch—potholed and neglected—winds off to the south. We bumped along this track for five kilometres before arriving at a ledge overlooking the cliffs of the Valley of Kedron, a deep, arid canyon of wind-eroded chalk-like rock. At the top of the far side of this ravine stands a domed Greek Orthodox church, enclosed by a towering wall. Before I did anything else in Palestine—and certainly before I headed on to Mar Saba for the night—I knew I had first to make a pilgrimage to this shrine.

The driver parked in front of the gatehouse and I pulled at the rope; inside the enclosure, a bell rang. There was no answer. I rang the bell a second time and soon afterwards the wimpled head of a nun peered suspiciously down over the parapet and asked in Greek what I wanted. I explained what I had come for. After a few minutes there was a rattling of bolts and the great black gate swung open.

At the far side of the courtyard stood a gleaming new basilica with an octagonal dome, a bell tower and a red-tiled roof; around its edge ran the arcade of a cloister. The nun led me to a small cupola in the centre of the courtyard, and taking a huge bunch of keys from her pocket unlocked a door. Then she lifted a storm lantern from a niche and, lighting it, led me down a flight of ancient stairs. From the dark below seeped a dank smell of musty air tinct with the sweet scent of burning oil-lamps.

As we sank deeper underground, masonry gave way to the living rock of a cave wall, and we entered a wide, echoing underground cavern. A pair of recesses at the far side of the cave were illuminated by the dim, flickering light of a cluster of lamps placed in front of two gilt icons each depicting a heavily-bearded Byzantine saint. Another group of lamps flickered at the bottom of the stairs, under an ancient icon of the Magi. To one side of it stood a huge pile of skulls.

'This was the cave where the Three Wise Men hid from King Herod,' whispered the nun, holding the storm lantern aloft. 'St Theodosius saw the cave in a vision and founded his monastery in this place to honour the Magi.'

'And the skulls?'

'They belong to the monks that were slaughtered by the Persians when they burned the abbey.'

'When?'

'Not so long ago,' she said. 'Around 614 A.D.'

The nun held the storm lantern above the charnel so that the light picked out the sword-gashes cleaving the crania of the topmost skulls. 'What you have come to see lies over there,' she said, pointing at the lamp-lit recesses in the far side of the cave.

I walked over towards the lamps. As I drew nearer I could see that the lamps rested on a pair of Byzantine grave slabs. On both the tomb-slabs had been carved in shallow relief an intricate design of equal-armed Byzantine crosses, some set in diamonds, others in circles. Between the crosses were carved inscriptions in clear Byzantine Greek. That on the left read Sophronius; that on the right bore the name of John Moschos.

'St John Moschos died in Constantinople,' said the nun, 'but his dying wish was that he should be brought back here to the Lavra of St Theodosius. He regarded this as his home: this was where he was first tonsured, and where he spent most of his life. But the Holy Land was still occupied by the Persians and it was not until much later that St Sophronius was able to fulfil his promise to bring back John Moschos's body and to rebuild the monastery.'

'And the monks?'

'Before the slaughter there were seven hundred elders here,' said the nun. 'It was the most celebrated monastery in the Holy Land. There was a hospital for lepers and a rest house for pilgrims; also an inner monastery for those driven insane by the rigours of their asceticism. There were four separate churches. Monks came here from as far away as Cappadocia and Armenia ... But after the Persians the monastery never recovered. It has never had as many monks ever again.'

'And now?' I asked. 'How many of you are there today?

'What do you mean?' said the nun. 'There is only me. I am the last. A priest is supposed to come from Jerusalem once a week to celebrate the liturgy, but he is old and sometimes he forgets.'

The nun bent forward and kissed the icon of Moschos: 'I will leave you,' she said. 'If you have come all the way to see the grave of St John Moschos you will want to be alone with him. Bring the lantern with you when you have finished.'

Holding the lamp aloft, I looked around the crypt and paused for a second before the macabre pile of skulls. I had read so much about the monks of St Theodosius in the pages of *The Spiritual Meadow* that I felt I must know some of the men who had been slaughtered by the Persians, men whose anonymous bleached bones now lay piled in front of me. They were characters like Brother George the Cappadocian 'who was pasturing swine in Phasaelis when two lions came to seize a pig'; rather than running off 'he seized a staff and chased them as far as holy Jordan'. Then there was Moschos's friend Patrick, 'the native of Sebastea in Armenia, who was of very great age, claiming to be one hundred and thirteen'. He had once been an abbot but 'being very humble and much given to silence' had given up his position 'saying that it was only for great men to shepherd the spiritual sheep'. What had been the fate, I wondered, of another of Moschos's companions, Brother Christopher the Roman? Every night he deprived himself of sleep, performing a hundred prostrations on each of the steps that led down into the cave-crypt, never stopping until the bell rang for matins.

I left the skulls and stood before the grave of John Moschos, the man whose writings had brought me on this journey, and in whose footsteps I was travelling. On top of the slab rested a modern icon of the man, shown old and grey with a scroll in one hand and a quill in the other. So, I thought, this was where he started off and where, after all his travels through the width and breadth of the Byzantine Levant, he ended up.

Prompted by the example of the nun, and despite having half

dropped the habit, I began to pray there, and the prayers came with surprising ease. I prayed for the people who had helped me on the journey, the monks who had shown me the manuscript on Mount Athos, the frightened Syriacs of Mar Gabriel, the Armenians of Aleppo and the Palestinian Christians in the refugee camp at Mar Elias in Beirut. And then I did what I suppose I had come to do: to seek the blessing of John Moschos for the rest of the trip, and particularly to ask for his protection in the badlands of Upper Egypt, what undoubtedly would be the most dangerous part of this journey. Then I rose, climbed the stairs, and emerged blinking into the bright light of the Judaean midday.

*   *   *

The Monastery of Mar Saba lies ten miles from that of St Theodosius, a little to the North of the Dead Sea. Around St Theodosius, the soil is still grudgingly fertile and the olive trees stand out against the terraces cut into the hard white hillsides. But as you drive the cultivation recedes. Passing the last village, we entered the desert; the *locus horrendae et vastae solitudinis* of the Bible. Below us the barren shale hills fell away towards the lowest point on earth, the Dead Sea, a quivering drop of mercury in the far distance. Straight ahead, a pair of small rectangular Byzantine watchtowers rose vertically against the lip of a deep wadi. In the forty miles of landscape visible from the hilltop, those two towers were the only buildings in sight.

It was only when you passed underneath the machicolation of the nearest tower that you caught your first glimpse of the great monastery that lay hidden in the lee of the sheer cliff-face below. Despite its massive rocky solidity, the monastery's implausible position on a cliff face in the midst of the wilderness somehow gave the whole place a fantastic, almost visionary appearance, like one of those castles in children's fairy tales capable of vanishing in the blink of an eye.

At the time of John Moschos, the wastes of Judaea had become so densely filled with monks and monasteries that, according to one chronicler, 'the desert had become a city'. Yet of the one hundred and fifty monasteries founded during the Byzantine rule, only six are still lived in, and of those only one, Mar Saba, still supports enough monks to really qualify as a living monastery. It has been occupied continuously since its foundation in the late 5th century: apart from a two-week hiatus following the massacre of the monks by the Persians in A.D. 614—the same raid that devastated St Theodosius—divine office has been sung in the rock chapel of St Sabas every morning for the last 1,380 years. As in St Theodosius, the skulls of the hundreds of monks killed by the Persians, along with those subsequently murdered by marauding Bedouin, have been carefully kept in the abbey church, stacked in neat rows as nonchalantly as other churches might stack their hymn books.

Mar Saba, I quickly discovered, remains the most austere of monasteries. If it is now remarkable mainly for the terrible severity of its asceticism, it was once famous for its scholarship, and despite the monastery's extreme isolation it was nevertheless one of the intellectual and philosophical powerhouses of Byzantium. When the Anglo-Saxon pilgrim St Willibald visited the monastery in the early 8th century he remarked on the fact that all the monks were busy copying out manuscripts and composing hymns and poems. The monastery's library, now kept in the Greek Orthodox Patriarchal Palace in Jerusalem, is almost unrivalled amongst mediaeval collections in the esoteric breadth of its interests and the number of languages represented; it is also evidence of the extraordinary quality of the copying and calligraphy produced in the Mar Saba scriptorium.

Here Cyril of Scythopolis wrote his *History of the Monks of Palestine*, an unusually critical and intelligent work of hagiography. Mar Saba's hymnography, the work among others of Romanos the Melodist, was, according to the great Byzantine scholar Brehier, 'the most original manifestation of the poetic genius of the mediaeval Greeks'. Moreover it was in a cell in Mar Saba that St John Damascene wrote his great *Fount of Knowledge,* undoubtedly the most sophisticated and encyclopaedic work of theology produced anywhere in Christendom until the time of Thomas Aquinas; indeed, Aquinas drew heavily on John's theology and wrote that he read a few pages of John Damascene's work every day of his adult life.

I spent the afternoon of my arrival in my cell reading John Moschos's stories of the monks of the Judaean desert. Together, the stories in *The Spiritual Meadow* form a detailed picture of one of the strangest periods in the region's history. For around two hundred years, the deserts of the Holy Land were filled not only with 150 fully functioning monasteries, but also with countless cave-dwelling hermits and great herds of 'grazers', nomadic monks who, according to Moschos 'wander in the desert as if they were wild animals: like birds they fly about the hills; they forage like goats. Their daily round is inflexible, always predictable, for they feed on roots, the natural products of the earth.'

Today it seems inexplicable that so many people— many of them highly educated—from across the width of the civilised Byzantine world would give up everything and travel for thousands of miles to live a life of extreme hardship in the discomfort of the desert; yet to the Byzantine mind nothing could have been more logical. While Moschos never underestimates the hardship involved in living the life of the desert fathers, he is also well aware of its joys. Indeed one of the principal themes of his writing is that by living their life in utter simplicity and holiness, the monks were returning to the conditions of the Garden of Eden, in harmony both with the natural world and its Creator.

Mar Saba (28 October)

Over the days that followed I explored many of the caves, cells and chapels which honeycomb the cliffs within the great boundary walls of Mar Saba. If you look hard enough, many fragments of the Byzantine monastery known to John Moschos still survive. The great cave chapel 'Built by God' stands as bare and austere as it would have done in the early Byzantine period. But the most interesting chapel of all is that built around the tomb and hermitage of St John Damascene.

John Damascene is certainly the most important figure ever to have taken the habit at Mar Saba. He was the grandson of the last Byzantine governor of Damascus, a Syrian Arab Christian named Mansur ibn Sargun. Ibn Sargun was responsible for surrendering the city to the Muslim general Khalid ibn Walid in 635, just three years after the death of Muhammad. Despite the change from Christian to Islamic rule, the family remained powerful. John's father, Sergios ibn Mansur, rose to become a senior figure in the financial administration of the early Umayyad caliphate, whose accounts, significantly enough, continued for many decades to be kept in Greek. Because of this John grew up as a close companion of the future Caliph al-Yazid; the two youths' drinking bouts in the streets of Damascus were the subject of much horrified gossip in the new Islamic capital. In due course John assumed his father's post in the administration and remained throughout his life a favourite of the caliph. This relationship made him one of the very first Arab Christians capable of acting as a bridge between Christianity and Islam, even if, like so many who attempt to bring together two diverging cultures, he eventually ended up being regarded with suspicion by both: dismissed from his administrative job after Caliph Yazid's death and falsely accused of collusion with the Byzantine emperor, he was nevertheless regarded with great mistrust in the Byzantine capital, where he was dubbed *Sarakenophron* or 'Saracen-Minded'.

John was in an excellent position to write the first ever informed treatise on Islam by a Christian, and when he retired to Mar Saba he dedicated his declining years to writing doctrinal homilies and working on his great masterpiece, a refutation of heresies entitled the *Fount of Knowledge*. The book contains an extremely precise and detailed critique of Islam, which, intriguingly, John regards as a form of Christian heresy related to Arianism. It never seems to have occurred to him that Islam might be a separate religion. Although he looked on Islam with considerable suspicion, he nevertheless applauds the way Islam converted the Arabs from idolatry and writes with admiration of its single-minded emphasis on the unity of God.

If a theologian of the stature of John Damascene was able to regard Islam as a new—if heretical—form of Christianity, it helps to explain how Islam was able to convert so much of the Middle Eastern population in so short a time, even if Christianity remained the majority religion in the region until the time of the Crusades. Islam was as much a product of the intellectual ferment of Late Antiquity as Gnosticism, Arianism and Monophysitism, and like those heresies it had greatest success in areas disgruntled with Byzantine rule. Many Syrians expressed opposition to Byzantium and its ruthless attempt to impose its rigid imperial theology by converting *en masse* to the heterodox Christian doctrine of Monophysitism; later they greeted the conquering Arab armies as liberators and many converted again, this time to Islam. No doubt they regarded the Arabs' new creed as a small step from Monophysitism; after all the two faiths started from a similar position: that God could not become fully human without somehow compromising his divinity.

Whatever the reason for its success, Islam certainly appealed to the former Monophysites and within a century of the Arab conquest Syria was a mainly Muslim country. By contrast, the inhabitants of Palestine, who had done well out of Byzantine patronage of the Holy Places, never showed much interest in converting either to Monophysitism or to Islam, and Jerusalem remained a predominantly Orthodox Christian city until the time of the Crusades.

In his own lifetime, however, the most influential part of Damascene's *Fount of Knowledge* was not the section on Islam; instead it was John's attack on the heresy of iconoclasm. For at the same time as John was becoming a monk, Byzantium was being engulfed by a wave of image-smashing. All the icons in the Empire were ordered to be smashed and their painting was henceforth banned. The reason for this may well have been the rise of Islam and the profound soul-searching which the loss of the Levant provoked in Byzantium. Many came to the conclusion that God was angry with the Byzantines for their idolatry, and for this reason gave the Muslims success in their wars.

Just as John's public life demonstrates the astonishing political tolerance of the Umayyad caliphate in its willingness to employ a Christian in a senior administrative role, despite almost continuous hostilities with the rest of the Christian world, so his retirement demonstrates the surprising degree of intellectual freedom it permitted. For under the Umayyads John was able to do what no Byzantine was permitted to attempt: to write and distribute a systematic defence of images, in which he provided the fundamental theological counterblast to iconoclasm. John argued that although no man has seen God at any time, nevertheless, since Christ deigned to take upon himself the human form, it was necessary to worship the human face of God in the sacred icon.

Earlier this afternoon, after I had woken from a siesta, the monastery guestmaster, Fr Theophanes, took me to John Damascene's old cell: a tiny cave, its ceiling cut so low as to make standing virtually impossible.

'Imagine,' said Theophanes. 'St John spent thirty years in this place.'

Left alone in the cell by the guestmaster, I pondered the probability that if John Moschos came back today, it is likely he would find as much familiarity in the practices of Islam—with its fasting, prostrations and open prayer halls, as well as in its emphasis on the wandering holy man—as in those of modern Western Christendom. In an age when Islam and Christianity are again said to be 'clashing civilisations', supposedly irreconcilable and necessarily hostile, it is important to remember, on the one hand, Islam's very considerable debt to the early Christian world, and on the other, the degree to which it has faithfully preserved some elements of our own early Christian heritage long forgotten by ourselves.

Old City of Jerusalem (4 November)

In the days that followed as I walked around the Christian Quarter talking to the Palestinian Christians, I found that the inhabitants of the Old City were overwhelmingly gloomy about the long term prospects of a Christian presence surviving in Jerusalem—at least as long as it remained under Israeli rule. Rightly or wrongly, the Palestinians all seemed to believe that there was a concerted campaign to drive them out, or at any rate to make their life so difficult that the majority would opt to leave of their own volition. In 1922, 52 percent of the population of the Old City of Jerusalem had been Christian; now Christians made up just under 2.5 percent of the population of the municipality. There were now more Jerusalem-born Christians in Sydney than in Jerusalem; those that remained could be flown out in just nine jumbo jets. The Old City of Jerusalem ceased to be dominated by Christians in the 1940s; now everyone agreed that it would probably soon have no permanent Christian presence at all.

All this is part of the most dramatic decline in a Christian population to have taken place anywhere in the modern Middle East, with the single exception of Turkish Anatolia. There the progressive campaign of massacres and deportations, culminating in the 1915 Armenian genocide and the 1922 Greco-Turkish transfer of population, left only a few thousand Christians where at the turn of the century there had been well over four million. In Palestine the decline of the Christian population over the course of this century has been more gradual, but no less overwhelming.

In 1922, twenty-six years before the creation of the State of Israel, Christians made up around 10 percent of the population of British Mandate Palestine. The Christians were wealthier and better educated than their Muslim counterparts, owned almost all the newspapers and filled a disproportionate number of senior jobs in the Mandate Civil Service. While numerically they dominated the Old City of Jerusalem—as indeed they had done almost continuously since the 4th century A.D.—their leaders and merchants had already moved out from the narrow streets around the Holy Sepulchre and the Via Dolorosa, to build fine villas for themselves in the West Jerusalem suburbs of Talbieh, Kattamon and Bak'a—now home to the better-off Israeli businessmen and Knesset MPs.

The exodus of the former inhabitants of these houses began

in 1948, during the war which followed the withdrawal of British troops from Mandate Palestine. In the fighting, some 55,000 Palestinian Christians—around 60 percent of the total community—were driven from their homes, along with around 650,000 Muslim Palestinians. After the Israeli conquest and occupation of the West Bank during the Six Day War, a second exodus took place: between 1967 and 1992 around 40 percent of the Christians then in the Occupied Territories—a further 19,000 men, women and children—left their homes to look for better lives elsewhere.

The great majority of Palestinian Christians now live abroad, in exile: only 170,000 are left inside Israel and the West Bank, compared with the 400,000 living outside the Holy Land, either in squalid refugee camps in Lebanon or elsewhere. The Christians now make up less than a quarter of 1 percent of the population of Israel and the West Bank. Moreover their emigration rate remains very high, double that of the Muslim Palestinians, not because the Christians suffer any worse indignities than the Muslims, but because being better educated they find it far easier to emigrate and get jobs abroad. So far, the stumbling peace process has done little to stop this flood of emigrants. A recent survey by Bethlehem University showed that around a fifth of those Palestinian Christians still remaining in their ancestral homeland hope to emigrate in the near future.

All this matters very much. Without the local Christian population, the most important shrines in the Christian world will be left as museum pieces, preserved only for the curiosity of tourists. Christianity will no longer exist in the Holy Land as a living faith; a vast vacuum will exist in the very heart of Christendom. As the Archbishop of Canterbury recently warned, the area, 'once centre of a strong Christian presence', risks becoming 'a theme park' devoid of Christians 'within fifteen years'.

The future looks particularly bleak for Christian Jerusalem as Jewish settler organisations focus their energies on the Holy City. Rings of new settlements are springing up all around East Jerusalem, while within the Old City radical settler groups continue to try to buy up land within the Muslim, Christian and Armenian Quarters of the

Old City. Within ten years of the Israeli conquest of East Jerusalem, 37,065 acres of Arab land had been confiscated and settled; today only 13.5 percent of East Jerusalem remains in Palestinian hands. Less assertive but equally insistent is the Muslim claim to the place they call Al-Quds (the Holy City), as the Jordanians and the Palestinian Authority compete for the right to protect the Muslim Holy Places. Amid these two competing claims, the Christians' stake in Jerusalem seems almost irrelevant.

The various Churches in Jerusalem are more than aware of the seriousness of their situation. Traditionally, the forty-seven different Christian denominations represented in the Holy City were famous for their pointless and petty squabbling: year after year newspapers across the globe would celebrate Easter with some light Paschal story about the Greek Orthodox feuding with the Roman Catholics over the cleaning of such-and-such a windowsill in the Holy Sepulchre. But since 1989 the patriarchs and archbishops of the major Churches have come together—possibly for the first time since the First Crusade in 1095—to issue an annual joint statement 'to make known to the people of the world the conditions of life of our people here in the Holy Land who experience constant deprivation of their fundamental rights ... [and to] express our deep concern and alarm for the growing feeling of insecurity and fear among our people and churches ... [which constitutes] a serious threat to the future of Christianity and its rights in the Holy Land.'

*   *   *

The archaeologist I most wanted to meet to discuss all this with was Fr Michele Piccirillo of the Studium Biblicum Franciscanum. Piccirillo is an Italian who has lived in Jerusalem since 1960 and who since then has single-handedly rediscovered much of the monastic world described in *The Spiritual Meadow*. In a series of remarkable excavations, the Franciscan uncovered many previously unknown Byzantine monasteries, chapels, churches and villas dating mainly from the 6th to the 8th century, and in the process brought to light a breath-taking treasury of late antique floor mosaics, including some of the finest mosaic work ever discovered in the Levant. I had seen some of them as I passed through Jordan on my way to Palestine, for the finest set of all lie around Madaba and Mount Nebo, immediately above the Allenby Bridge, the frontier post leading into the Occupied West Bank.

The importance of these new discoveries goes beyond mere aesthetics and art history. Perhaps the most unexpected aspect of it is the astonishing degree of continuity that has been revealed. According to Piccirillo, the Arab conquest of the 7th century is archaeologically invisible: the rulers changed, but life went on exactly as before. Indeed much of the finest 'Byzantine' work he has dug up dates from the period immediately *after* the Arab conquest when order was better kept, trade was flourishing and the area was released from the crippling taxes imposed by the Byzantine exchequer: 'The archaeologist who searches for a break between the pre- and post-Muslim conquest searches in vain,' wrote Piccirillo in the book which summed up his life's work. 'Archaeology demonstrates an uninterrupted continuity between the two periods.'

After the conquest, the local population soon adopted the Arabic tongue and over the centuries many converted to Islam, but the conquerors' armies were not large and initially provided little more than a military caste superimposed on the existing population. There was no wholesale exchange of population. The Palestinians we see today—and especially the Palestinian Christians—are therefore likely to be the descendants of the same mix of peoples Moschos saw on his travels through this region in the 7th century: an ethnically-diverse blend of the many races that have passed through this area since the earliest periods of prehistory.

Piccirillo's evidence is very important, for official Israeli histories still paint a picture of pillaging nomad conquerors, sweeping in from the desert, massacring or wiping out the indigenous population and leaving the area a depopulated desert—until the birth of the Zionist movement in the 19th century. Despite the fact that no serious historian, in Israel or elsewhere, would even begin to try to defend such a crude distortion of Palestine's mediaeval history, this version still possesses a curious half-life in government propaganda. *Facts About Israel*, for example, is an information book produced by the Israeli Ministry of Foreign Affairs which is prefaced by a fifteen-page account of 'the history of the Land of Israel'. Here, following an extremely detailed account of the biblical Israelite kingdoms, fourteen hundred years of the region's Islamic history is written off in just one paragraph, a small section entitled 'Arabs in the Land of Israel': 'Arab migration in and out of the country started at the time of the Arab conquest of the Land in the 7th century, fluctuating thereafter with economic growth and decline. Towards the end of the 19th century, when increased Jewish development stimulated economic and social revival in the Land, many Arabs from surrounding countries were attracted to the area by its employment opportunities, higher wages and better living conditions.'

I rang Piccirillo and arranged to come around for tea that afternoon. We sat in his small cell in the Studium Biblicum Franciscanum and talked for a long time about his work, in the course of which he confirmed everything he had written. He concluded:

> All the sites I have excavated call into serious question the old view that the Arab invasions resulted in the destruction of Christian buildings, that the Arabs persecuted the Christians and prohibited the building of new churches. The sheer number of Christian mosaics dating from the Umayyad period constitutes *very* strong evidence not only for the continuity of the Christian presence but also for the tolerance of the new Islamic rulers.

It was only at the very end of our conversation that I asked him about the accusations I heard of anti-Christian and anti-Islamic bias in the Israeli archaeological establishment. He was quite clear in his response. Whatever the situation in the early years of the state, he said, current Israeli archaeological methods were thoroughly professional: in his opinion the historical sites of Israel were excavated impartially without regard to religion. But he was equally adamant about the serious disparity in the presentation of those finds, he said:

> The conservation of Christian remains is systematically less good than the treatment accorded to Jewish remains. Of course conservation is a problem everywhere. But here where it so easily becomes a political issue the Israelis should be doubly careful. The fact is that the Holy Land has many communities. Each has its rights and if a state wants respect it should respect others.

'How does this neglect show itself?' I asked.
Piccirillo replied:

> Synagogues they look after beautifully. They cover them with shelters and stop people standing on the mosaics. But newly excavated churches or monasteries they can quite easily bulldoze as they did with those discovered in 1992 outside the Damascus Gate. They would never dream of doing that to a synagogue, and the religious establishment would never let them. But with Christian buildings, if they don't bulldoze them, they leave them just as they find them. In Jordan every single mosaic I have excavated is now under specially built shelters, even specially built museums. But there are churches with good mosaics open to the air all over Israel.

'Does that matter?' I asked.

'It matters very much. If these Christian sites are not guarded they can get attacked.'

This was certainly true. I had recently seen a report of one such attack in the *Jerusalem Post* of the 23 October 1994 which noted an assault on an unguarded Byzantine church at Mamshit near the Israeli nuclear facilities at Dimona. 'The vandals, suspected *haredim*, pulled apart colourful mosaics and shattered columns that held up the church's ceiling,' read the report, which said the incident was one of a series over the previous fortnight which included the vandalizing of another Byzantine church at Sussita on the Golan Heights. The *haredim* who were apparently responsible were said to be against archaeological excavations in general, and so were not setting out specifically to target Christian sites; nevertheless Christian sites did seem to figure especially prominently on their hit lists.

'But you see,' continued Piccirillo. 'It's not just a matter of protecting from vandals. A mosaic ...'

The friar broke off and searched for words: 'A mosaic which is not looked after is like a rosary whose string is cut. Once one or two tesserae have gone the whole mosaic falls apart. In a short time everything—*everything*—is lost.'

The Anglican Hostel, Nazareth
(20 November)

Around 570 A.D., after he was first professed as a monk at the Abbey of St Theodosius, John Moschos withdrew into the wilderness and spent ten years in the remote cave monastery at Pharan, to the north of Jerusalem.

Pharan, the modern Ein Fara, is reputedly the oldest abbey in Palestine. It was founded in the early 4th century by the great Byzantine hermit, St Chariton, who, it is said, settled in a cave above a pool of pure spring water. There he gathered a community of like-minded ascetics around him, living a life of silence, self-abnegation and severe fasting, interspersed with long hours of prayer. But Moschos appears to have been drawn to the site less by its antiquity than by the wisdom of its then *hegumen*, Abba Cosmas the Eunuch. In a crucial passage in *The Spiritual Meadow*, Moschos credits Cosmas with first giving him the idea to collect the sayings of the fathers: 'whilst he [Abba Cosmas] was speaking to me about the salvation of the soul, we came across an aphorism of St Athanasius, Archbishop of Alexandria. And the elder said to me 'when you come across such a saying, if you have no paper with you, write it on your clothing'—so great was the appetite of Abba Cosmas for the words of our holy fathers and teachers.' It was advice that was eventually to lead Moschos to compiling *The Spiritual Meadow*, and so preserve the otherwise largely unrecorded history of the monks of Byzantine Palestine.

I found a Christian Palestinian driver, Sami Fanous, who agreed to take me to see the cave at Ein Fara. I very much wanted to see the ruins of the *lavra* where fourteen hundred years earlier, John Moschos had retired to spend a decade of his life in silent meditation. Other than the bare hermits' caves, only a little survived of the monastery that Moschos had known. There were some crumbling cell walls, a cistern, a few stretches of Byzantine stonework, the odd staircase and a little sagging terracing where the monks had once, presumably, grown vegetables. A Byzantine mosaic was said to survive in the cave church at the top of the honeycomb of interconnected caverns, but it was impossible now to reach it without a rope or step ladder. After an hour poking around, clambering into some of the more accessible cave-cells, I set off up the hill again.

When he lived here during the last days of Byzantine Moschos must have known that his whole world was crumbling. But I wondered whether even he realised the extent to which he was witnessing the last days of the Golden Age of the Christian Middle East.

Soon after his departure on his travels, Jerusalem was to fall to the Persians. Briefly recovered by the Byzantines, it fell again in 641 A.D., this time to the Muslims. The Christian population that Moschos knew and wrote about—the monks and the stylites, the merchants and the soldiers, the prostitutes and the robber chiefs—all the strange and eccentric characters who wander in and out of the pages of *The Spiritual Meadow* ended their lives under the rule of Islam, their numbers gradually whittled down by emigration, intermarriage and mass apostasy. With occasional periods of stasis, such as the early Ottoman period, that process has persisted ever since, greatly accelerating this century with the creation of the State of Israel.

The ever-accelerating exodus of the last Christians from the Middle East means that *The Spiritual Meadow* can now be read less as a dead history book than as the prologue to an unfolding tragedy whose final chapter is still being written. Today, Christians are a small minority of fourteen million struggling to keep afloat amid 180 million non-Christians, with their numbers shrinking annually through emigration resulting from oppression, persecution, or simply to live a better life in the West. This process of decline is an historical continuum that began during the journeys of Moschos and whose disastrous final chapter I have been witnessing on my own travels some fourteen hundred years later. Christianity is an Eastern religion which grew firmly rooted in the intellectual ferment of the Middle East. John Moschos saw that plant begin to wither in the hot winds of change that scoured the Levant of his day. On my journey in his footsteps I have seen the last tendrils in the process of being uprooted. Moschos saw its beginnings. I fear that I have seen the beginning of its end.

HEARTS WITH ONE PURPOSE:
MY JOURNEY WITH
THE PEOPLE OF PALESTINE
Elaine Kelley

My pilgrimage to the Holy Land began ten years ago. It was a journey going deep into old stone, a kind of spiritual archaeology into God's secret hiding place. Oh, I remember those days when I first believed there was such a place and the thrill of setting out to look for it. Then I went to Jerusalem to see what I would find there. In Bethlehem, there in the cave deep beneath the Nativity Church, we prayed before the altar of St Joseph and shared what we had seen and felt on that day. I said to my fellow pilgrims, 'I'm coming back to live here,' and I believed that it was true. Back home in Oregon after my pilgrimage nothing could ever be the same. I was changed, 'all changed, changed utterly, a terrible beauty is born' (W B Yeats, 'Easter, 1916'). Life then travelled on a new course for me, and I continued to search. A year later, 3 February 1990, on the Feast of St Blaise who removed a bone from the throat of some poor creature many centuries ago, I entered the Sisters for Christian Community during Mass, in front of all the people gathered there, and I spoke as one whose mouth had been opened. After making my vows I was free to search some more. Another year passed but I had not forgotten where I had seen the most beautiful things. I read about the Holy Land and ancient Palestine where Jesus Christ had lived. I made inquiries about volunteer opportunities in the Church there, but nothing concrete transpired. So I consoled myself with the idea that some day I would go back. God had dangled the pearl on his fishing hook before me. It was my Holy Land! Beauty is the bait; and it will pull you in on its barbs.

St Francis Catholic Church in Portland, Oregon, is a haven for the homeless, for peace and justice activists, and would-be saints who live on the fringe. Daniel Berrigan, Cesar Chavez, maybe St

Francis himself would feel at home there. This is my parish. There I met Larry and Mary Hansen, fellow pilgrims who were to become good friends and a bridge over to Bethlehem. They had also been to the Holy Land, but their experience had taken them beyond the perfunctory visit to holy sites to a meaningful encounter with the living stones of the Holy Land, the Palestinians. At first it was the fervour of Christian pilgrims sharing stories about the Holy Places that brought us together every Sunday after Mass. We talked about our longing to return, to spend more time in the land called 'the Fifth Gospel' and to be immersed in the earthly life of Jesus. Later they told me about the people they had met during their pilgrimage, including a Palestinian priest, Fr Peter Madros, the pastor of the Catholic Church in the West Bank town of Beit Sahour, the site of the biblical Shepherds' Field, located on the hillside and valleys below Bethlehem. My friends had accepted his invitation to 'meet some terrorists,' he said, an allusion to the Western media stereotyping of all Palestinians. The terrorists turned out to be his friends who lived in an old home in East Jerusalem. They were ordinary people with extraordinary stories to tell. They told Larry and Mary about their heritage as Palestinian Christians, about the military occupation and the *Intifada*, which at that time was raging in the West Bank and Gaza. Larry and Mary had got more than they had bargained for on their pilgrimage, and returned to Oregon transformed, determined to enlighten their own Christian community about everything they had seen and heard. What they shared with us was not a travelogue with slides of the old churches and holy sites, beautiful as they are. They shared, instead, the story about an ancient people in an ancient land whose culture and very existence was under threat, about the Mother of All Churches and a little-known remnant called the Palestinian Christians whose ancestors were among those first disciples who formed the original Christian communities of 1st-century Palestine.

Larry had made an arrangement with Catholic Near East Welfare Association in New York for funds raised in Oregon and elsewhere around the country to go to Fr Peter's project to provide jobs for parishioners with severe economic hardships. I had worked in many fund-raising projects for justice and peace campaigns, environmental groups and Church organisations like the Jesuit Volunteer Corps where I was then employed. So how could I say 'no' when Larry asked me to help with a project that would keep me tangibly connected to the Holy Land while working with new friends for such a worthwhile cause? As a veteran of anti-war demonstrations during the era of Vietnam and El Salvador, I had some understanding of the Palestinian/Israeli conflict, and my gut feeling was that the Israelis had become exactly what they hated. They were now the oppressors, the aggressors controlling an unarmed civilian population. I remembered brief glimpses during my pilgrimage of Israeli soldiers outside the window of the tour bus at the military checkpoint as we passed into the West Bank to visit Bethlehem. I remembered seeing some of the *Intifada* boys, too, with their *keffieh*-covered faces, and recognised that image from television news stories about terrorism in the Middle East. It was the only image of the Palestinians our American media had to offer at the time. Our tour guide was an Israeli woman, very informed on the history of the Christian Holy Places, and making no apologies for the Israeli military presence all along the way, the delays at checkpoints, the security measures to protect us all from the dreaded 'terror' of Palestinians. The politics of the Holy Land was but a fleeting curiosity in those days, however. Later, when I was living among them, their sufferings would become very personal.

When the Gulf War started in January 1991 we got caught up in the anti-war effort. 15,000 strong, we marched in downtown Portland to protest the bombings of Iraq. Larry and Mary were there, and many others from St Francis Church. But it was a short-lived movement for the masses of people, and the bombings continued as the protests diminished, leaving only a small group at St Francis to form an ongoing peace and justice action group. During that time I was getting an education on Middle East history and US foreign policy from the writings of leading Palestinian intellectuals and activists—Edward Said (1992; 1994; 1996), Naim Ateek (1989) and Fr Elias Chacour (1985), to name a few. For several months I continued working with the Hansens to raise the awareness of our Churches on behalf of Palestinian Christians in the Holy Land, and to solicit contributions to CNEWA for Fr Peter's jobs project in Beit Sahour. Larry, an eloquent speaker on many issues, spoke out on Iraq and Palestine wherever people would listen, in churches and schools, at the archdiocese, writing letters to local newspapers, challenging national, state and local officials, and forcing Christians to re-think their endorsement of the bombing of Iraq and US economic support to the State of Israel.

All the while I had not forgotten the Holy Land. I dreamed of returning, wanting only to be there, just to pray in the ancient churches, to sit in the shade of an old olive tree, to place all my senses into the environment of stone and breeze and fragrance that held the treasure of the earthly life of Jesus Christ. Meanwhile I comforted myself with the work I was doing while nurturing the thought that I would go back 'some day'. I had no idea how soon that day would come.

It was Holy Week, 1991. After Mass Larry told me he had spoken to the Palestinian priest on the phone. 'Fr Peter says you can come and live in Beit Sahour,' Larry told me. And I was reeling, from dream to reality in an instant. 'I'm going!' 'I'm going!' And I could scarcely believe it, though I knew that it was true, and even before I could catch my breath, I was planning and packing and telling everyone. There were times during the next six months when I had butterflies about what I was about to do: moving to a foreign country, alone, where I did not know anyone, did not speak the language, did not know anything about what it was like to live in a Palestinian town on the West Bank in the midst of one of the greatest political struggles of our time. This was the real thing. And it was clearly an answer from God. You are going!

Fr Peter told Larry I would have to raise my own money for air-fare, food and housing, as the Church in Palestine had no funds for such things. So we envisioned a Middle East peace project of public speaking and fund-raising for my work in Palestine as a peace volunteer in the parish of Our Lady of Fatima in Shepherds' Field. By the end of October I had an airline ticket and $10,000 raised from over 300 individual donors and religious communities in a special savings account set up for me by the Jesuit Volunteer Corps, and a pledge for more if I needed it. On 11 November 1991, I boarded a plane and was on my way back to the Holy Land.

Divine madness is more commonplace than Christians might think, a form of grace occurring in varying degrees according to our capacity to receive and God's own wisdom in giving. I remember the intensity of prayer, the desire to live for God, the half-discerned promises of love, the wilful deliberations of a soul that does not yet know itself. It is an energy which is itself a source of strength, not our own, given to help the spiritually immature, to help us on the long road back to God. And I was going back, to that earthly place where Jesus Christ lived and still walks among the quiet places. My life's course was flowing back to those dry desert edges, a fish way out of water to be set down in history's flood of human events.

How many books had I read on Palestinian history and culture and politics before actually experiencing it? Just one day in Palestine was more of an education. And I recall that intense year in flashes of names and faces and events. It was my 'year for living dangerously', for hearing the noise of battle close by and the news of battle far away, as Jesus himself put it, a year of walking through the fire of the Palestinian/Israeli political conflict, and experiencing it in passionate, personal terms. I learned how to be a guest, the object of many gracious invitations into people's homes, to drink sweet tea or strong Arab coffee, because that is what one does in Palestine. And I learned so much more. It was a total immersion in the language, the original old-time Christian religion and the Arab culture of profound community, where one family can have thousands of members sharing the same last name and where neighbours live in immediate proximity.

I arrived, or shall I say landed, on a new planet, in a world of steep hills of stone with houses and churches of stone, and everything so old, including the people who were as old as the hills, and it was hot and dry. So I exchanged my corduroy jumper for a summer dress and began my new life. Fr Peter arranged for me to stay initially with a Palestinian Greek Orthodox family—Lamia and

Sabba and their four young children—Nadeen and Nadeem (seven-year-old twins), Nada (six years) and Faddie (just one year old) and their extended family who lived in houses nearby. The warm welcome and genuine hospitality I was shown exceeded anything I had read about. Lamia was the housekeeper at Our Lady of Fatima Church, cooking and cleaning for the two priests who lived there, after cooking and cleaning for her family. She spoke enough English for us to communicate and helped me find my way in my new environment.

And what an environment it was! I was a time traveller on winding roads and ancient narrow ways made for donkeys and holy ones who go on foot. Walking up and down and all around through a maze that seemed to have no beginning and no end, I lost myself in the spiralling gyre of old Beit Sahour, like the cycles of history that shift with time but return to where they began. A tour guide could get lost in these old streets. On a high road you can see the town spread out beside biblical Shepherds' Field, like the psalmist of repose in verdant pastures. The most striking features are the church spires and the mosques. Moonlight reveals yet another view, with a skyline of stone-contoured white buildings, cross-topped configurations of terraces and porticoes all stacked tightly together on the hillside in a breathtaking silhouette against the sky. Beit Sahour is an old village, about 800 years old, a town of about 15,000 in 1991, predominantly Christian (over 80 percent) with the Greek Orthodox forming the largest population, followed by the Latins (Roman Catholic), the Melkites (Greek Catholic), then the more recent Anglican, Lutheran, Baptist and Methodist communities. The people are multi-lingual, speaking and storytelling and gossiping in Arabic, English, French and German, and sometimes even Hebrew. Yes, it is a famous little place, mentioned in the Gospel of Luke, where angels announced the birth of Christ to two shepherds, the first two known Christians. The people claim that God chose this place to announce the birth of Christ because of their propensity for gossip. They say God knew that if He told the people of Shepherds' Field they would tell the whole world.

Beit Sahourians are among the most educated of Arabs in the Middle East, more affluent, more connected to the West because of their ties to the world-wide Church. Yet, in 1991, and throughout the *Intifada* years, they experienced an unemployment rate of about 60 percent. Those among them with the best education, financial resources and with family members abroad were the most likely to leave. Since 1948 almost half of the Christians of Palestine have emigrated to other countries. It is a Diaspora of great proportions and every family in Beit Sahour has some story of separation. They go looking for a better life, education for their children, a career, an income to support their families.

Though traditional and conservative, Palestinian society is not homogeneous. Diversity is in bloom in urban Palestine, with donkeys, sheep and goats sharing the same road with cars and trucks, church bells and muezzins often clashing simultaneously, stone houses built centuries ago standing alongside newer high-rise apartments made of prefabricated blocks from a nearby quarry. There are women in slacks who have jobs and drive cars and veiled women wearing the traditional long dress called a *thaub* who stay at home with five, six, or ten children. There are real shepherds who look like they came right off a Christmas card, and businessmen in Western-style suits and ties. Sometimes the differences do not mix well, like olive oil and water, but add a little salt of the earth, shake it up and you've got something you can dress a salad with, because this is a family, a large, extended Palestinian family, united like the dense intertwining roots of an ancient olive tree that go deep, deep into the land.

I walked everywhere. At every turn people would gaze in curiosity, noting a stranger in their midst, noting without fear of course, because God had sent me after all. *'Ahlain! Ahlain!'* the people said, one after another coming out onto their doorsteps to greet me, and I thought, 'How do they all know my name?', and I wondered about that for many weeks until I learned a few words of Arabic, including *'ahlain'* which means 'welcome'. I began to use more and more Arabic words and phrases. The more mistakes I made, and they were legion, the more people would laugh and enjoy it. One nice woman said she would invite me for lunch every day if I promised to speak Arabic. And so I did.

My first days in Palestine fell in the midst of celebrations for Palestine Independence Day, held every November since 1988. Thus began my initiation into the heartbreaking politics of the Holy Land. Every night there were demonstrations, hundreds of masked young men (*shabab* in Arabic), their faces covered in black and white chequered *keffiyehs*, their bodies wrapped in home-made camouflage of plastic and paper, marching through the streets of Beit Sahour, drumming ancient rhythms on the *tabala* drum and moving in militant formation, while their families and neighbours, women and young children, emboldened them on the sidelines with steel-wool flares, hurling them in fiery circles, and cheering them on with chants and singing, '*Biladi, biladi, biladi, lakee hubbi w'fou'addi*' ('My country, my country, my country, to you my love and my loyalty'). This was the army of Palestine, the 'shake-off' called the *Intifada*, a revolution of teenagers armed with stones and Molotov cocktails, carrying out a struggle for freedom long abandoned by their parents who had lost the fights of 1948 and 1967. It was a ritual street dance, the sacramental allure of fire and drum, oppressed humanity marching in the throes of heroic resistance. And in the beating of the drum I again heard the words of Yeats and the terrible beauty he describes:

> Hearts with one purpose alone
> Through summer and winter seem
> Enchanted to a stone
> To trouble the living stream.

Nearby, in the shadows, the army of Israel watched and waited, an army with jeeps, deadly machine-guns and teargas, rubber bullets and real bullets, an army of young arrogant men under the command of the Bethlehem Military Administration with total, unchecked authority over the inhabitants of the West Bank. Demonstrations were illegal under Israeli military law and the army typically responded with night raids, arrests, teargas, shooting and curfews.

It is a harsh place to live even without war, a daily flagellation of heat and noise and pushing crowds of angry, frustrated people. Sometimes it is so hot it takes an effort to focus, to feel really alive. Mind and body submit to inertia under the hot sun and you want to sleep and just dream again of being here, undaunted by the physical reality, perhaps to view it all as in a movie theatre, reclining cool with popcorn and a coke through the passion and climax of *The Last Temptation of Christ* It is a strife- and stone-strewn Holy Land, adverse to the comfort of all living creatures. It is the spiritual made tangible through suffering.

The weeks and months passed and I had many new friends who invited me back again and again, to have tea, to listen to their stories, and to laugh when I tried to speak Arabic. I discovered a closeness and warmth I had never known before, and learned to enjoy people, perhaps because I could not understand anything they were saying. But I soon realised that ordinary people asking very little from life and trying desperately to cope in a hostile environment can be the friendliest and most hospitable of people. They draw you in. They seem to know better than the rest what is important in life. They tell you what you do not know and what you need to know to be a part of them, and you want to be a part of them, for there is nothing more beautiful than people who have nothing and no one but you to tell about their pain. Maybe that is why God loves those who pray. In an endless curfew, when the electricity is cut, when one of them has been taken away in the night and no one knows where, when the siren blows and soldiers yell through the loudspeaker and schools have been closed for weeks, when a child is overcome with teargas and I was often the only one free to go outside to get a doctor. It was an abject lesson in people needing each other to survive.

The value of my witness to the Palestinian tragedy is, I believe, in the firsthand stories I tell about those whom I have known and loved. And as an American, and a member of a Catholic religious community, my witness can have even more credibility, more power to move hearts than reports coming from the Palestinians themselves who have lived and suffered through all of this. I have no ulterior motive, no political axe to grind or poignant personal loss to convey, and my identity does not slant and otherwise fog the truth with bias. Neither is there much value to be found in any secular topical discussion of Palestinian/Israeli politics. Our spiritually hungry world is overfed with daily servings of death and destruction on the pages of every newspaper. The story of the Palestinians is no less than the ongoing story of the cross of Christ, not the only story, certainly, in our sad world of war and genocide, of Kosovo and East Timor, but a story that stands out in the annals of 20th-century history and continues unresolved into the 21st. And the only spiritual lesson to be wrought from this suffering, our own as well as others', is in seeing what Simone Weil referred to as 'the possibility of loving, divine love in the midst of affliction'. What other value has this suffering than to open our eyes to that possibility and to inspire our hearts to respond to the command we have received as Christians to act with compassion.

I remember the night the priest woke me up because a member of the parish had been shot and I had to see, he said, to know the truth about life for Palestinians in the Holy Land if I was to be of any use at all. Wa'el Badra had been shot in both legs that night and left bleeding beside the road. His family took him to Mokassad Hospital in East Jerusalem. Now they were telling the priest in Arabic what had happened and the priest was telling me in English so I could write a report to human rights groups and tell the world outside and maybe do some good. Wa'el had borrowed his father's car to drive the short distance to visit his fiancé who lived near Shepherds' Field. It was dark. Wa'el saw headlights and slowed down; then, realising that the two men in the car were Jewish settlers, with guns, he wheeled the car around quickly to try to escape, but the settlers got to him first. They pulled him out, threw him down and shot him in both ankles. Terrified, Wa'el somehow managed to get up and run on two wounded legs, jumping into the darkness of a ravine and under a tree where he hid until the settlers drove away. Wa'el's father eventually came looking for him, found the car with bullet holes all over it and found his son, seriously wounded but alive. We filed reports about the shooting to no avail, and the guilty parties were never punished or even searched out.

Gunfire seemed to occur mostly at night. Soldiers would come into town and storm someone's house, dragging the young and the old out of bed, grabbing anyone between fifteen and twenty-five, accusing and questioning, and finally leaving with a son or a brother, taking him away, sometimes for days, sometimes for years. And it was not always men who were treated in this manner. Issa was seven when the *Intifada* started. His house is situated at the foot of a long flight of stairs that served as a favourite escape route for *shabab* running away from soldiers in jeeps. One day Issa was playing outside his house just at the foot of these stairs when two soldiers came running down looking for stone-throwing boys who had already run past. Accusing Issa of being one of the stone-throwers, a soldier hit him in the head with the butt of his rifle, picked him up and threw him over the side of a steel fence to the concrete floor twenty feet below. Issa sustained a broken leg and broken wrist, and the scar on his forehead is still visible after twelve years. His little sister Jane was three when the *Intifada* began. She and her father were rushed to a hospital after teargas canisters were hurled by soldiers through their front window. Everyone in Palestine is an expert on teargas, including me. It is a vicious weapon which can burn the lining of your lungs and cause permanent lung damage if you get a big enough dose of it. It can cause instantaneous miscarriage and sometimes death. After experiencing it myself I am amazed the world thinks it needs nuclear weapons. Tear gas is so painful I would think it could stop any army dead in its tracks. At least it stopped me. One time I was walking through the vegetable market when I saw in the distance two soldiers beating a man. I hurried my steps in order to challenge the soldiers to stop what they were doing. But a few steps further and I felt the intense burning of my eyes and skin. It was an involuntary response to turn and run and run and run until I was sufficiently far away from the stuff.

You always knew right away when someone had died because the church bell would toll its slow, sad bong, bong, bong, and like a brush-fire on a dry weary land the news would spread to every house throughout the village. That is what happened the day seven-year-old Monar was struck and killed by a speeding car. The news reached clear to Jericho within the hour. I was spending the day there with a distant relative of Monar's family. We were walking in the streets of the oldest city on earth when a young boy came running up and in obvious distress told Buthaina to call home. We ran to someone's house to use a phone. Buthaina told me what had happened, that everyone was being summoned home. By the time we got to Beit Sahour little Monar's body had already been retrieved from the hospital and she was in her house in a casket, in the centre of the room, held in the arms of her inconsolable mother and surrounded by hundreds of women sitting in concentric circles all around them, weeping and praying and seemingly holding mother and child close to their collective bosom. It was an expression of the entire community's grief and it went on for days, with thousands more women coming to the house to shed their share of tears and help absorb the pain, while the men were doing the same in another house close by. The funeral was a collective event, too. You could scarcely get near the Greek Orthodox Church at the centre of Beit Sahour, so many people were there. Monar's mother had to be carried in. Weeks later we learned that it was a Palestinian from Beit Sahour who had accidentally killed Monar, an Israeli collaborator, the people said, who disappeared forever, presumably into the relative safety of Israel, never to return to his hometown again.

The death of a child by a speeding car is a deep personal tragedy. The death of a young unarmed college student shot in cold-blood by soldiers is a tragedy with long-term political consequences. On 2 May 1992, I was fixing supper in my little stone house near the church when I heard gunfire and a loud commotion. I went outside where neighbours told me that a man had been shot. Jeeps were driving up and down ordering everyone to remain in their houses; a full curfew was in force. It was Anton Shomaly, a student at Bethlehem University, a Christian resident of Beit Sahour and member of Our Lady of Fatima parish. Neighbours who saw what had happened said that soldiers had come to town to disburse a small group of *shabab* who were building street fires and throwing stones. The soldiers went driving through town and spotted Anton whom they chased on foot. They chased him down and caught him on the street above my house. Witnesses said that, even though Anton had already surrendered, the soldier shot him twice in the side, then threw him down some stairs on the side of the road, leaving him for dead. Others took him to Mokassed Hospital. In spite of the military patrols and the curfew, people in Beit Sahour were waiting in the streets to hear news of Anton. When word came that 22-year-old Anton was dead, the bell tolled and the muezzin called out for the whole town to hear that a Christian martyr of Beit Sahour was coming home and everyone was to go to the Latin Church for the funeral. Thousands defied the curfew to walk to the church, moving up the steep hills in silent procession. Inside the church it was chaos, weeping and screaming, with Anton's bloody body lying on the altar waiting for the priest who could not be found. The impatient crowd finally lifted Anton up into a coffin over their heads and carried him to the Latin cemetery. In the night you could hear gunfire in the distance and there was no mistaking the burning sensation of teargas. There were men and women, some children and elderly people too. After they buried Anton in a five-minute ceremony we began our long quiet walk to the outskirts of town to pay respects to the Shomaly family. At a corner we turned into the headlights of an oncoming jeep, and in the darkness it was difficult to know if the gunfire was coming straight on or going up into the sky. We ran, like sheep without a shepherd, in all directions to escape the bullets. I stooped down onto the ground as people ran past me, and I was afraid. Then two young Palestinian women lifted me up and we ran together and hid behind a stone wall where we waited for the guns to stop. A Palestinian man came running into the yard where we were hiding and, not seeing us, picked up a large stone which he hurled full force against the side of an oncoming jeep. He ran, but the jeep then slowly backed up toward us. A search light came over the gate into the yard but did not detect us. Finally, the jeep moved away and the three of us ran inside the house where about fifty others were hiding.

There followed a week of strict curfew, night raids, house searches and arrests. Another man had been shot and an artist beaten, his entire household searched for political posters made from a painting of Anton he had done as a gift to the Shomaly family. We learned that the authorities had tried to confiscate Anton's body from Mokassad Hospital in order to bargain with his parents over how many would be allowed to attend the funeral. They feared another insurrection over the martyrdom. But the Shomaly family had immediately taken Anton's body away to Beit Sahour for a quick burial. As is the custom in Palestine, people from every household in Beit Sahour went to pay their respects to the family, sitting in large circles in plastic chairs borrowed to accommodate the crowds. Also during that week the women in town organised a Mothers of the Martyrs March. Dressed in black, thousands of women walked from the Orthodox church to the Shomaly home, in full view of army patrols, but with an escort from the United Nations representative's office in Jerusalem. On the seventh day after Anton's death, a funeral Mass was held in the Shomaly home to avoid a confrontation with soldiers at the church. The Consul General of Belgium was called to personally escort Fr Peter to the house, as even he was confined to his rooms at the church during the curfew. My neighbours asked if I would go with them in their car to the Shomaly home. They said that the company of an American offered them a little security from the potential danger of being caught disobeying the curfew order. So we piled into the car and found a way over unpaved back roads to the Shomaly house.

In spite of daily occurrences like this, somehow daily life went on. If schools were closed by military order, class would be conducted in someone's house. If shops were prohibited from opening, including the neighbourhood bakery, there was a system for dealing with it. One of the kids would sneak through the alleys, under the trees, across an olive grove, even over rooftops, to reach the home of the baker. Doctors made house calls, often without compensation. It was common in those days, and still is, for all the neighbouring women to work together on a community lunch, saving time and resources while enjoying each other's company.

In the midst of troubles there were also occasions for celebrations. Weddings were as ubiquitous as the children that followed, though reduced to a bare semblance of the normal fanfare associated with a Middle Eastern wedding, to conform to the *Intifada* standard of a nation in mourning. The release from prison of a hometown boy was a major event with a feast prepared for the whole town. People would line up for a chance to welcome the prisoner home, with kisses and tears. There was dancing and loud music, prayers of thanksgiving, clapping and yodelling and singing words of praise for the brave warrior who had returned. I remember the day Tarik came home after two years in an Israeli political prison. He came home with permanent kidney damage from so many beatings. And I interviewed George and Iman, brothers released from Ansar III, a political prison in the Negev Desert whose very existence violates international laws and the Geneva Convention. From them I heard unbelievable stories of torture. Even more unbelievable is how typical the stories are. These men were amazed that I was shocked by what they told me.

That first year in Palestine lives in my memory like the dream adventure of Dorothy in *The Wizard of Oz*, complete with enemies, danger, beloved friends and incredible beauty in a strange and wonderful land. When I finally woke up in my home in Oregon a year later I could not forget the people and all that had happened in Palestine. The experience had branded itself on my heart forever. For the next four years I would fly back and forth several times, maintaining my connection to people in Palestine while working in Oregon to help develop a connection between our Christian communities. I returned to the Holy Land again in August 1998 to live in Bethlehem and to work in the development office of Bethlehem University.

Seven years have passed since the end of the *Intifada* and the beginning of the Middle East 'peace process'. Yes, there has been change in Palestine, and it is a different world now, a world divided between those who support the peace process and those who do not. There is a frenzy of economic development going on with funds from foreign governments for Bethlehem 2000, for new hotels, restaurants, souvenir shops, even a theatre. Everywhere there is building and planning to accommodate the thousands of pilgrims and for a future time when there will be peace and a functioning independent Palestinian economy. All of this is a sign of hope that the future will be better for the Palestinian people. Yet, some things have not changed that continue to dull that hope. Checkpoints still prevent free access to Jerusalem, settlement expansion and new construction are rampant, and new by-pass roads will effectively isolate the Palestinian people once and for all from the international community of pilgrims and tourists, cutting them off in their impoverished enclaves similar to the Jewish ghettos of Eastern Europe and the Bantustans of South Africa. In Bethlehem a new road with a new checkpoint will open soon, establishing one route for Palestinians to use and another for the rest of humanity. And at the entrance to Bethlehem Israelis are planning a number of new hotels so visitors do not have to bother any more with going all the way into Bethlehem to find a room at the inn.

As I write, it is December (1999) and it has not yet rained. Christians and Muslims all say that God is angry with the people and is withholding his rain from them. It is an ancient belief that resonates in this Great Jubilee year on the eve of a new millennium. If it does rain soon it will be a mixed blessing, for the roads are still piled high with earth and rubble from development projects that started too late, and a good rain would send the mud flowing down the hills all around. If it does not rain soon the olive harvest will be ruined, and there will be insufficient water for domestic uses for a third consecutive year. Those with a sense of humour are calling this whole development and marketing scheme 'Bethlehem minus 2000', or complain that the project should have been named 'Bethlehem 3000', so that they could have another thousand years to prepare for what the world has been waiting and watching for, which is peace in the Middle East and a reason to celebrate the 2000th Christmas in Bethlehem and the beginning of a new millennium. Some look back with nostalgia to the days of the *Intifada*, while others believe the last days are upon us. We are like the people who have seen the earth and the sky and can predict the weather, but we do not know the meaning of the present time. Yet we are called to search for that meaning, to seek after justice and peace and the truth that has been told. And we know this land is our Palestine, the place we call home. It is the Holy Land, a real place here on earth and a place for the dreams that live in our hearts. It is a holy land; but it is not yet heaven.

LIVING STONES AND LIVING FAITH
Duncan Macpherson

The pattern of the contributions to this book is one of autobiography. They show how the encounter with the Holy Land changed previous perceptions of Israel and the Palestinians. They then go on to chronicle subsequent activity arising from this eye-opening experience. As with other conversions, however, change is frequently a matter of process rather than a blinding flash of light. This was certainly the case for me.

A pilgrim comes home

One summer evening in 1981 I arrived at St George's College in East Jerusalem to follow a course on 'Palestine in the Time of Jesus'. Curiously, although this was my first visit to Jerusalem I did not feel that I was a stranger to the place. My father had served here with the British Army under General Allenby in 1917. For all I knew, remote ancestors had been here centuries before, as warriors or pilgrims, or both. Above all, however, I was coming home to where Christianity began. I left my bags in my room and, after a brief conversation with some sixty-something year-old Americans on the same course, I went directly to the Church of the Holy Sepulchre. I know that many people feel disappointed or alienated by their first visit, but I was fortunate. The church was almost deserted. I went into the shrine of the tomb of Christ and found myself to be quite alone except for the Greek monk on duty. I knelt at this holiest of places in the Christian world and was profoundly moved.

      The politics of the Israeli-Palestinian conflict could not have been further from my mind as I began this visit. This is surprising perhaps, since the decade preceding my arrival in Jerusalem had been dominated by politics. Although I had been teaching theology since 1967, at what was then a College of Education, my intellectual interests and preoccupations had not been limited to religion but had included an active interest in radical politics and trades' union struggles. Influenced perhaps by Marxist books and companions my own allegiances as a Catholic and as a Christian had come to seem increasingly problematic. For me, coming home to Palestine also marked new beginnings: the beginning of a renewal of faith and, concurrently, the beginning of a growing involvement with the cause of justice and peace for the Palestinians in the land where the Christian faith began.

Developing perceptions

I suppose my earliest childhood impressions of the Palestinian-Israeli conflict included the stock notions of plucky little Israelis fighting off cruel and cunning Arabs. In the culture of my childhood Jews were stereotypically mean and Arabs were stereotypically dirty, but it was always much easier for British people to identify with the Jews, especially when they were far away and engaged in the kind of pioneering colonising at which the British themselves had excelled. In my years as a boarder at a minor English public school I had been an avid reader of G A Henty's Victorian tales of adventure in the swashbuckling days of the British empire. The Israelis fitted well into the same sort of model. As a sixteen-year old I remember being wildly enthusiastic about the 1956 collusion between Israel, Britain and France which led to the invasion of Suez.

At university, while studying theology with the intention of becoming an Anglican priest, the growing influence of Christian values on political judgements made me more guarded and thoughtful. I was influenced too by a Jewish friend on the same landing in my hall of residence. He regularly held forth to me on the Middle East. According to his perspective Israel was a buccaneer state. That it should claim to be acting on his behalf just because he was a Jew, he regarded as considerable cheek.

Ten years later I had become a Roman Catholic. I was by now, married with four young children, teaching courses on world religions to future teachers. My views on Israel and the Palestinians were now, again, influenced by anti-Zionist Jews, who situated the Jewish state firmly within the Marxist framework of understanding to which I was generally sympathetic. However, although I had been a political activist, neither I nor those who had influenced my thinking gave much attention to the cause of the Palestinians. Our main focus was on the struggle of industrial workers in Britain. In the list of international causes we engaged Palestine came a long way behind Vietnam, South Africa, Northern Ireland, or Central America. The fact that I became involved with the cause of the Palestinians was largely a matter of chance.

The tutor on the course at St George's College in 1981 tried to be even-handed in his treatment of 20th-century political issues in the land of Jesus. Nonetheless he was a good educator, and unadorned facts have power. Just to point out the sites of former Palestinian villages is more persuasive than any number of polemical diatribes. The group experienced something of the latter from a senior Palestinian Anglican, and the impression of anger and self-pity was entirely counter-productive for winning over anyone to the Palestinian cause. However, the decisive influences in my conscientisation about Palestine were external to the course programme at St George's.

Pilgrimage to a Palestinian university

Many of the group were charismatic Christians, and I was somewhat uncomfortable with their brand of spirituality, and found the frequent prayer meetings a burden. However, they were nice people, and most of them retired early, leaving me free to wander around the Muslim Quarter of the Old City in time for evening Ramadan celebrations. The contacts I made were first with shopkeepers, and then with a student from Bir Zeit University who came into one of the shops to smoke and to chat with the shopkeeper. He was a serious young man with a phlegmatic personality that completely belied the common stereotype of a Palestinian. Culturally a Muslim, he had a wide knowledge of Marxist theory as well, as of the literature of the Arab-Israeli conflict. He had experienced several periods of detention without trial, and told me in a very matter-of-fact fashion about his experiences of torture at the hands of the Israeli security forces. Despite these experiences he was eager to read more about the experiences of the Jews under the Nazis, as he felt that this might help him to understand the mind-set of his enemy better and enable him to hate them less. After several agreeable evenings discussing Palestinian and Israeli politics, Marxism, Islam and Christianity, he invited me to visit Bir Zeit. This visit was to mark another milestone in my involvement with the Palestinian cause.

The university had already been pointed out to the students of St George's College by our tutor-guide from the road some two miles away, and some of us had got down from the coach to take photographs. We were informed that the students were highly politicised and that the university was subject to frequent disturbances followed by closures imposed by the Israeli army. The prospect of visiting it provoked both apprehension and excitement. The journey itself was an education since it was my first experience of travelling in vehicles with blue West Bank number plates. The shared taxi-service to Ramallah and the bus to the old campus in Bir Zeit village were both subject to delays and questioning by security forces at check points. My political activities in London had placed me on picket lines and on demonstrations facing rows of policeman on horseback, but this was the first time I had found myself alongside a frightened civilian population harassed by a heavily armed occupying power.

At the university I was introduced to Albert Aghazarian who ran, and still runs, the Department of External Relations at the university. This was the beginning of another friendship that was to last through the years. By virtue of his job Albert is well known throughout the world to journalists and politicians. With the kind of extrovert personality that made Antony Quinn's performance in *Zorba the Greek* seem like Andy Pandy, Albert's enthusiastic advocacy of Palestinian academic freedom is matched only by his persuasiveness when arguing the wider issues of the Palestinian cause. Albert outlined to me the system operative at Bir Zeit by which students were obliged to obtain credits in practical community work to be eligible to graduate. One way in which this could be done was by active involvement in an annual summer camp in which foreign volunteers participated in socially useful work in villages and refugee camps. I immediately began to explore with him the possibility of bringing a group of my own students on a special volunteer programme in the following spring.

Before I left we had agreed that I should attempt to organise charitable funding for an exchange programme between a student group from my own college and students from Bir Zeit.

University closure

To my astonishment I was back a few months later with a party of more than forty students and staff from my college. However I found that I was in 'over my head'. At Heathrow Airport we heard that the university had been closed and was under curfew until further notice!

Anxious for the security of my group I worked closely with Albert to devise an alternative programme. I was not reassured by the experience of coming out of a restaurant in Ramallah to find myself a yard away from an Israeli civilian firing his pistol after a Palestinian child who had apparently just hurled a stone at the windscreen of a bus. Such episodes were, I was told, only too commonplace.

The university arranged accommodation for my group in East Jerusalem and we were given the privilege of meeting and being entertained by a Palestinian folk-dancing troupe and other students from the university. They danced and sang and talked endlessly of their experiences and aspirations. My students were not at all politicised, and, although they sang their own songs and taught the Palestinians the Conga, they received much more than they could give as they listened open-mouthed to the description of life in a world so different from their own.

Eventually we left Jerusalem with our friends to participate in a building project in Galilee for Father Elias Chacour, Greek Catholic priest and Palestinian leader of Gandhian stature, who was working to better the lot of Palestinians living inside the 1948 borders of Israel. On arrival we found that there had been a violent incident involving the wounding of the Greek Orthodox priest by a man in Israeli military uniform. Father Chacour advised us to move on and we proceeded to Tiberias where we stayed in an Israeli government hostel. Since most of the students had West Bank identity cards they ran the risk of imprisonment by spending the night in Israel, but the leader of their party spoke fluent Hebrew and the warden of the hostel assumed that they were all Israelis!

No room in Bethlehem

On the return journey we visited Beit Sahour, the Shepherds' Field, near Bethlehem. Here a Christian Palestinian family had experienced collective punishment. Two young lads had thrown stones at an Israeli jeep. They had been arrested and held without trial and the Israeli army had demolished the family home. The mother, heavily pregnant, sat with two little girls on a plastic settee under an awning, while the father and two students began the laborious task of rebuilding their house. We were all silent in the face of the pain and the injustice suffered by this family. There and then, I made a commitment to try to make people at home aware that such things happened and I asked one of the Bir Zeit students to convey this resolution to the disconsolate family.

The first visit by the *dubka*, or Palestinian folk-dancing troupe from the university took place some months later and was a major triumph. Students from the college arranged hospitality for the Palestinian dancers, and ferried them around the country to rapturous receptions at the Universities of Sussex, Oxford, Cambridge, Durham, Essex, Warwick, Aston, Edinburgh, Manchester, Dundee and Glasgow. At each venue Albert spoke movingly of the music and dance as the irrefutable evidence of the irrepressible vitality and spirit of the Palestinian people. For myself and my students this seemed self-evident and our involvement with the Palestinian cause was by now an irreversible process.

In the summer of 1983 I combined organising the participation of more than thirty students from my college with taking a small group of councillors from the London Borough of Hounslow to meet elected local government officials in the West Bank. Most of these were under house-arrest and all but one had been deposed from office by the Israeli authorities. The object of this exercise was to consolidate a twinning between Hounslow and Ramallah and El-Bireh. During the course of this visit we met Karim Khalef, mayor of Ramallah, and Basam Shak'a, mayor of Nablus, both of whom had been crippled by Israeli terrorist car bombs. Both evinced a quiet dignity, determination and generosity of spirit towards their enemies.

We were also impressed by the testimony of the Reverend Audeh Rantisi, Anglican priest and deputy mayor of Ramallah. He described how he and the other inhabitants of Lydda, together with the many refugees who had taken refuge in the town, had been expelled at gun point from their homes in 1948. Some had died at the hands of the Haganah as their possessions were looted, and many more had died on the bitter trek eastward to Ramallah. At that time such eyewitness accounts of what happened were not generally known either to the Israeli public or to the world. Significantly they gave the lie completely to the official Israeli line that the Palestinians had left of their own free-will as part of an Arab conspiracy to destroy the nascent Jewish state.

In 1984 a second visit to Britain took place by a folk-dancing group from Bir Zeit University. This time the student minibuses not only took them to universities and colleges around Britain, but also to

Amsterdam and Bremen. One of the most amusing memories that I entertain of this trip is the effect of the thirty Palestinian dancers pouring onto the floor of the disco on the North Sea ferry on our journey between Hull and the Netherlands!

Each year after that I was involved in taking parties of students and pilgrims to the Holy Land and they all included visits to Bir Zeit. Individuals from Bir Zeit came to visit my college, but nothing occurred on the scale of these two original university exchange visits.

Their purpose had been in large measure achieved. Hounslow twinned with Ramallah. The College Student Union twinned with Bir Zeit Student Council, and a number of other twinnings took place between Bir Zeit and various universities or other student unions. Our efforts had contributed to the end of the university's isolation and had also benefited other Palestinian universities, in particular Bethlehem and Al-Najah in Nablus. My own involvement with Bir Zeit now expressed itself in the work of Chair to the British charity, Friends of Bir Zeit University.

Living Stones

Under the influence of Christian Palestinians of the stature of Elias Chacour and Audeh Rantisi, and encouraged by my colleague Michael Prior, I became increasingly concerned to make British Christians more aware of the existence of the Christian Palestinian minority. This is turn had the potential of raising the wider issue of justice for the Palestinian people as a whole. As my own personal pilgrimage drew me more and more towards a renewal of Christian commitment it seemed unreasonable that British pilgrims should appear to be so indifferent to their fellow Christians. Most groups had only Israeli guides. They stayed in Israeli hotels, worshipped only with their own priest or minister, visited traditional sites and archaeological ruins and completely ignored 'the living stones' of the land; the indigenous Christians through whose ancestors our own ancestors had first received the faith.

Our committee first met in 1984 and we took great care that the organisation should be fully ecumenical. The membership of the committee and the spiritual patrons included Anglican, Free Church, Eastern Orthodox, Roman Catholics and Quakers. We inaugurated a journal and established a pattern of annual services and conferences often inviting leading Palestinian Christians as speakers.

In 1987 we organised an ecumenical pilgrimage to establish a pattern of what would characterise a *Living Stones* pilgrimage. The day we visited Bethlehem University a demonstrating student was shot dead from a distance by an Israeli sniper. I wrote up an account of this episode in *Middle East International* under the title 'Letter from Bethlehem' (19 December 1987).

In the next year I went to Jerusalem to meet with Christian leaders in the city and successfully solicited their support for the *Living Stones* project. On the last day I went to Bir Zeit to see the university vice-president and I was given the services of the university's chauffeur and car to take me to the airport. The car had, of course, a blue number plate and I was grabbed by Shin Bet secret police before I could get through the glass doors! One officer flung down a pad and asked me to list people I had been meeting in East Jerusalem. Quite truthfully I was able to give him the names of only the Christians leaders I had visited. 'These people are bishops,' he remarked scornfully. 'Can you explain to me what interest Christianity has in Jerusalem?' I replied that there was once a very famous Jew who lived in Jerusalem and who was highly thought of in the Christian religion. No flicker of a smile delayed the next, completely unrelated, question.

More opposition followed in 1990 when I was able to give more publicity to the *Living Stones* concept in the regrettably short-lived Sunday newspaper, *The Sunday Correspondent* ('Pilgrims' Progress in the Holy Land' April 19, and 'The Holy Land of Ambiguity' June 10). My own activity on behalf of the Palestinians, the role of *Living Stones*, the initiatives of my friend and colleague, Michael Prior, and even *The Sunday Correspondent* all received unfavourable mention in a well known Jewish newspaper. I also began to receive repeated and offensive phone calls day and night in my home. It is to be expected that standing up for the rights of the oppressed will provoke opposition. I have been harassed at airports and even physically attacked by an Israeli doctor when I protested at racial bullying, but the most distressing injustice is to be accused of antisemitism. According to the logic of this approach any Gentile who is concerned for the Palestinians is a covert Jew-hater, and, if he or she is Jewish, a self-hating Jew. I also had to contend with the assumption that Christian faith is incurably anti-Jewish. To anyone not too prejudiced to listen I have always tried to explain that opposition to racism and sectarianism is indivisible, and that the Gospel and the teaching of the contemporary Catholic Church should exclude anti-Jewishness and anti-Judaism just as much as it should exclude racism against Arabs and prejudice against Islam. The Christian record of anti-Judaism and anti-Islam is real enough and can only be understood against the background of history. Nonetheless the oft-stated contention that there is a straight line between the New Testament and Auschwitz is unworthy of serious consideration. Certainly sacred texts have to be read with care and this applies just as much to the readers of the Pentateuch and the Book of Joshua as to St John's Gospel.

The decade of the 1990s was to involve more activity on behalf of Friends of Bir Zeit University (FOBZU) and of *Living Stones*. Supported by a small group of enthusiasts, including a number of former students from my own college, we managed to rebuild FOBZU from a small lobbying group arranging occasional visiting lectures to a medium-scale charity managing projects requiring and obtaining five figure corporate grants.

FOBZU successfully launched a fund to provide scholarships for Palestinian women from poor backgrounds, in villages or refugee camps. These grants enable them to continue their university studies when they would not otherwise be able to do so. British government funding was obtained for a university centre to monitor food contamination in the West Bank and a lottery grant was obtained for a university programme to train social workers in Gaza and the West Bank.

Meanwhile *Living Stones* continued to disseminate information in Britain on responsible approaches to pilgrimage. It does this working closely with the Middle East Council of Churches and other Christian communities. It needs to be explained that *Living Stones* pilgrimages are not necessarily organised by the organisation itself. A *Living Stones* pilgrimage is a pilgrimage organised along *Living Stones* principles. *Living Stones* is in association with Churches Together in Britain and Ireland, and has as its stated purpose the promotion of understanding between Christians in Britain and those in the Holy Land and neighbouring countries. It also tries to act on behalf of Christian communities where their interests are threatened. Although primarily concerned with establishing links between Christians we also encourage dialogue and encounter with all other religious communities, especially Jews and Muslims. All this finds expression in a twice-yearly magazine and we aspire to providing a useful source of information. At the time of writing, we are preparing the publication of a 'Pilgrimage Guide' for the third millennium to appear in March 2000.

Conclusion

All of the achievements of Friends of Bir Zeit University and of *Living Stones* have been based on team efforts, and there is no way in which I can claim more than a small part of the credit for them. Nevertheless, the cause of the Palestinians has filled a large part of my personal canvas since 1981. I would like to end this autobiographical note by expressing hopes for the future of peace and justice in the region. Unfortunately the grounds for optimism are not good, at least in the short term. Nevertheless if a genuinely democratic Palestinian state does emerge one day it will be due in no small part to institutions like Bir Zeit. The life of the university already embodies the essential elements of a pluralistic civil society. Likewise, if opinion in the West is ever galvanised to bring pressure on Israel for a just and permanent settlement it will be due in some measure to a number of different organisations like *Living Stones*. Each such organisation can perform a vital role of conscientisation within its particular constituency. In the case of *Living Stones* this constituency is the Christian community in Britain.

The pilgrimage of spiritual renewal that I trace back to its beginning in the Church of the Holy Sepulchre in 1981 developed in parallel with my pilgrimage of solidarity with the Palestinians. I was encouraged to become a permanent deacon in the Roman Catholic Church and I was ordained by Cardinal Basil Hume in the College Chapel in 1996. This has given me a valued opportunity to preach the Gospel, but it is, in part at least, to the Palestinians that I owe the insight that there is no coming home that is indifferent to the homelessness of others. Likewise there is no authentic piety that does not seek for justice.

A TALE OF TWO BOOKS:
MY JOURNEY INTO ISRAELI-
PALESTINIAN ISSUES
Rosemary Radford Ruether

I was nine-years old in 1945. Like many kids I spent Saturday afternoons at the movies. Newsreels were a common feature of movies in those days. At the end of World War II the death camps that had slaughtered millions of Jews were 'discovered' by the victorious allied armies and images of the piles of corpses as well as the living skeletons of the survivors were broadcast on the movie screens. Those images shocked my consciousness; I still have a vivid recollection of them. These experiences, together with a sense of relation to the Jewish community through the Jewish side of my family, sparked a concern with antisemitism.

This concern grew as I studied Church history. In 1970, having completed my doctoral studies in Patristics and the history of Christian thought, I decided to research a book on the Christian roots of antisemitism. This was published in 1974 under the title, *Faith and Fratricide: The Christian Theological Roots of Antisemitism*. In this book I explore the New Testament beginnings of Christian polemic against Jews in the context of the division of Christianity from Judaism, and the elaboration of the themes of Christian anti-Judaism in the *Adversus Judaeos* literature of the Patristic period. I then trace the continuing pattern of anti-Jewish ideology and practice in Christianity and its conversion into racial terms in modern Europe, culminating in the Holocaust. The final chapter proposed ways of revisioning Christian theology, particularly Christology, to free it from its anti-Judaic 'shadow side'.

This book was initially not welcomed by the Christian side of Jewish-Christian dialogue movements that were just beginning at that time. Many Christians involved in dialogue wanted to distance the New Testament and the core of Christian theology from the problem and were not pleased when I made it central. The American Jewish community was very appreciative of the book. I soon found myself invited to speak in synagogues and dialogue conferences on this subject. In these gatherings I found myself quizzed about current Christian politics in relation to the State of Israel. For example, I was often asked (this was 1975-80) why the pope did not recognise the State of Israel. I was at first mystified by these questions since I did not regard myself as privy to the pope's policies on this or any other subject. But it gradually became evident to me that a connection was being made between Christian repentance for antisemitism and wholehearted support for the State of Israel. A Christian leader who was not so supportive of the State of Israel was, by implication, still clinging to antisemitic views.

In my book I had not made any connection between Christian antisemitism and policies toward the State of Israel. I had regarded antisemitism as a problem for Christians to deal with, theologically and socially, in Western Christian lands and cultures. I knew nothing about the Middle East, Israeli or Palestinian. But it became evident that I had better learn something in order to sort out the meaning of these questions. So I began to read about the history of Zionism, Israel and the Arab world.

In 1980, I had an opportunity to travel to Israel with a group organised by Jewish women from Montreal that was billed as an opportunity for dialogue between Jewish, Christian and Muslim women. The stated goal was to foster better understanding between these communities, on the presupposition that women talking to women might make some breakthroughs in communication. The idea sounded promising and I signed on to go. But as we travelled around Israel from the Lebanese border to the Gaza Strip, it became evident to me that we were only seeing the Israeli side. We never actually went into Palestinian areas or communicated with Palestinian Christians or Muslims. The one Muslim in our group, a Canadian of Egyptian background, felt so betrayed that she left the group after the first two days in Israel. Clearly something was wrong with this picture.

Three of us who felt most keenly that we were getting only one side of the story, myself, Charlene Hunter-Galt and a Hispanic woman from New Mexico, decided to plan our own excursion to the Palestinian side. I called Raymonda Tawil, whose book, *My Home my Prison*, I had read. She was then working from a news centre in East Jerusalem and quickly agreed to set up a day trip. On the next to last day of our tour, the day set aside for shopping, the three of us slipped away from the main tour, took a five-minute taxi ride to Raymonda's office in East Jerusalem and quickly realised that we were indeed in a different world, a world of which we had been given no real glimpses at all in the official tour, despite the objective of dialogue.

In the news office we spoke to Palestinian Arabs, and also Israeli Jews but with a very different point of view from those we had heard until then. We then travelled to Ramallah to interview the mayor, whose legs had been blown off by an Israeli undercover assassination attempt, visited a refugee camp and the Palestinian women's project, *El-Nash el-Usra*, led by the indomitable Umm Kahlil. When we returned to the hotel in West Jerusalem where the official tour was staying, it was clear that the organisers were furious with us, although no word was spoken. Their anger was expressed by extreme coldness.

This experience revolutionised my perceptions of the situation. I can only compare it to my later experience in South Africa; the stark difference between the world views of White South Africans who accepted *apartheid* and the world of Black and Coloured South Africa. The difference was that the White South Africans who had invited me on that trip in 1989 expected me to spend most of my time on the Black side, while the organisers of my trip to Israel seemed to want to keep the Palestinian side invisible, while giving us the impression that we had heard 'both sides'.

This trip to Israel, with its brief clandestine visit to the Palestinian world, was a profoundly disturbing experience. I felt manipulated in order to bring my work on Christian antisemitism into line with pro-Israel propaganda. I began to read much more, now intentionally to see the Palestinian experience. In 1986 I and my husband, Herman Ruether, a political scientist and student of Islam, arranged for sabbatical leaves to study at Tantur, an ecumenical centre on the Bethlehem road situated literally at the border between Israel and the West Bank.

There it became evident to us the extent to which biblical and theological material was being garnered by both Western Christians and Israeli and Western Jews to make the case for Israel, both based on divine election and the donation of the land by God and as compensation due for Christian antisemitism. I taught a course on the Holocaust, the State of Israel and the Palestinians, while Herman Ruether taught a course on Islam.

The result of this work was a second book, published in 1989, *The Wrath of Jonah: The Crisis of Religious Nationalism in the Israel-Palestinian Conflict*, co-authored with Herman Ruether, who worked particularly on the sections on Middle East political history and on Islam. For me, then and today, the two books, *Faith and Fratricide* and *The Wrath of Jonah*, are complementary. The same basic principles underlie both, namely that justice is due on both sides of human conflicts, and that religion should be used to foster justice and mutual flourishing of both communities, not the domination of one over the other. When religious and ethical values were misused to promote domination, such misuse needs to be unmasked and denounced and alternatives proposed in order to promote genuine reconciliation based on truth and justice.

I continue to use both of these books together in my teaching. For example, I regularly teach a course on the Holocaust, the State of Israel and the Palestinians, where the students first read *Faith and Fratricide* as well as books on the Holocaust, view videos such as the powerful French film on the death camps, *Night and Fog*, and also read on diverse forms of Zionism, on the history of Arab nationalism, and the Palestinians, using *The Wrath of Jonah*, as well as Jewish and Palestinian sources. Usually the course is followed by a trip to Israel/ Palestine designed to allow students to interact with differing perspectives on both the Israeli and Palestinian sides.

But I quickly discovered that those, both Western Christians and Jews, who loved my first book, *Faith and Fratricide*, regarded the second book as a renunciation of the first. Reviews denouncing it ignored the first book, or suggested that either I was insincere in the first book or had 'changed my mind'. I was now a pariah, excluded from Christian-Jewish dialogue groups. For example, an invitation for me to speak on the Christian antisemitism material at a conference at Northwestern University, Illinois, sponsored by the National Council of Christians and Jews was abruptly cancelled.

A woman working in the National Council office in Chicago was so disturbed by this that she leaked me the memo from the local *B'nai Brith* in which it was advised to cancel my invitation on the grounds that I was an 'enemy of the State of Israel'. I immediately protested this cancellation to the Christian and Jewish leaders of the conference. The Catholic and Episcopal bishops replied with concern, and a rabbi tried to set up a dialogue between me and the *B'nai Brith* instigators of the action, but, instead, the whole conference was cancelled. No dialogue took place.

I tell this tale of two books, not to focus on my story as one of mistreatment. Indeed I feel well supported by an emerging community of Palestinians and Western and Israeli Jews who are working on a different relation to each other. I recount it to illustrate how the issue of Christian critique of antisemitism and the Holocaust has been co-opted into a pro-Israel stance that silences the Palestinian story. Concern for the first is regarded as excluding concern with the second. Western Christians who want to stay in official 'ecumenical' relations with Jews avoid talking about Palestinians, indeed even avoid learning anything about them, lest they transgress the boundaries of this dialogue and even be marginalised and vilified. Such Christians seem incapable of imagining that there might be a way of being concerned about justice for the Palestinians that would at the same time be an expression of positive regard for Jews and for the welfare of the State of Israel. This is the set-up that Jewish liberation theologian Marc Ellis has called 'the ecumenial deal'.

Having stated my own view that the theologies of my two books, *Faith and Fratricide* and *The Wrath of Jonah* are complementary, that each rests on the same underlying principles, and indeed I see it as necessary for students of the issue to understand both stories, I would like to relate this view of a necessary interrelation of the two to the biblical theme of Jubilee, as found in Leviticus 25.

Genuine justice that can found real Israeli-Palestinian co-existence must be based on a very different sharing of the resources of the land than that envisioned by the so-called 'peace process', as constructed by the Labour Party and the United States in 1993, and continued in a fashion ever more prejudicial to Palestinian wellbeing under the present Israeli and US regimes. The terms of this so-called peace plan are basically an *apartheid* scheme designed to give only local control in some small regions, about 10-12 percent of historic Palestine, into hands of the Palestinian Authority.

In return the PLO are called to function as 'native police' to repress Palestinians under Israeli military control who surround these regions, cutting them off from access to each other or to Jerusalem, while consolidating and legalising Israeli settlements in an expanded Jerusalem and the West Bank and Gaza. A third partition of Palestine, the partition of the West Bank and Gaza, is thereby legitimated, with the Israeli settlement areas eventually annexed, the Palestinian zones cut off from real economic or political self-determination, and an intermediate zone 'shared' by Israeli and Palestinian authorities under extremely unequal terms.

Such an arrangement is unjust. It does not allow for minimum daily wellbeing of Palestinians. Rather, they are denied access to adequate land, water, markets and other means of economic maintenance, constantly harassed by curfews, work and travel restrictions, enforced by military checkpoints that turn their small areas into sealed ghettos. The situation breeds an endless cycle of grievance and violence. Each explosion in which some Palestinians, spontaneously or planned, lash out at Israelis justifies another round of restrictions, incursions, killings or imprisonments of Palestinians, refusal of 'concessions' by the Israeli government, until the Palestinian

Authority can guarantee a definitive end to Palestinian resistance. This goal is unattainable and can only make more Palestinians see the Palestinian Authority itself as puppets, corrupt tools of repression under the Israelis and Americans.

Real peace and co-existence in minimal justice demands a fundamental change of consciousness. Such a change of consciousness must recognise that the dream of a Jewish state purged of Arabs is itself the problem and must be foregone for a just sharing of the land by both communities. This just sharing must concede adequate resources in land, water and autonomy to Palestinians, and seek a coexistence of two communities living together as neighbours within political configurations that give equal citizenship to both.

There can be several ways of organising such a relation, and I do not attempt to discuss them here. The point is that the Israeli and the Palestinian *apartheid* dreams of separation of Jew and Palestinians into mutually exclusive nation-states must go. The fundamental perception that whatever is good for one side must be at the expense of the other must be changed into a quest to live together as neighbours based on a relation in which the wellbeing of one depends on the wellbeing of the other. This transformation must be constructed by an interlinked process of change of attitude *and* change of social, political and economic relations.

The biblical Jubilee vision is vital to this hope for peace through justice because it envisions a process of periodic dismantling of the structures of oppression by which some have taken the lion's share of the land, while reducing others to landlessness, debt and slavery. Unlike the apocalyptic-millennialist traditions that have dominated Christian, Zionist and Islamic political theologies, including liberation theologies, that seek a once-for-all show-down between the 'good guys' and the 'bad guys', where one side is defeated so the other side can reign supreme over the earth, the Jubilee calls for dismantling both excess power and excess powerlessness in order to right the balance, although not in a perfect or final way.

This process is not once-for-all, but must be renewed every two generations, continually reconstructing relations of just relation that overcomes the endemic human tendency to construct relations of domination by some over others. Every fifty years we must dismantle the resultant excess power imbalances by forgiving debt, releasing prisoners, freeing slaves, restoring adequate land to each family, letting the land rest and be renewed, so one can begin again with relations of people and land that found basic wellbeing for all.

I think this vision is crucial to justice and peace in the Israeli-Palestinian case. Indeed it is the only vision that gives real hope of peace. The competitive idea in which one wins at the expense of the other, in which one side celebrates when those from the other side are wiped out, recreate an endless cycle of violence. The issue is not whether the Jubilee was ever observed fully or at all in ancient Israel, or indeed whether the ancient texts envision this being done between Jews and non-Jews in the land. What is at stake is being able to imagine *today* the other as neighbour rather than enemy, and beginning to construct both the psycho-spiritual and the political-economic relations to make this concrete in real experiences of Jews and Palestinians living side by side in communities of mutual wellbeing in a shared land.

THE CHURCH OF SCOTLAND AND JERUSALEM—A CHANGE OF DIRECTION
Colin Morton

The Middle East had never much figured within my mental horizons. Born of Scottish missionary parents in north-eastern China when it was under Japanese occupation, I was brought up in England and Scotland and became a minister of the Church of Scotland in 1959. For the best part of the next thirty years I served as a parish minister in industrial, working class parishes in central Scotland. I was and am a member of the Iona Community which, along with its other disciplines, places an emphasis on not separating the spiritual and material, and on exercising one's faith by social and political action. In 1983, I was asked to stand as a Labour Party candidate for Lothian Regional Council, which had a wide range of responsibilities including education and social work. Although my Conservative Party opponent happened to be the present Earl of Balfour, the question of Israel never arose in the contest; it is likely that voters had other things on their minds and thought that the noble earl might have had insufficient understanding of their immediate problems. At any rate they gave me a useful majority.

For the next five years I combined being a parish minister with being a councillor, liking the different perspectives involved in my relationships with people. During that time I was working out a race relations policy for the Region and was active in the Community Relations Council, largely funded by the Regional Council. This brought me into close contact with the immigrant communities in and around Edinburgh. I found this challenging and enjoyable. However, once the Labour Party gained a majority and took over the administration, the pressures on my time became excessive and I was not sure what to do. I did not want to give up either of my roles, as if admitting that they were incompatible. As my wife, Carol, and I had been fifteen years in the parish of Prestonpans it was probably time to move; a change would surely be good for the parish, if not for me. No move seemed attractive enough to energise me. Then Carol saw that a minister for the Scots Kirk in Jerusalem was being sought, and I applied for the job; after all there was plenty of politics and of religion in Jerusalem. For reasons which are obscure to me I was appointed, and in the summer of 1988 we found ourselves on the plane.

I have always been interested in the relation between politics and religion. Religion (and certainly Christianity) has to do with the whole of life; the spheres of law and justice, of social and economic relations, of work and trade, all belong to God, as much as those of worship and of religious duties more narrowly defined. All our choices, all our actions and inactions, have their religious and political implications whether we recognise them or not. However, there are still two kingdoms, the Church and the State, both authentic, and it is harmful if they get too close. The State requires worldly power to do its proper business, to protect the people, to regulate the economy and to administer justice. Power corrupts, and if the Church gets interested in seeking power it becomes corrupt. The proper limits of political power are obscured, and the Church forfeits its prophetic role in calling the State and the powerful, to account when false gods, such as those of racism or nationalism, are idolised, or when truth is suppressed, or when justice is perverted from protecting the weak to serving the interests of the powerful or of one particular group. So it is right that all Christians should play as active and responsible part as they are able in the common and political life of a nation, guided by the faith and wisdom God gives them. Their participation is a religious duty and, allowing for the human fallibility even of religiously committed people, it should generally be for the health of the nation. On the other hand, religious institutions should not be involved in political power-play and such things as religious political parties are a mistake.

In my earlier life the questions posed by Israel and Zionism had not pressed on me very hard, nor had I known any Palestinians. I had been with many Jews when studying economics at university, and in the political and economic debate the one aspect of Israel which I remember being a hot subject was the idealistic socialism of the kibbutz movement. When I went on to study theology at Edinburgh in 1956 the Suez crisis was arousing passions and dividing Britain; a number of us disturbed the academic peace of New College with our involvement in opposition to our government's actions. We were treated to the verbal and intellectual fire-power of Professor T F Torrance, a theologian of very considerable weight and renown, arguing not only that Israel deserved Britain's support and protection, but also in effect that the Jews had a God-given right to the land. In common with most people around I felt a strong sympathy for the Jews, but I could not see how that sympathy and an awareness of European guilt had given us, or anyone else, the right to give another people's land to them; nor was it the business of Sir Anthony Eden, the Prime Minister at the time, to be the arbiter of theological disputes, even if such considerations were in his mind at all in his dealings with Colonel Nasser, which seemed unlikely.

During the next thirty years I was pretty much absorbed in the more local matters of the parish, of church and society. The international issues which appeared to demand personal judgement and some engagement were those of colonialism and neo-colonialism, world poverty and development, nuclear arms and the Vietnam War. All these were not unconnected with the Middle East, but that seemed less obvious then. The Middle East was a complicated part of the world, evoking conflicting sympathies. There were enough complications without it. In church circles those who were most interested in Israel seemed to me to be opting out of the more pressing and immediate demands of the Gospel for the Church of Scotland.

For similar reasons I felt no temptation to visit the Holy Land. However, in 1984, our daughter, Lucy, needed time to find a new direction in her life and went as a volunteer to Kibbutz Gonen in Upper Galilee. It was a good experience for her, sharing its communal life and, for part of the time, being entrusted with care for a severely and multiply handicapped young boy. She had her twenty-first birthday while she was there, and Carol and I went out to celebrate it with her.

We found that for the kibbutzniks and for other secular Israelis, whom we met through friends of ours, it was a time of crisis and soul-searching. The Lebanese War was seen by them as the first non-defensive and indefensible war that Israel had fought. Up to then, army service had always been a noble and virtuous duty; now it was highly questionable. The original kibbutz ideals were proving impossible to maintain through the passage of time and changing conditions, and the best of the younger generation were leaving. It was fascinating to be present in this very articulate ethical debate when myths were beginning to be questioned. I noticed, but did not fully register at the time, that Israel's earlier years were still seen as a golden age and that Palestinians were a non-subject for most people.

Like innocents Carol and I arrived at St Andrew's in West Jerusalem in 1988 when the *Intifada* was in its early stages. It was not altogether clear what purpose the Church of Scotland had in Israel and Palestine (the words 'Palestine' and 'Palestinians' were taboo in West Jerusalem then). The church and hospice (guest-house) in Jerusalem had been built as a memorial for those who had died in the Palestine campaigns of 1917-19, and had largely served the British military and civilian personnel during the Mandate years, and later the growing number of pilgrims and visitors. The rest of its work in the country, mostly medical and educational on an evangelical basis, dated from earlier times, and had been undertaken by the Jewish Mission Committee. After 1948 the institutions that continued under the Church of Scotland, apart from St Andrew's, were a school in Jaffa and a hospital in Tiberias, which was converted into a church centre when the hospital was no longer required. So its work was all in Israel proper and not in the Occupied Territories. St Andrew's was just over the Green Line in West Jerusalem, and had been cut off from the other churches centred in the Old City and East Jerusalem. Those who took responsibility for it were those who formerly were interested in Jewish missions, but latterly were engaged more in Christian-Jewish dialogue. The Church of Scotland was seen both in Scotland and in Israel as being very supportive of the State of Israel, but there was a growing sense that this fairly uncritical support did not represent the opinion of the Scottish Church as a whole, and indeed shortly before we arrived there had been the first contacts between the Church of Scotland and the Middle East Council of Churches. The changes in the name of the responsible committee are revealing, first the Jewish Mission Committee, then the strangely named Committee for Relations with Israel and Other Faiths, then the Middle East and North Africa Committee.

We found Jerusalem a totally divided city. St Andrew's had a host of contacts on the Israeli side and among expatriates, but very few with Palestinians from East Jerusalem or the West Bank, whether Christian or Muslim, apart from our own staff. The staff included Jews and Muslims, but most were Christian Arabs from the Bethlehem area who had all worked at St Andrew's for many years. This was the time of protest, stone-throwing and commercial strikes throughout the Occupied Territories. The response on the part of the government was to crush the protest by whatever means, the breaking of bones, ordered by Defence Minister Rabin, tear-gas, shooting, mass arrests into administrative detention, torture, and constant humiliation. Almost every Palestinian family had a member in prison at one time. In Gaza the Community Mental Health Project found that well over 90 percent of children had witnessed a family member being beaten up, an experience more psychologically traumatic than suffering oneself. The death toll among Palestinians mounted daily. Despite the curfews and harassment our staff struggled to keep their hours pretty well, and we gained through them an insight into the pressures these ordinary families endured.

We were able to build up relationships with people from East Jerusalem, and were deeply impressed by their strength and spirit. What struck me forcibly was the wealth of ability and tradition, the diversity, and the cultural richness of Palestinians. This was so different from the general picture painted back in Britain. The redoubtable Doris Salah, Director of the YWCA, bringing us to meet the people in Jalazoun Refugee Camp, and strong figures in the indigenous Christian leadership. Archbishop Lutfi Laham of the Melkite Church, Bishop Samir Kafity, Revd Audeh Rantisi and Canon Naim Ateek of the

Episcopal Church, people like these—there are too many to name—in their speaking, writing and actions deeply challenged us Western Christians as to whether we could stay uninvolved with any integrity. Al-Haq, the human rights organisation, was producing a wealth of well-researched material and legal background. We were able to get to know Mahdi Abdul Hadi, the Director of PASSIA (the Palestinian Academic Society for the Study of International Affairs) which was producing very valuable material, not least its annual diaries full of information.

I saw that we had a basic responsibility to the truth and to make information available, to report what was happening and to enable concerned visitors to see for themselves, and to meet a range of people involved in the conflict. Jerusalem, however, is not an easy place in which to be impartial, or to be credited with objectivity. Everything has a political message: the place-names you use, the wine you serve, the colours you display, all these things declare you to be on one side or the other. Whose side are you on? That was always the question. Even if you wanted to be neutral you could not, and those who set out with that intention found themselves 'placed' within a few days. Situated as we were, I felt myself to be in a delicate position. If we were identified as being pro-Palestinian (and therefore seen *ipso facto* as anti-Israeli, if not antisemitic), that could upset some members of the congregation who were definitely pro-Israeli, and some of our many Jewish guests at the hospice. It might complicate life for our staff and for others associated with St Andrew's. The Church of Scotland as a whole was divided on the issues and it might serve my own conscience, but not be very helpful, if I did not have the support of the Church I represented.

Most expatriates in Jerusalem are identified with one community or the other. Where they live and work inevitably influences them. Short-term visitors move freely from one side to the other. Long-term ones find it more difficult emotionally, although even they, as opposed to local people, have no practical impediment. We were a bit different. On the one hand, we were in West Jerusalem and had inherited a network of relationships at St Andrew's; on the other, we more and more saw our purpose as support and advocacy for the Palestinians and, especially, solidarity with the Christian community. This gave us an uncommon experience. I am concentrating more on reflections on my experience on the Jewish side, as my experience was more unusual. I will not do justice to what Palestinians went through. This is not to say that seeing it did not have a huge impact and influence both on me and on those whom increasingly we helped to see it too. But I know that Carol is covering that aspect more in her contribution to this volume. Moreover, I came to believe that deteriorations or improvements in particular human rights of occupied people, however important to the lives of the people concerned, did not affect the basic situation. No occupation, no expropriation, no assumption of complete authority by one people over another can be humane, moral or justified for any length of time. Even if the occupiers are paragons of virtue and humanity—which the Israelis are not, being weak human beings like the rest of us—it is impossible.

As for the Church in Scotland things went well. Robin Ross, the Middle East Secretary, arranged for six Palestinian Christians to visit Scotland so that we could discuss with them our future policy. It was a great group: Sami Geraisy, a most distinguished Orthodox layman from Nazareth, head of the International Christian Committee in Israel, and his wife Adele, Naim Ateek and Shehadeh Shehadeh from the Episcopal Church, Doris Salah, a Latin Catholic, and Wassef Daher, a warm friend and able worker whom the Scots took to as one of their own, calling him Jimmy. That was a key event, changing perceptions in Edinburgh. Because of it we worked to establish a partnership with the Episcopal Church and gained so much from working with the likes of Bishop Kafity, Canon (now Bishop) Riah Abu el-Assal, Naim, Shehadeh and others. The Church was still divided, and there was always opposition to the change of direction expressed in the annual General Assembly, when some of the things that were said could appal the delegates who came over from the Episcopal Church. At first the outcome of debates seemed uncertain and was faced with some trepidation, but later the opposition came to be negligible.

Back in Jerusalem the conflict went on, and efforts to suppress not only Palestinian protest, but also the name and the culture were being forcefully practised. I remember the occasion in the New Year of 1990 when there was an entirely peaceful demonstration. Jews, Palestinians and foreigners joined hands all around the walls of the Old City to be met with police charges, mounted and on foot, with water cannon armed with green dye. The picture stays in my mind of a girl holding in her hand four coloured ribbons, black, white, red and green, the Palestinian colours, trying to hold them tight while six soldiers surrounded her, held her and pulled them away. The Christian village of Beit Sahour was practising non-violent non-co-operation, refusing to pay taxes and seeking to be self-sufficient by growing their own food. The Rapprochement Centre was opened, and Israelis were welcomed to meet and discuss. The leaders of the centre, including Dr Jad Isaac, were imprisoned, the whole village was declared a closed military zone and was put under siege, with soldiers entering houses to seize or wreck household goods and the equipment used by people for their livelihood. On Christmas Eve, Archbishop Desmond Tutu came to preach at the annual Carol Service in the Shepherds' Field. The siege was relaxed for the day; it was not seen as politic to close the Shepherds' Field to the Christian world on Christmas Eve. It was a dark night; it seemed that all Beit Sahour came out for this brief day of freedom; the army was in full force; and Archbishop Tutu spoke devastatingly and almost hilariously, detailing one act of inhumanity after another, every time saying, 'Of course, I am speaking about South Africa.' Then a conference was organised bringing together Christians in conflict from South Africa, Northern Ireland and Palestine. It was sobering to hear those from elsewhere saying that the Palestinian situation was worse than theirs. All the time, my suspicion grew that religion, and not least Christianity, was providing cover for crimes and oppression.

Meanwhile the Church of Scotland was being seen by some as changing its direction in Israel. Through Carol's work there were Palestinian crafts on sale at St Andrew's. The heads of the main indigenous Churches and the Middle East Council of Churches came out with statements that were seen as objectionable by the authorities, and published a prayer to be used on Palm Sunday 1990. I thought it a good prayer, and used it in our Service. One, who had already resigned in protest from the Kirk Session, walked out slamming the door, and reported us to the authorities. I was called in to the Ministry of Religious Affairs and hauled over the coals. It was explained to me that the Church of Scotland was similar to the United States of America! We had been good friends to Israel. If we deserted Israel, it would be like America doing so. I should not be political, or associate with the politicised Palestinian Church leaders. I said that it seemed to me a religious duty not to shut my eyes to the suffering and oppression of people, whether they were my people or not, whether they were Christians, or Jews, or Muslims. We then discussed what 'political' meant. I differed from his view that criticising the government was political, while supporting it was not. I said that neither I nor the Church of Scotland was anti-Israel. We were friends of Israel, but the occupation was bad for the Palestinians, and in the end as bad, or even worse for Israel. The Director later told me that the government had ordered a campaign to separate Western Christians from the local Churches.

An American Jew who had stayed at St Andrew's wrote a letter to the *Jerusalem Post* complaining about some of the literature which was available in St Andrew's. The paper published my reply in defence. The result of this small matter was that I found much less reserve in the attitude of Palestinians towards us, as I had stated a case publicly in West Jerusalem. We did get some pressure, intimations that life would be easier if we played the game, anonymous phone calls that our staff would suffer. On the whole, though, we found our Jewish guests and friends quite easy to deal with; it was mostly the more liberal and peace-orientated who would come to St Andrew's, many of whom were very critical of their government, and did not find it strange that we should be supportive of our fellow-Christians; this despite the fact that propaganda was such that some generally well-informed friends thought that all Western Christians shared the dispensational theology of the 'Christian embassy'. The ones who were more difficult were Christian supporters of Israel from abroad who could be very virulent in their attacks on what we were doing, and hated all things Palestinian.

Israeli society is so diverse that every generalisation is right and every generalisation is wrong. I found it an exciting society, and would have found it congenial were it not for one crucial factor, which makes possible the one incontrovertible generalisation, and which has brought Israel into a moral morass. It has been said often enough that Israel needs a common enemy to keep it together; if it ever lacked one it would fall apart. With surprisingly few exceptions even among the most enlightened and peace-minded, of whom there are many, Israeli Jews are unable to see Arabs or Palestinians as human beings (Teddy Kollek's great success was that he appeared to, not that he ever did anything for them). The depth of their lack of knowledge is startling. They know much more about Tibet or Thailand than the West Bank or Gaza. With Israel having a citizens' army a great number of Israelis will have served in the Occupied Territories, but occasional books and articles appear telling of life there as if they were about Mars. There was a news item in the *Jerusalem Post* about the dreadful hardship endured by the inhabitants of the Jewish settlement of Beit-El who were suffering occasional half-hour breaks in their water supply, at a time when people in Bethlehem had had no water for three weeks. It may be a mixture of fear and a hidden sense of guilt which demands such a process of denial. Israelis seem at a loss as to why Palestinians do not appreciate them, and ascribe their enmity to inhuman malice, and not to any understandable motive. They do not see what is so glaringly obvious to others—that they have caused the Palestinians grievous harm. I remember being at a small gathering when Queen Beatrix of the Netherlands asked Ashkenazi Chief Rabbi Lau how it could be that Jews with their whole history and tradition could so deny other people's human rights. His answer was that it was the duty of Jews to live. This argument could justify any act, or crime, and has been used to justify many.

During the Gulf War it became even more clear how the Palestinians, including our staff, were treated as non-humans, denied gas masks and placed under house curfew for six weeks, with only very occasional and very short breaks to buy food at shops that were empty. I have never seen people so traumatised as our staff after that experience. At St Andrew's we were flooded out with Israeli refugees from Tel Aviv; but unlike the Palestinians of 1948 they were later able to return to their homes. The Palestinians were being excoriated for cheering the Scud missiles when they went over. One night, as we were all eating together, the radio announced that a missile had landed in the West Bank. The Israelis all spontaneously cheered, until they realised what they themselves had been saying ten minutes before; silence fell. How easy it is deny ordinary human emotions to the other.

'Peace' in the Gulf came with its promise of overall resolution in the Middle East: there would be regional disarmament and the exclusion of all weapons of mass destruction from the area. These were hypocritical parts of the UN resolution which there was never any intention to attempt. The Madrid talks followed, and then Oslo, with the high hope that things would move forward to a reasonable fulfilment of UN resolutions. What has happened since has been depressing—increased and massive expropriation of land, settlement and road-building, closures for goods and people, and economic disaster for most Palestinians, with their average income going down sharply, being now less than a tenth of that of the Israelis. There have certainly been some gains—less physical confrontation and fewer deaths and disablements, and there has been a growing recognition among many that Palestinians exist—it is possible to use the word 'Palestinians' in Israel now. There is a long, long way to go. In the end there can only be two possibilities, but neither seems possible in the short run. Either there will be two states, Israel and Palestine, both viable and in control of their agreed borders—that is far from being on offer. Or, there will be in effect one state—but it is unthinkable that one state could continue with roughly half the people able to travel, to buy and sell, to build and to enjoy other rights, while the other half is unable to.

Under pressure to clarify where I stand, and why, I found particularly helpful, belonging as I do to a Reformed and biblical tradition, firstly, Colin Chapman's, *Whose Promised Land?*, and later Peter Walker's, *Jesus and the Holy City*. Michael Prior's searching criticism of the way biblical material has been used is invigorating (*The Bible and Colonialism*, and *Zionism and the State of Israel*). Miroslav Volf's *Exclusion and Embrace,* although it does not deal with the Israeli-Palestinian issues, contains most important insights into the questions of justice, identity, and the way of peace and reconciliation. As for God's particular relationship with the Jewish people, I am sure that it implies respect for the God-given particularity of other peoples as well.

The Church in the Middle East faces great difficulties and threats to its continued presence, which is so vital both for the region, and, I believe, for the world. It will survive, given strength by the endurance of its faith and its tradition. But does it try to find its place in the present power system, which is more or less holding for the present in the region, and which may produce an unequal and temporary agreement between Israel and the Palestinian Authority? If it does this at a time when the only potent opposition to the present order is the more extreme Islamic one, it could help lead to a deeper religious conflict. Does it risk the dangers of unpopularity with the powers of the present order by embracing more of a liberation theology? At any rate, I hope that it may be able to build up, in partnership with many in Islam, the institutions of a civic society on lines which may not follow those of the West exactly. I hope, too, that the West may not place obstacles in the path, a hope that is not easy to sustain, given that in the Middle East the West has never encouraged democracy, human rights or the observance of international law, but, instead, has offered protection to any leader who will repress any opposition that might harm its interests.

There is now less myth and more history concerning the founding of the State of Israel, and I have become more critical of Zionism than I was, of its very basis now, as well of the way in which it has been put into effect. I find it difficult to see how you can separate the two, and am not sure if its purpose could ever have been fulfilled without gross injustice. Given the time and circumstances of the growth of the idea it may not be for the like of me to condemn it. At any rate, Israel is a fact, and it cannot and will not be undone. I hope that there may be among Jews a reappraisal of the future of Israel and its place in the continuing story of the Jewish people, and I have been impressed by the thinking of Professor Marc Ellis with his criticism of European Christian domination, and his perception that Jews through Zionism have turned from being with the disadvantaged, to making an alliance with those who oppressed them in the past and who go on oppressing. Certainly Christian-Jewish dialogue could be harmful unless it includes oppressed people.

Benjamin Beit-Hallahmi in *Original Sins* notes how Zionism has failed to the extent that the majority of Jews in the diaspora have always chosen to go elsewhere than to Israel, if they had the choice. He goes on to say, 'We might claim that Zionism has not met two of its three challenges. It has not succeeded in creating an alliance with either the Jewish people, those it was trying to save, or in reaching an accommodation with Arab West Asia, into which it was projecting itself. The only complete success of political Zionism was in creating an alliance with Western world powers' (Beit Hallahmi 1992: 204). We in the West do have a responsibility to reappraise our attitudes and policies towards both Israel and the Islamic world; particularly the Churches have to do so, for it was Christian opinion which to a great extent underlay these attitudes and policies.

Since returning to the United Kingdom I have been acting as 'focal person' of the Middle East Forum of the Churches' Commission on Mission, which is part of Churches Together in Britain and Ireland. I have also been involved in forming the Scottish Palestinian Forum, bringing together different organisations and individuals concerned with Palestinian issues and have kept up my interest in promoting alternative tourism in Palestine and Israel.

WOMEN'S OCCUPATION:
JUST TRADING IN THE HOLY LAND
Carol Morton

Friendly ghosts of times past have recently been haunting my days and nights, unexpectedly surfacing into consciousness as and when they pleased—an outcome of my having been invited to contribute to this volume. Once familiar or loved faces smile through their pain, tempting me to recall that previous moment when our lives intersected and stories were shared. Those stories gradually wove themselves into a strong fabric which clothed and shielded me from future accusations of too great emotional involvement with Palestinian people and issues, and from the rebuffs of other Christians whose temperament was of a more Zionist persuasion. Recounting these stories and recording the situations I witnessed will constitute the greater part of my contribution to this volume.

In the summer of 1988 my husband Colin was appointed by the Church of Scotland to be minister of St Andrew's Church and director of the Hospice. I resigned my work as Scottish Regional Adviser for Traidcraft, a UK Christian fair trade organisation, and went along for the ride, which as it turned out, lasted nine and a half years. My work had been concerned with issues of justice in trade, women's development, income generating projects; my responsibilities included recruiting volunteers, providing educational and practical support and managing a small shop.

My limited knowledge of the situation of Palestinians in the West Bank and Gaza led me to believe that there might be an opportunity to do similar marketing work in Jerusalem. The extent to which this proved not only to be possible but also to fill a real need for co-operative and self-help income generating projects in the West Bank, Gaza and Israel could not have been anticipated at the time. The marketing work culminated in the establishment of a non-profit-making company, Sunbula, which was granted *amouta* (charity) status in Israeli law in 1996 and became a member of the International Federation of Alternative Trade.

Our only previous visit to the land was in April 1985 to a kibbutz in Galilee, where we helped celebrate the twenty-first birthday of our daughter Lucy, volunteering there. We knew little about local Christians, and the Church of Scotland centres we visited in Jerusalem and Tiberias were not directing their guests towards any fuller understanding of the situation or contact with the indigenous Christian community. We did see Palestinians used as cheap labour in the kibbutz, and knew that much of the idealism and work ethic of the early movement had burnt out.

We moved into the manse of St Andrew's in July 1988, six months into the *Intifada*. While I knew there were historic events in 1948 and 1967 which were at the base of the current uprising, I had little in-depth knowledge of the circumstances in which Palestinians were living in the West Bank and Gaza, or of the various forms of discrimination suffered by those living in Israel. As for Jews, I had grown up with them in Massachusetts, hardly noticing them in their assimilated state. Zionism? Probably I had lingering visual images, having seen the film *Exodus* and read the book. A steep learning curve is the usual description for what followed.

Two of the books I read early on were *The Third Way* by Raja Shehadeh, and Raymonda Tawil's *My Home My Prison*. Both were centred around life in Ramallah and dealt with events leading up to the explosive situation, which needed for ignition only the spark provided by the incident in Gaza, which inflamed the Strip and began years of uprising, which became known as the *Intifada*. Shehadeh detailed the Palestinians' stance of *Samud*—being steadfast and persevering despite intolerable pressures. Palestinians must stop leaving the land. It was the beginnings of my appreciation of the value placed by Palestinians on land and place, familiar development issues but here intensified and twisted. Bells rang—'land is life' postcards for Australian Aborigines; a craft project for Bihari refugees in the slums of Dhaka visited during a study tour to Bangladesh in the early 90s.

Raymonda Tawil's story told of the way Palestinian society had been fragmented by repressive policies by which, for instance, there could be no meetings with more than a few men present. Institutions had been closed, men deported. Because of her political activity organising women to do things men were prohibited from doing, she eventually was issued with orders confining her for long periods to her home. Women's roles were to continue to change dramatically in the following years, as the national demand necessitated. The two issues raised in these books, land and women's development, dominated my thoughts and work in the next ten years.

Colin's induction took place in September 1988. St Andrew's lies just over the Green Line in West Jerusalem. While life went on as usual in the Western part of the city, those in the East were staging daily strikes at the command of the leadership of the *Intifada*. All shops and businesses closed daily at 1 p.m., and often whole days in addition if there were some particular protest, or the commemoration of a martyr, or some violent incident.

Some of the parishioners were Palestinians, having been cut off in 1948 from their own churches by the wall bisecting the city. By 1967, when it became possible again to cross the city, they had become comfortable at St Andrew's and continued worshipping in a West Jerusalem Presbyterian climate. Rizek Abusharr was our Session Clerk. In 1948, as the Jewish forces overran the city, he had sheltered in a Jerusalem convent for six months, three of them in total hiding— a mini Anne Frank story in reverse. He and Alice, his wife, are two of the few Palestinians who still live in their home in West Jerusalem; their families did not flee the city as so many did. Friends in Bethlehem remember leaving their home in Jerusalem, taking the key and thinking they would be back in a few days. Fifty years later they are still in Bethlehem. For them the 'Peace Process' means loss of any right to return. They need permits to enter the city of their birth; if permitted, they cannot drive cars as now virtually no private West Bank or Gaza vehicle is permitted through checkpoints.

The Palestinian staff at St Andrew's told of the daily humiliations, children denied education, arrested, tortured. All schools including universities had been closed by the Occupation forces and remained closed for up to three years. Underground efforts tried to compensate for the worst effects on the students. The eventual problems on reopening, for instance trying at beginners' level to accommodate the needs of those who had just started but had their schooling interrupted, topped by two years' worth of five-year-olds who had never had the chance to start formal schooling, was an almost impossible task.

During the reception following Colin's induction to St Andrew's I chatted with one of the church elders. Dave at that time worked with the Co-operative Development Project, funded by US AID to encourage the development of co-operatives in the West Bank and Gaza. When I mentioned my previous work, he said that the most pressing problem for women's co-operatives at that time was that of marketing. Cupboards were crammed full of heavily embroidered items. Projects were located in areas of political conflict. Marketing had often depended on bazaars and an 'old girls' network' both local and abroad; but the level of violence, together with the demand to close early every day, meant stocks were not moving. Certainly no foreigners or tourists would be able to travel in these areas, much less find the entrance which, if it had any sign, would be written in Arabic. Many of the products being made were not of the quality Westerners would buy, nor suitable for their tastes. Product codes and labels were non-existent. Dave promised to introduce me to a few co-ops.

Shortly after that we met with Doris Salah, a strong, articulate Palestinian refugee who heads the YWCA (the Y) in East Jerusalem. The Federation of Charitable Associations in East Jerusalem, to which the Y and 105 other societies belonged, had been closed down for a year on 28 August. She complained, 'Why should Palestinians pay the price for what the Germans did to the Jews?' With her we went to see the Y's work in Jalazoun Refugee Camp, north of Ramallah. We were welcomed into houses with rooms punitively sealed, and saw others entirely demolished. In the home of a camp resident we asked how things were this year compared to last. A young mother replied that this year it was much worse. 'Last year they beat only the men; this year they beat women and children too. Last year we had a home. This year the army blew it up and we went to live with my uncle. Now his house was blown up too.' Palestinian costume dolls and nativity scenes made at the Y centre in Jalazoun were soon sold at St Andrew's.

There followed visits to Kalandia Camp Co-operative and the Holy Land Handicraft Co-operative Ltd., Beit Sahour, with Dave. Subsequently much of my time was spent driving the church car, with its yellow number plates, into Occupied East Jerusalem and the 'hostile' blue plate country of the West Bank. Several times the car was stoned, windows broken, shards of glass sprinkled over the whole of the inside. This seemed a small though uncomfortable price to pay compared to that being exacted from the people I visited.

Soon there were contacts with Surif Co-operative (through Mennonite Central Committee), Al-Shurooq School for the Blind, Bethlehem Arab Society for the Physically Handicapped (BASH) and the UNRWA camps in Gaza. Stock levels soared and we commandeered a cupboard in the library and staged a small bazaar in November 1988. The next year we converted the men's toilet (a space 2 x 3 m.) into an area with selling and storage space, with a cash/desk in a corner at the back. After church, whenever a group phoned, or even when more than three customers came into the shop we had to decamp and put stock on tables in the entrance hall. The word spread and people came: foreigners and Jews to learn and talk about what was happening in the West Bank and Gaza, Palestinians to buy bits of their own culture as they could no longer travel to the producers.

Then the crunch came: there was no space to display carpets from an Oxfam-funded income-generating project for women in Lekiya, near Beersheba. The Israeli government has a policy of separating the Bedouin from their land and concentrating them in seven townships where there is very little employment. Women lost what status they had working on the land and few receive education past primary school. Earning income from spinning, dyeing and weaving brought income, with it status and perhaps a chance for their daughters to receive a better education. So we kept the carpets, and, our enterprise, after five years in the men's loo, progressed to the library.

Craftaid, as it became known, also sold selected books and cards. In 1989 we were the only place in West Jerusalem which stocked al Haq's courageous first annual report, *Punishing a Nation: Human Rights Violations During the Palestinian Uprising December 1987—December 1988.* This volume substantiated and codified all the stories I had been hearing as it documented the increase in the punishments Palestinians had already been suffering for years under the Occupation. Chapters include:

> Use of Physical Force (204 deaths in the West Bank
>   alone during the first year of the *Intifada*),
> Obstruction of Medical Treatment
> Settler Provocation and the Use of Excessive Force
> Administrative Methods (deportation, detention, house
>   demolition)
> Curfews and Other Forms of Isolation
> The Administration of Justice
> Economic Sanctions
> Repression of Education
> Repression of Organisational Activity
>   (Al Haq 1989: i-v)

Another book we stocked was *Children of Bethlehem* (1989) by Patrick White, Brother Patrick of Bethlehem University, which had been closed in 1987. From October 1988 the closure was intensified—only the resident Brothers, some of the Sisters and essential maintenance staff were allowed on the property. Patrick became a regular visitor, delivering stocks of the Christmas cards he had had printed from his remarkable series of watercolours depicting

Bethlehem and surrounding areas. Our advance order and payment had to some extent enabled the project to go ahead. Each visit he seemed more profoundly sad. Sometimes we just sat in that back corner of the 'shop' and looked at each other. Finding it impossible to articulate ever more gruesome tales, the only adequate communication seemed the tears which simply welled up in our eyes. Daily more horrific stories were coming to us both, but I was quite sheltered in my West Jerusalem comfort; he lived it first hand:

> ... yesterday when I was walking through New Gate in the Old City of Jerusalem ... I witnessed the appalling treatment the young male Palestinians suffer. Green beret Border Police, a tough element in the Israeli security forces, were stationed by the gate, interrogating young Palestinian men, taking their identity cards and lining them up against the wall. They were then threatening the men and taking them one by one into the small toilet in the wall just to the left of the gate. Here, and I stood and witnessed it, they beat the Arabs with their fists and batons. I had known this was going on for some time but had never actually witnessed it (White 1989: 111-12).[1]

'Settlement Tours' were being organised in the late 80s by Kathy Bergen who worked for MCC. One day Kathy drove us north, east and south, showing how the city of Jerusalem was gradually being cut off from the surrounding areas of Palestinian population by modern suburban housing schemes termed 'settlements'. The western side of Jerusalem is all part of the State of Israel and so completes

---

[1] An interesting note to this comes from a conversation with a Californian Jewish woman who was staying at St Andrew's in 1991 researching conflict resolution programmes. She also was working with, amongst others, members of the green beret police. They harboured deep resentment at being given all the dirty jobs to do, especially since they were paid less than other police units.

the ring around the city. Kathy ended her tour at Mohanna's dilapidated bus on the edge of Gilo, the large settlement to the south of Jerusalem. Mohanna and his aged father lived with no amenities, refusing to leave the scrap left of their land after their home had been destroyed during the building of Gilo. He showed us his letter from Jerusalem Mayor Teddy Kollek, granting him compensation which had never come. Mohanna was a tailor and our growing craft outlet gave him some business making up cushion covers from pieces of embroidery from Gaza.

Kathy pointed out to us other sources of Palestinian discontent and resentment. These did not always have Israeli origins. She maintained that expatriates working for some of the growing number of international NGOs and UN organisations were paid, in salary and benefits, ten times what local Palestinians' salaries were. They exacerbated the serious shortage of housing in Jerusalem, causing rents to skyrocket for local people. The role of NGOs in Palestinian society and nation building deserves deep analysis at some future point. Certainly one could detect areas where definite dependencies were being created and project funding paid salaries of citizens of the donor country, rather than those of the local population. Although expatriates fulfilled the role of travelling through checkpoints and roadblocks, critical to communication and project completion, this too could also be resented by Palestinians unable to travel in their own land.

My first of many trips to Gaza was with Elizabeth Tykal-Barnhart. Working with the Middle East Council of Churches, she took minibus loads full of people down the Tel Aviv highway, south at Latroun and through the lands where cacti still delineate boundaries of some of the 418 Palestinian villages destroyed in 1948. We were met at the Eretz checkpoint by staff from the Near East Council of Churches, and given a tour of their premises, and of some of the refugee camps, and of parts of Gaza City. Costa Dabbagh, head of the Near East Council of Churches, told us of the conditions in Gaza. During and after the 1948 war, 200,000 refugees had fled to Gaza, inundating the 80,000 residents. Forty (now fifty) years later the refugee number had risen to about 600,000, over half of them living in one of the eight camps, making Gaza vie with Bangladesh for the title of the most densely populated area on the earth. We saw the huge pool of sewage in Jabalya Camp, contiguous with Gaza City itself.

Two memories from later visits to Gaza stand out. In about 1991, I was leading a group on a fact-finding tour. We were travelling in a minibus belonging to the United Nations Relief and Works Agency (UNRWA) through Beach Camp (Shati), when suddenly we heard rapid repeating gunfire and loud sirens. Our driver speeded up, driving even more erratically than he had already been when trying to negotiate the pot-hole ridden muddy lanes which pass for streets in that camp. Detouring to avoid passing by the spot where an Israeli soldier was taking pot shots from the roof of one of the camp houses, we swerved around a corner into a more open area. Suddenly the driver screeched to a halt as a young masked Palestinian ran in front of the van, put up his arms signalling us to stop. Another youth ran up and threw open the side door of the minibus, where I was sitting, and indicated I should get out or move over. Being in charge of the safety of those on this vehicle, I hesitated, and was just beginning to panic, when I saw the reason for this hijacking of our bus. Two other masked men ran up from behind, carrying a small girl with blood streaming down her face. She had been shot by a rubber bullet, the kind we had seen at Ahli Arab Hospital on our first Gaza visit. The matron had pointed out that the innocent sounding missile was in fact a thin coating of rubber over a good-sized metal ball. We were told they were particularly aimed at the eyes of children, and, in fact, through the years we saw several blinded in this way. Our driver was directed to take the girl and the lad holding her to the UNRWA clinic in the camp, which we swiftly did, and then left the scene.

Another Gaza visit was made in 1990, with an extremely improbable group of four women driven in the foreign registered car of Ingunn, a Norwegian social worker attached to BASH. She needed to make some contacts with the Early Childhood Resources Center in Bureij Camp. I had made arrangements to meet the director of the

ECRC, Mary Khaas, and talk about marketing of children's toys being made in a related project employing Gaza women, working on machines only ever previously worked by men. An American/Israeli Jewish woman, Judy, who was a strong supporter of *Shalom Achshav* (Peace Now), begged to come and see Gaza for herself, wanting to speak to whomever she could to say there were other kinds of Israelis than the ones they see daily as Occupation forces. A fourth, Najla, a Beit Sahour Palestinian who worked at St Andrew's, pleaded to come, having never been to this area only about sixty miles from her home. At that time very occasionally West Bank Palestinians were allowed into Gaza if they were accompanied by foreigners. I have a photograph of Ingunn, Najla and Judy in the centre, looking at a few of the books which were in shelves entirely covering the wall of a deserted classroom with a cement floor. Two-thirds of the shelves are empty and a few books and pamphlets struggle to support each other in the bays of the remaining shelves. The staff were proud of this first centre in Gaza and wanted to resource other areas of the Strip.

Mary was fierce with Judy who approached her in the kindest way possible, talking about Peace Now. Mary rounded on her and shouted, 'Don't come back here until every one of you peaceniks refuses to serve in Gaza. You come wiping my tears away with one hand and stab me in the back with the other!' Mary was referring to the *Yesh G'vul* ('There is a Limit') movement of Israeli soldiers who refuse to serve in the Occupied West Bank and Gaza. Many have consequently been imprisoned. Others believe that by serving in these places one might be able to be a positive influence and persuade other soldiers to behave in a more humane manner.

Mary, a Quaker, had returned from Haifa to Gaza where her family had land, preferring to witness there under Occupation. She had seen how impossible it is to accomplish this ideal, given peer pressure and crowd mentality. Her stories that day were vivid. In the past she had seen Israelis in helicopters dropping rubble on crowds of people, including a funeral procession; now it had progressed to snipers aiming and shooting from above at innocent people below. She had seen a soldier on a street corner with a whip, applying it indiscriminately to passers-by. Her grandchildren had nightmares and were bedwetting because of repeated intrusions in the middle of the night by soldiers requiring the whole household to line up on the street for no reason, then ransacking the house. During the whole *Intifada* Gaza was under curfew every night from sundown to sunrise, with large families entombed in small stifling rooms, tensions mounting and domestic violence breeding.

The woman I saw most in Gaza was Lilian, Women's Programme Officer at UNRWA. Through her we marketed the embroidery done by women in camps and centres throughout the Strip. She told us that in fact had we not ordered consistently from their shop in the difficult times before, during and after the Gulf War in 1990, the project would have closed because it was not covering its costs. Now about 400 women earn income through this means. On one occasion we visited a group embroidering, sitting around a circle on the veranda of a building in Dir al-Balah camp centre. Two of the older women, sisters, had never married, which they explained meant they had no children to support them in their old age, so were embroidering for income. Another was a Muslim (Gaza is 99 percent Muslim, 1 percent Christian) whose husband had divorced her to take another wife because she had produced three daughters and no sons. She had no other way of earning money. The youngest embroiderer, a girl of about eleven, was an orphan and was learning the craft as the only way of earning any money in her spare time.

The instructress brought us into the adjoining room to show us evidence of the previous evening's visit of the Israeli army (IDF). Sewing machines, old fashioned and non-electric to be sure, but the only means for women to learn to sew and make basic garments for their families, had been pushed over and trashed by the army. What possible excuse could there be for this? No excuse, no reason is necessary. I asked if there was not some complaint system: after all, this was United Nations property. She replied that they fill out forms and submit them; they receive an acknowledgement but never any compensation.

As happens with so many Palestinian families, particularly Christian, Lilian's two sons now lived abroad. They had gone to America to study, married American girls and settled in the States. Both she and Mary Khass, her friend, in fact, had the means to leave Gaza did they so wish, and I asked them if they considered it. They both looked at me and smiled: 'Why would we leave? Gaza is like our baby. If your baby is sick you don't leave it.' In the academic world, Bernard Sabella of Bethlehem University was alerting people to this decimation of the Christian population which is still continuing.

Palestinians have a disarming way of personalising a place, showing how intimately connected they are with it. Hala Sakakini, whose *Jerusalem and I: A Personal Record* (1990) tells the story of the Israeli conquest of the Katamon area of Jerusalem where they lived—their privations, the fierce fighting in the area, fleeing to Cairo, then in 1953 returning to settle in Ramallah. In 1967 they, with Ramallah, came under Occupation, but were able for the first time in nineteen years to visit their former home. 'It was a sad encounter, like meeting a dear person whom you had last seen young, healthy and well-groomed and finding that he had become old, sick and shabby. Even worse, it was like coming across a friend whose personality had undergone a drastic change and was no more the same person' (Sakakini 1990: xi). Printed at the back of the book is Hala's illuminating map, detailing what she remembered of where Palestinian families lived pre-48 in Katamon.

Living in West Jerusalem, we also had a great deal of contact with Jews, both Israeli and expatriate. Some were courageous in voicing opposition to government policies. A Canadian couple, parents of an Edinburgh friend, had made *aliyah* after 1948. They were two of the most distressed Jewish citizens whom we came to know, and they became our best Jewish friends. We felt deeply their loss when finally in 1993, losing hope in any justice ever coming in the land, they returned to Canada for their later retirement years. They told of how they had been brought up in Jewish youth movements, had come to Israel after the war in order to help build up the state for the returning victims of the Holocaust. They shared with us their disillusionment with what they felt the Jewish state had become, and how Jews had become the perpetrators of persecution and had institutionalised evil. Their son had been arrested for his work with an alternative news agency. Our compulsive reading of the English weekly version of the Arabic language newspaper, *Al-Fajr,* began from their recommendation.

Another Jewish friend, the lawyer Lynda Brayer, a convert to Roman Catholicism, worked in the human rights area. She felt that particular cases of blatant injustice—imprisonment, torture, land seizure, house demolition, etc., should be challenged through the court system. Some redress would come; justice must triumph. She founded the Society of St Yves to pursue this work. Sadly, through the years of battle in court, Lynda came to believe that there was in fact no justice to be had through this channel, it being often impossible even to obtain the basic details of a case because of the security blackout.

Other Jews also gave us hope. One was Marc Ellis with his *Towards a Jewish Theology of Liberation* (1989). I first heard him in the early 90s addressing a packed audience of women at the YWCA. The room was electric when he actually advocated that Israel acknowledge the injustice it had done to Palestinians and ask forgiveness. Women in Black were demonstrating every Friday at 1 p.m. in French Square, a busy intersection in the heart of West Jerusalem. They mourned not only for the Palestinians, but also for the Jews: occupation defiles the occupier even more than the occupied. Michael and Shulamit, both active in the Association for Civil Rights in Israel, stood beside us in Silwan when settlers occupied homes in this Palestinian village just outside the Old City. Organisations like *B'tselem* issued hard-hitting reports which we sold. But the Occupation went on and still goes on.

A major consequence of the Israeli policies for Palestinian society was outlined for me one day shortly after the Gulf War. I was working at the desk in the back of the shop when a Scandinavian social worker came in. She had been doing a follow-up study on a previous project in Bethlehem area villages and camps. Previously she had witnessed a vertical, generational disintegration of Palestinian society, often because of the humiliation of their elders in front of the young. Their obvious impotence caused lack of respect by the young, whereas traditional Palestinian society had honoured elders. Now, however, she said that something more insidious was happening. During imprisonment, under torture, some youths would break and become informers; some became drug dependent. No one knew who had turned collaborator, and trust between peers evaporated. Community life and solidarity suffered sometimes irreparably; the culture of individual survival was taking over. Hanna, the cook at St Andrew's, reinforced this when he came in very dejected one day. He said the poverty of the people had led to thieving from old widows. He had never seen this before in Palestinian society, and was desolate.

For nine and a half years I had the amazing privilege of working with Palestinians who were struggling for survival—their own personal survival, that of their nation and of their land. St Andrew's' staff jested that I had earned the right to have a *hawiyyah*, or identity card. Issued by the Israelis, it is essential for the most basic of human activity. Lose it, or have it confiscated at your peril.

Through listening and witnessing I came to know what others learn through research or study. How could a Western Christian not be affected by these daily encounters with the pain—and often the joy—of a people who, Muslim or Christian, had a living faith of *Allah karim*—God is generous. To those who reject Jewish and Palestinian liberation theology, especially to Zionist Christians, I can only say, 'Your God is Too Small'. The cries of the oppressed will indeed be heard. Their living faith encourages us to unite with Christian, Muslim and Jew who struggle toward the only kind of peace which will endure— that based on justice.

Since returning to Scotland in December 1997 I have been involved in the Scottish Palestinian Forum as secretary and treasurer and also continue marketing informally the Palestinian crafts which taught me so much of life in Palestine.

STUDYING THE BIBLE
IN THE HOLY LAND
Michael Prior, C.M.

As well as being an absorbing academic pursuit, my engagement with the Holy Land has had something of the quality of a moral imperative. I would have been spared some pain had Providence not dictated that significant portions of my postgraduate biblical studies be undertaken in the Land of the Bible. Although the focus of my engagement was 'the biblical past' I could not avoid the modern social context of the region. As a result, my studying the Bible in the Land of the Bible provoked perspectives that scarcely would have arisen elsewhere.

As a boy and young man, politics began and ended in Ireland, an Ireland obsessed with England. It was much later that I recognised that the history I absorbed so readily had been fabricated by the new nationalist historiographers, who refracted the totality of Ireland's history through the lens of 19th-century European nationalisms. Although my Catholic culture also cherished St Patrick and the saints and scholars after him, the real heroes of Ireland's history were those who challenged British colonialism in Ireland. I had no interest in the politics of any other region—except that I knew that Communism, wherever, was wrong. Anyhow, the priesthood beckoned.

The intensive training programme in spirituality within the Vincentian Community, which I joined in 1960, prided itself on its detachment from 'secular affairs'. Already in 17th-century France, our founder, St Vincent de Paul, being aware of the divisiveness of political preferences among his disciples in different nation states, cautioned against engaging in 'the affairs of princes'. In any case, much of my time was taken up with the study of experimental physics and mathematics: indeed, while Krushchev's missiles were speeding to Cuba on the showdown day in 1961, I was working in the laboratory in University College, Dublin.

In the seminary, piety and theology were portrayed as being of a somewhat metahistorical order, above any set of particular social or political circumstances. However, I was excited by Pope Paul VI's encyclical *Populorum Progressio*, with its bold analysis of contemporary polity, its criticism of nationalism, and its advocacy of a transnational world-order. While Liberation Theology was gestating in the womb of Latin America, what passed for a distinctive Irish theology operated within a static ideological framework, reposing in the jaded marriage between a triumphalist and self-assured Irish Catholicism and a revolutionary nationalism which by then had become totally 'routinised'. All the while, social unrest was simmering in 'the Six Counties' of Northern Ireland, but I had not been 'up north' up to that time.

The Six-Day War

Prior to the 5-11 June 1967 war, I had no particular interest in the State of Israel, other than an envious admiration for Jews having constructed a nation state and restored a national language. In addition to stimulating my first curiosity in the Israeli-Arab conflict, Israel's conquest of the West Bank, the Golan Heights, the Gaza Strip and Sinai brought me 'face to face', via TV, with wider, international political realities. I recall rushing through the seminary supper each evening to see how diminutive, innocent Israel was faring against its rapacious Arab predators. All my sources of information projected it as a classic conflict between virtuous David and despicable Goliath. The startling, speedy, and comprehensive victory of diminutive Israel produced surges of delight in me. And I had no reason to question the mellifluous mendacity of Abba Eban at the United Nations, delivered in that urbanity and self-assurance characteristic of Western diplomats, however fraudulent, claiming that Israel was an innocent victim of Egyptian aggression.

Later that summer in London, I was intrigued by billboards in Golders Green, with quotations from the Hebrew prophets, assuring readers that those who trusted in biblical prophecy could not be surprised by Israel's victory. Up to then I had never encountered an association between contemporary events and biblical prophecy. Biblical prophecy, the academy insisted, related to the period of the prophet, and was not about predicting the future. The prophets were 'forth-tellers' for God, rather than foretellers of future events. I was intrigued that others thought differently.

I was to learn later, in the 1980s and 1990s, that the 1967 War inaugurated a new phase in the Zionist conquest of Mandated Palestine, one which brought theological assertions and biblical interpretations to the very heart of the ideology which propelled the Israeli conquest and set the pattern for Jewish settlement. After two more years of theology, ordination, and three years of postgraduate biblical studies, I made my first visit to Israel-Palestine at Easter 1972, with a party of postgraduate students from the Pontifical Biblical Institute, Rome.

Seeing and believing

Although my visit was concerned exclusively with the archaeological remains of ancient civilisations, it also provided the first challenge to my favourable predispositions towards Israel. I was disturbed by the ubiquitous signs of the oppression of the Arabs, whom later I learnt to call Palestinians. I was witnessing some kind of 'institutionalised oppression'—I cannot recall whether 'apartheid' was part of my vocabulary at the time. The experience must have been profound since, when the Yom Kippur War broke out in October 1973, my support for Israel did not match my enthusiasm of 1967. I had no particular interest in the area for the remainder of the 1970s, but I recall watching on TV the visit of Egypt's President Sadat to the Israeli Knesset in November 1977, an initiative which would culminate in a formal peace agreement in 1979. Things changed for me in the 1980s.

In 1981 I went with a party from my university to visit Bir Zeit University in the Israeli-occupied West Bank. Because the campus was closed by the military just before our arrival, carefully planned programmes had to yield to Palestinian '*ad hoc*-ery'. Bir Zeit put a bus at our disposal, and a mixed group of Palestinian and British students constituted a university on wheels. I was profoundly shocked when I began to see from the inside the reality of land expropriation and the on-going Jewish settlement of the West Bank. I began to question the prevailing view that the Israeli occupation was for security reasons, but even with such obvious evidence I could not bring myself to abandon it.

Although I was researching the Pauline Epistles during my sabbatical year in the École Biblique in 1983-84 day-to-day life in Jerusalem sharpened my sensitivities. I was beginning to suspect that the occupation was not for security reasons, but was an expansion towards the achievement of 'Greater Israel'. One incident in particular alerted me to the religious dimension of the conflict. On a spring morning in 1984, the Voice of Israel radio reported that during the night a Jewish terrorist group had been caught in the act of attempting to blow up the Dome of the Rock and the Aqsa Mosque on the Haram al-Sharif (the Temple Mount), only a few hundred metres south of the École. Subsequently the newspapers published a picture of one of those convicted of the offence, wearing the typical dress of the religious settler movement *Gush Emunim*. He had the Book of Psalms in his hand as the judge read out the verdict. That an attempted act of such enormous international and inter-faith significance sprang from religious fervour shocked me. Settler Jews performed other acts of terror during that year, and the name of the overtly racist Rabbi Meir Kahane was seldom off the headlines, further underlining the link between aggressive settlement activity and biblical piety.

I can date to that period also voicing my first displeasure at my perception that the land traditions of the Bible appeared to mandate the genocide of the indigenes of 'Canaan'. At the end of his public lecture in Tantur, I suggested to Marc Ellis, a young Jewish theologian who was developing a Jewish Theology of Liberation with strong dependence on the Hebrew Prophets (see Ellis 1987), that it would be no more difficult to construct a Theology of Oppression on the basis of other biblical traditions, especially those dealing with Israelite origins that demanded the destruction of other peoples.

I had more pressing academic demands when I returned to London after my sabbatical, but I did record some reflections on my year in the journal of the Catholic Biblical Association of Great Britain, of which I was then editor (Prior 1984). Soon after his visit to Palestine in the autumn of 1984, Duncan Macpherson told me of the plea of Abuna Elias Chacour to Christian pilgrims from the West to meet the Christian communities, 'the living stones' of the land, and not be satisfied with the 'dead stones' of archaeological sites. Soon a group of interested people in London established the ecumenical trust, *Living Stones*, which promotes links between Christians in Britain and the Holy Land, and appointed me chairman. In 1985 I co-led a study tour to Israel and the Occupied Territories, and led a group of priests on a 'Retreat through Pilgrimage' in 1987 (Prior 1989) and made other visits in 1990 and 1991.

Earlier in 1991, I had participated in an International Peace Walk from Jerusalem to Amman, and although I did not reach the destination, I gained the acquaintance of several groups of Israeli soldiers and police, enjoyed detention twice, and faced what appeared to be an inevitable spell in prison. Officially, my crime, in the first instance, was to have trespassed into 'a closed military zone' on the outskirts of Ramallah, and in the second, to have refused to leave a similarly designated area on the way from Taybeh to Jericho. The real purpose of such designations was to halt the silent walk of some thirty 'peaceniks' from about fifteen countries. Our presence was having a decidedly energising effect on the Palestinians, who did not dare protest so forthrightly. My singing of Psalm 119 (118) in my *bel canto* Irish-accented Hebrew, a favourite of Jews at Passover, had an obviously disturbing effect on the young soldiers detaining us. Formal arrest, and several hours interrogation in Jericho followed. The peace walk experience illustrated to me how easily the noble discourse of jurisprudence, designed to protect the vulnerable, can legitimise oppression.

It took some time for my experiences to acquire an ideological framework. Gradually I read more of the modern history of the region. In addition to bringing a university group in 1992, I spent August in the École Biblique, and while there interviewed prominent Palestinians, including the Latin Patriarch of Jerusalem, Michel Sabbah, the Greek Orthodox Archbishop Timotheos, the Anglican Bishop Samir Kafity, Canon Naim Ateek, and the Vice-President of Bir Zeit University, Dr Gabi Baramki.

I made three visits in 1993, one at Easter to prepare the Cumberland Lodge Conference on Christians in the Holy Land (see Prior and Taylor 1994), one for study in August, and the third to bring a group of students. Although my academic concentration in that period was on the scene of Jesus in the synagogue in Nazareth (Luke 4.16-30), my growing unease about the link between biblical spirituality and oppression stimulated me to examine the land traditions of the Bible, and so I began to read the narrative systematically with that theme in mind. Already I had written a number of articles on the Holy Land (Prior 1990; 1992; 1993a; 1993b; 1993c; 1994). With my manuscript on Luke 4.16-30 completed on 22 July 1994 (see Prior 1995a), I could give my whole attention to the land traditions of the Bible in the École Biblique in August.

Yahweh and ethnic cleansing

What struck me most about the biblical narrative was that the divine promise of land was integrally linked with the mandate to exterminate the indigenous peoples, and I had to wrestle with my perception that those traditions were inherently oppressive and morally reprehensible.[1]

---

[1] See, for example, Exodus 3.8; 6.2-4; 23.23-33; 33.1-3; 34.11-15; Numbers 21.1-3, 21-35; 31; 33.50-56; Deuteronomy 2.33-34; 3.3; 7.1-11; 9.1-5; 20.16-18; Joshua 6.21-27; 8.2, 19-29; 9-11; Psalm 78:54-55; 80.8; 105.43-44.

Even the Exodus narrative was problematic. While it portrays Yahweh as having compassion on the misery of his people, and as willing to deliver them from the Egyptians, and bring them to a land flowing with milk and honey (Exodus 3.7-8), that was only part of the picture. Although the reading of Exodus 3, both in the Christian liturgy and in the classical texts of liberation theologies, halts abruptly in the middle of v. 8 at the description of the land as one 'flowing with milk and honey', the biblical text itself continues, 'to the country of the Canaanites, the Hittites, the Amorites, the Perizzites, the Hivites, and the Jebusites'. Manifestly, the promised land, flowing with milk and honey, had no lack of indigenous peoples, and, according to the narrative, would soon flow with blood.

After the King of Heshbon refused passage to the Israelites, Yahweh gave him over to the Israelites who captured and utterly destroyed all the cities, killing all the men, women, and children (Deuteronomy 2.33-34). The fate of the King of Bashan was no better (3.3). Yahweh's role was central:

> When Yahweh your God brings you into the land that you are about to enter and occupy, and he clears away many nations before you—the Hittites, the Girgashites, the Amorites, the Canaanites, the Perizzites, the Hivites ... and when Yahweh your God gives them over to you ... you must utterly destroy them ... Show them no mercy ... For you are a people holy to Yahweh your God; Yahweh your God has chosen you out of all the peoples on earth to be his people, his treasured possession (Deuteronomy 7.1-11; see also 9.1-5; 11.8-9, 23, 31-32).

In the rules for the conduct of war, if a besieged town did not surrender, the Israelites should kill all its males, and take as booty the women, children, livestock, and everything else in the town (Deuteronomy 20.11-14). It was some shock to realise that the narrative presents 'ethnic cleansing' as not only legitimate, but as required by the divinity (20.16-18). The book ends with Moses' sight of the promised land before he dies (34.1-3). Although Moses was unequalled in his deeds, he left a worthy successor, Joshua, who, after Moses had lain his hands on him, was full of the spirit of wisdom (34.4-12). So much for the preparation for entry into the Promised Land.

The first part of the Book of Joshua (2.1-12.24) describes the conquest of a few key cities, and their fate in accordance with the laws of the Holy War. Even when the Gibeonites were to be spared, the Israelite elders complained at the lapse in fidelity to the mandate to destroy all the inhabitants of the land (9.21-27). Joshua took Makkedah, utterly destroying every person in it (10.28). A similar fate befell other cities (10.29-39): everything that breathed was destroyed, as Yahweh commanded (10.40-43). Joshua utterly destroyed the inhabitants of the cities of the north as well (11.1-23). Yahweh gave to Israel all the land that he swore to their ancestors he would give them (21.43-45). The legendary achievements of Yahweh through the agencies of Moses, Aaron, and Joshua are kept before the Israelites even in their prayers: 'You brought a vine out of Egypt; you drove out the nations and planted it' (Psalm 80.8; see also Psalms 78.54-55; 105.44).

By modern standards of international law and human rights, what these biblical narratives mandate are 'war-crimes' and 'crimes against humanity'. While readers might seek refuge in the claim that the problem lies with the predispositions of the modern reader, rather than with the text itself, one could not escape so easily. One must acknowledge that much of the Torah, and the Book of Deuteronomy in particular, contains menacing ideologies, and racist, xenophobic and militaristic tendencies. The implications of the existence of dubious moral dispositions, presented as mandated by the divinity, within a book which is canonised as Sacred Scripture invited the most serious investigation. Was there a way of reading the traditions which could rescue the Bible from being a blunt instrument of oppression, and acquit God of the charge of being the Great Ethnic-Cleanser?

In that August of 1994, the École library had just received a *Festschrift* consisting of studies in Deuteronomy. In addition to articles covering the customary source, historical-critical, and literary discussions, it contained one by F E Deist, with the intriguing title, 'The Dangers of Deuteronomy', which discussed the role of that book in support of *apartheid* (Deist 1994). It dealt with the text from the perspective of its reception history, especially within the ideology of an emerging Afrikaner nationalism. During that month I also read A G Lamadrid's discussion of the role of the Bible and Christian theology in the Iberian conquest of Latin America (Lamadrid 1981). The problem, then, went beyond academic reflection on the interpretation of ancient documents.

The Bible as instrument of oppression

It was clear that some biblical narratives had contributed to the suffering of countless indigenous people. The traditions of Deuteronomy had provided intellectual and moral authority for the Iberian devastation of 'Latin America' in the late medieval period, for the Afrikaner exploitation of non-whites in southern Africa right up to the 1990s, and was continuing to do so in the ongoing Zionist ex-spoliation of the Arabs of Palestine. Not only did these narratives have the capacity to infuse exploitative tendencies in their readers, but my research was confirming how in practice they had fuelled virtually every form of militant colonialism emanating from Europe, by providing allegedly divine legitimation for Western colonisers in their zeal to implant 'outposts of progress' in 'the heart of darkness'. When I got back to England I wrote an article, 'The Bible as Instrument of Oppression', giving the three case studies of Latin America, southern Africa and Palestine (1995b; see also Prior 1995c). Apart from the surprise at seeing my photo and a synopsis of my message appearing on the *Catholic Times* there was little sign that my fifteen minutes of fame was about to descend on me. The subject, I judged, deserved a fuller investigation, but before embarking on a more substantial monograph it would be prudent to examine the situation in Old Testament scholarship.

Western scholarship and the Holy Land

Somebody must have addressed the moral question before, I presumed. Back in Jerusalem for August 1995, I realised that this was not the case. Even though Gerhard von Rad lamented in 1943 that no thorough investigation of 'the land' had been made (1966:79), no serious study of the topic was undertaken for another thirty years. But surely W D Davies' seminal studies had compensated for the neglect hitherto (1974; 1982; 1991)! Davies acknowledged later that he had written his *The Gospel and the Land* (1974) at the request of friends in Jerusalem, who just before the war in 1967 urged his support for the cause of Israel (1982: xiii). Moreover, he confessed that he wrote *The Territorial Dimensions of Judaism* (1982) under the direct impact of that war, and its updated version because of the mounting need to understand the theme in the light of events in the Middle East, culminating in the Gulf War and its aftermath (1991: xiii). I was intrigued by the frankness with which Davies publicised his hermeneutical key: 'Here I have concentrated on what in my judgement must be the beginning for an understanding of this conflict: the sympathetic attempt to comprehend the Jewish tradition' (1982: xiii-xiv).

While Davies considers 'the land' from virtually every other conceivable perspective, little attention is given to broadly moral and human rights' issues. In particular, he excludes from his concern, 'What happens when the understanding of the Promised Land in Judaism conflicts with the claims of the traditions and occupancy of its other peoples?'. He excused himself by saying that to engage that issue would demand another volume (1991: xv), without indicating his intention of embarking upon such an enterprise. I wondered whether Davies would have been equally sanguine had white, Anglo-Saxon Protestants, or even white Catholics of European provenance been among the displaced people who paid the price for the prize of

Zionism. Reflecting a somewhat elastic moral sense, Davies, although perturbed by the aftermath of the 1967 conquest, took the establishment of the State of Israel in his stride. Showing no concern for the foundational injustice done to the Palestinians in 1948, Davies wrote as if there were later a moral equivalence between the dispossessed Palestinians and the dispossessor Zionists. The rights of the rapist and the victim were finely balanced.

Walter Brueggemann's *The Land* (1977) brought me no further. While he saw land as perhaps 'the central theme' of biblical faith, he bypassed the treatment to be meted out to the indigenous inhabitants, affirming, 'What is asked is not courage to destroy enemies, but courage to keep Torah', avoiding the fact that 'keeping Torah' in this context demanded accepting its xenophobic and destructive militarism (1977: 3, 48, 60). By 1994, however, Brueggemann was less sanguine, noting that while the scholastic community had provided 'rich and suggestive studies on the "land theme" in the Bible ... they characteristically stop before they get to the hard part, contemporary issues of land in the Holy Land' (in March 1994: vii).

It was beginning to dawn on me that much biblical investigation—especially that concentration on the past which is typical of the historical-critical method—was quite indifferent to moral considerations. Indeed, it was becoming clear that the discipline of biblical studies over the last hundred years reflected the Eurocentric perspectives of virtually all Western historiography, and had contributed significantly to the oppression of native peoples. The benevolent interpretation of biblical traditions which advocate atrocities and war crimes had given solace to those bent on the exploitation of new lands at the expense of native peoples. While the behaviour of communities and nation states is complex, and is never the result of one element of motivation, there is abundant evidence that the Bible has been, and still is for some, *the idea* that *redeems the conquest of the earth* (see 1999b). This was particularly true in the case of the Arabs of Palestine, in whose country I had reached these conclusions as I studied the Bible.

By the autumn of 1995 I was well into a book on the subject. In the university mid-term in November I went to discuss with Sheffield Academic Press a draft manuscript on 'The Bible and Zionism'. Before I visited the press, however, I was pleased to celebrate Mass in St Vincent's Church. To a congregation hoping for spiritual nourishment, on the 29th Sunday (Year C), the lector read from Exodus 17.8-13:

> Then Amalek came and fought with Israel at Rephidim. Moses said to Joshua, 'Choose some men for us and go out, fight with Amalek. Tomorrow I will stand on the top of the hill with the staff of God in my hand.' So Joshua did as Moses told him, and fought with Amalek, while Moses, Aaron, and Hur went up to the top of the hill. Whenever Moses held up his hand, Israel prevailed; and whenever he lowered his hand, Amalek prevailed. But Moses' hands grew weary; so they took a stone and put it under him, and he sat on it. Aaron and Hur held up his hands, one on one side, and the other on the other side; so his hands were steady until the sun set. And Joshua defeated Amalek and his people with the sword.

The reading ended with 'This is the word of the Lord', to which the congregation replied, 'Thanks be to God'. Almost before I had time to wonder what this text could possibly mean for Sheffield Catholics before they even had their breakfasts, we had the formal response of Psalm 120, with its antiphon, 'Our help is in the name of the Lord ...' The second reading, from the Second Letter of Paul to Timothy, reminded the congregation 'how from childhood you have known the sacred writings that are able to instruct you ... All scripture is inspired by God and is useful for teaching, for reproof, for correction, and for training in righteousness' (3.14-4.2). Mercifully, the Gospel reading consisted of the narrative of the widow whose persistence in prayer wearied a certain judge (Luke 18.1-8). Being somewhat sensitive to the impact of the biblical narrative on human behaviour, I wondered whether the 'Amalekites' of Sheffield would be safe for another three years before this selection of readings would re-appear in the triennial Roman Catholic lectionary.

At Sheffield Academic Press later, the editor, apprehensive at my concentration on Zionism, persuaded me to use three case studies. The task ahead, then, would require further immersion in the histories of Latin America, South Africa, and Israel, as well as a more detailed study of the biblical narrative and its interpretation in the hands of the biblical academy.

Having had my moral being sensitised by the biblical mandate to commit genocide, I was amazed that scholars had a high esteem for the Book of Deuteronomy. Indeed, commentators conventionally assess it to be a theological book *par excellence*, and the focal point of the religious history of the Old Testament. In the 1995 Lattey Lecture in Cambridge University (14 November), Professor Norbert Lohfink argued that it provides a model of a utopian society in which there would be no poor (Lohfink 1996). In my role as the formal proposer of a vote of thanks—I was the chairperson of the Catholic Biblical Association of Great Britain—I invited him to consider whether, in the light of that book's insistence on a mandate to commit genocide, the utopian society would be possible only after the invading Israelites had wiped out the indigenous inhabitants. The protocol of the Lattey Lecture left the last word with me, and subsequently I was given a second word, being invited to deliver the 1997 Lattey Lecture, for which I chose the title, *A Land flowing with Milk, Honey, and People* (1997b).

The Little Bantustan of Bethlehem

The final revision of my study on the relation between the Bible and Colonialism (1997a) was undertaken while I was Visiting Professor in Bethlehem University and Scholar-in-Residence in Tantur Ecumenical Institute, Jerusalem (1996-97). My context was a persistent reminder of the degradation and oppression which colonising enterprises invariably inflict on their indigenes. I also became more aware of the collusion of Western scholarship in the enterprise.

Working against a background of bullet fire, and in the shadow of tanks, added a certain intensity to my research. Several bullets landed on the flat roof of Tantur on 25-26 September 1996. Two Palestinians, one a graduate of the university, were killed in Bethlehem, and many more, Palestinians and Israeli soldiers, were killed in the disturbances elsewhere in the West Bank. However, with no bullets flying in Jerusalem on the 26th, I was able to deliver my advertised public lecture in the Swedish Christian Study Centre, entitled 'Does the God of the Bible sanction Ethnic Cleansing?' By mid-December I was able to send the manuscript of *The Bible and Colonialism* to Sheffield Academic Press.

I preached at the Christmas Midnight Mass in Bethlehem University, presided over by Mgr Montezemolo, the Holy See's Apostolic Delegate, a key player in the signing of the Fundamental Agreement between the Holy See and the State of Israel on 30 December 1993. I reflected with the congregation that, not withstanding the Christmas rhetoric about God's Glory in the highest Heaven and Peace on Earth, the reality of Bethlehem brought one down to earth rather quickly. I assured them that passing by the checkpoint between Bethlehem and Jerusalem twice a day made me boil with anger at the humiliation which the colonising enterprise of Zionism had inflicted on the people of the region. I suggested that the birth of Jesus, however, symbolised that God would liberate those exploited by the powerful. The Christmas narrative assured Christians that life cannot be controlled indefinitely by forces of domination and exploitation. Tyrannies of emperors and local rulers would collapse. The Christmas narratives portray the ordinary people as the heroes and the rulers as the anti-heroes, as if assuring believers that the mighty will be cast down, and that God is working for the oppressed today. I would meet His Excellency again soon.

On 30 December, I listened to Mgr Montezemolo lecture in Notre Dame on the Third Anniversary of the Fundamental Agreement between the Holy See and Israel. The audience was composed exclusively of expatriate Christians and Israeli Jews, with not a Palestinian in sight. Well into the question time, I violated the somewhat sycophantic atmosphere: 'I had expected that the Agreement would have given the Holy See some leverage in putting pressure on Israel *vis-à-vis* the Palestinians, if only on the matter of freedom to worship in Jerusalem—Palestinians have been forbidden entry into even East Jerusalem, whether on Friday or Sunday, since March 1993.' His Excellency replied rhetorically, 'Do you not think that the Holy See is doing all it can?' At the reception afterwards, a certain Ambassador Gilboa, one of the Israeli architects of the Agreement, berated me in a most aggressive fashion for my question. Rather than assuming the posture of a culprit, I took the attack to him on the matter of the Jews having 'kicked out' the Palestinians in 1948. 'No, they were not kicked out', he, who was a soldier at the time, insisted. 'In fact helicopters dropped leaflets on the Arab towns, beseeching the inhabitants to stay put, etc.' I told him I did not believe him, and cited even the Israeli revisionist historiographer, Benny Morris, whom he dismissed as a compulsive attention-seeker. It was obvious all round the room that a not insignificant altercation was taking place. In the hope of discouraging him from trying to stifle the truth in the future, I assured him that he should have remained a soldier, because he had the manners of a corner-boy, and not what I expected from a diplomat. I went home righteous.

Academic life rolled on. My lecture on 'The Bible and Zionism' seemed to perplex several of the students of Bethlehem Bible College (28 February 1997). Most of the questions reflected a literalist understanding of the Bible, and I struggled to convey the impression that there were other forms of discourse than history. Having visited the Christian Peacemaker Team in Hebron as a gesture of solidarity on 6 March, I returned home for the Tantur Public Lecture on 'The Future of Religious Zionism' by the Jewish philosopher, Professor David Hartman, who gave a dazzling exegesis of the theme of covenant, from the Bible through the Rabbis to Zionism. It was an eventful occasion. My journal takes the matter up from the second half, devoted to questions:

> I made the fourth intervention, to the effect that in being brought through the stages of understanding of the covenant, from the Bible to Rabbinic Judaism, I was enchanted, and much appreciative. However, I was shocked to hear Zionism described as 'the high point of covenantal spirituality'. Zionism, as I saw it, both in its rhetoric and in its practice, was not an ideology of sharing, but one of displacing. I was shocked, therefore, that what others might see as an example of 19th-century colonial plunder was being clothed in the garment of spirituality.

Somewhat shaken, Professor Hartman thanked me for my question, and set about putting the historical record straight. The real problem was that the Arabs had not welcomed Jews back to their homeland. Moreover, the displacement of the Arabs was never intended, but was forced on the Zionist leadership by the attack by the Arab armies in 1948. Nevertheless, great developments in history sometimes require initial destruction: consider how the USA had defeated totalitarianism, although this was preceded by the displacement of the Indians.

On the following day, in the discussion time after my final session of teaching on *Jesus the Liberator* in Tantur, one of the Continuing Education students brought the discussion back to the previous day's deliberations. He was very embarrassed by my attack on 'that holy man'. There was a particularly lively exchange about the Lucan text, with several getting into the discussion. I was not aware that there were undercurrents about Zionism. Before getting to his question about Luke 4, a second student said that he was delighted with my question yesterday, and was sure that it represented the disquiet of many of the group. A third responded enthusiastically to my liberation ethic, saying that it disturbed him, but he had to cope with the disturbance. An American priest came to me afterwards, saying how much he appreciated my courage in speaking yesterday, and on a previous occasion, etc. His enthusiasm was not shared by everyone. After the class, an advertising notice appeared on the board from the overseer of the Scholar's Colloquium. It read, 'Dr Michael Prior presents a largish paper, "Zionism: from the Secular to the Sacred", which is a chapter from a book he is in the process of writing.' The next paragraph read,

> Zionism is a subject on which there are hot opinions—not least from the author himself. Some have suggested to me that this disunity is a reason why we should not discuss such matters at all. I believe the opposite: the quality of hot opinions is best tested in a scholarly discussion, where they must be supported by evidence and good argument. One can even learn something. Welcome!

The Swedish New Testament scholar, Bengt Holmberg chaired the Colloquium. The first scholar to respond to my paper, a US Catholic veteran of the Jewish-Christian dialogue, did so in a decidedly aggressive manner, accusing me of disloyalty to the Church, etc. The second was long in praise, but somewhat convoluted in content. The third, in a patronising fashion, intimated that there was nothing new in the paper, and rambled on about the Zionists' intentions to bring benefits to the indigenous population, etc. Losing patience, I asked him to produce evidence for his claims, adding that not only was there no such evidence, but the evidence there was showed that the Zionist ideologues were virtually at one in their determination to rid the land of Arabs. A fourth scholar, a Dutch Protestant veteran of the Jewish-Christian dialogue, chastised me for my audacity to address the question at all, insisting that I should be silent, because I was an outsider and a Christian. I rose to the challenge. Was I understanding him to say that having seen the distress of the Palestinian people I should now not comment on it? Was he asking me to deny my experience, or merely to mute my critique? I assured the Colloquium that as a biblical scholar, and an ongoing witness to what transpired in the region I considered it an obligation to protest at what was going on. The first respondent made a second intervention, accusing me of being a Marcionite, and assuring all that he had no trouble with a God who mandated genocide, after the fashion of Joshua. Once again, the admiring remarks were made in private later.

The proofs of *The Bible and Colonialism* arrived on Good Friday. I got my first taste of teargas in the vicinity of Rachel's Tomb on my way to Easter Sunday Mass at St Catherine's in Bethlehem. On 3 April, I delivered the Tantur Public Lecture, 'The Moral Problem of the Bible's Land Traditions', followed by questions, both appreciative and hostile. Uniquely for the series, the lecture was not advertised in the *Jerusalem Post*. In dealing with a trilogy of hostile questions I availed myself of the opportunity of saying that I considered Zionism to be one of the most pernicious ideologies of the 20th century, particularly evil because of its essential link with religious values.

Stars from the West studded the sky over Bethlehem for the celebrations of Tantur's 25th anniversary (25-28 May 1997). Under the light of the plainly visible Hale-Bopp comet, a frail Teddy Kollek was introduced at the opening ceremony as though he were the founder of the Institute. A choir from the USA sang, one song in Hebrew. Palestinian faces, not least that of Afif Safieh, the Palestinian Delegate to the UK and the Holy See, looked decidedly out of joint throughout the opening festivities. But the Palestinians were not altogether forgotten, being thanked profusely for their work in the kitchen and around the grounds. Moreover, for the lecture on 'Christians of the Holy Land' which was given later by an expatriate (27 Tuesday), prominent Palestinian savants were invited to speak from the floor. Although the lecture was billed to be presented by a distinguished expatriate scholar 'with local presenters', in fact the Palestinian savants had been invited only to the audience floor! Having excused himself from dealing with the political context, the lecturer delivered an urbane, accomplished historical perspective. The token Palestinians were invited to speak from the floor, first Naim Ateek, then Mitri Raheb, and then Kevork Hintlian. After two rabbis had their say also from the floor, I was allowed speak, wishing to make two points: that my experience with the Palestinians had impressed upon me their unity, rather than their diversity, and, secondly, that the Jewish-Christian dialogue had been hijacked by a Zionist agenda. After one more sentence had escaped from my mouth, the Chair stopped me short. I had broken the Solemn Silence. This was the third time that year I had been prevented from speaking in public. I paused, producing a most uncomfortable silence, thanked him, and sat down.

Saturday 31 May being the 28th Anniversary of my Ordination, I determined to do something different. Since it was the Feast of the Visitation also, I decided that I would go to Ein Karem, but on the way, I would call at Jabal Abu Ghneim, the hill opposite Tantur which, despite UN condemnation, was being prepared for an Israeli settlement. The teeth of the high-tech machinery had cut into the rock, having run down thousands of trees. The phrase, 'the relentless progress of our race' kept coming at me. On the way to Ein Karem, I visited Mount Herzl to see the grave of the founder of Zionism. Knowing that I would also visit the grave of Yitzhak Rabin, I was struck by the irony of the situation. Theodor Herzl was sure that Jews could survive only in their own nation state. Nevertheless, he died a natural death in Europe, and was re-interred in the new state in 1949. Prime Minister, Rabin, born in Palestine, was gunned down by a Jewish religious zealot in what was intended to be the sole haven for Jews.

On Sunday 29 June I began my meandering return, mixing holiday with journey, driving from the West Bank to London, via Haifa, Limassol, Patmos, Athens, Corinth, Patras, Venice, Udine, Aquilea, Miren, Ljubljana, Celje, Graz, Salzburg. Some 170 km from Salzburg I visited Dachau. I noticed a group of Israeli youngsters engaged in a commemoration ritual in a central area, with German students with whom they seemed to have constituted a group. Having spent my year with the victims of Israel's oppression I had disturbing emotions.

Back in England, I prepared the manuscript of the 1996 Amman Conference for publication, and by December 1997 we had a launch of *The Bible and Colonialism* (1997a), with *Western Scholarship and the History of Palestine* (1999) hot off the press. I had promised in *The Bible and Colonialism* (note 2, p. 259) that I would discuss elsewhere the more theological aspects of Zionism, and, while still in Jerusalem in 1997, I laid out my plans for writing the book I had really wanted to write some years earlier. I submitted a draft manuscript to a distinguished publisher in November 1997, and even though the anonymous reader found it to be 'a brilliant book which must be published', the press declined, because, I was informed orally, the press had 'a very strong Jewish list', and could not offend Jewish readers, who might as a result cut their links, which could bring about its collapse. While an American publishing company judged it to be 'a prodigious achievement of historical and theological investigation', and 'a very important work' it deemed that it would not really suit its publishing programme. Routledge, however, 'bit the bullet', publishing it under the title *Zionism and the State of Israel: A Moral Inquiry* (1999a).

On the basis of his having read my *The Bible and Colonialism* Professor Heikki Räisänen of the University of Helsinki invited me to address what is probably the most prestigious of the international biblical conferences, the *Society of Biblical Literature* International Conference in Helsinki-Lahti (16-22 July 1999) on the subject, 'The Bible and Zionism'. The session at which I was invited to speak dealt with 'Reception History and Moral Criticism of the Bible', and I was preceded by Professors Robert Jewett (USA) and David Clines (UK) on aspects of Paul and Job respectively. When my hour came, I invited biblical scholarship not to maintain an academic detachment from significant engagement in contemporary issues. I noted that 'the view that the Bible provides the title-deed for the establishment of the State of Israel and for its policies since 1948 is so pervasive even within mainstream Christian theology and university biblical studies, that the very attempt to raise the issue is sure to elicit opposition. The disfavour usually took the form of personal abuse, and the intimidation of publishers.' In the light of what happened next I might have added that one is seldom honoured by having the substantive issues addressed in the usual way.

After I had delivered my 25-minute lecture the official respondent, who had my paper a month in advance, said he would bypass the usual niceties ('A very fine paper, etc.'), and got down to his objections, which were so standard as not to deserve my refutation. Instead I suggested to the chair to open up the discussion. Some five Israelis in turn took up the challenge. 'Jews have always longed for the land.' 'They never intended displacing anyone.' 'The land was empty—almost'. I was wrong historically: Herzl never intended dislocating the Arabs. I interrupted, at that point, quoting Herzl's 12 June 1895 diary entry about his endeavour to expel the poor population, etc. I should not have raised a 'political matter' in an academic conference (despite the title): 'See what can happen when one abandons the historical critical method!' Another Israeli professor began by saying, 'I am very pleased to have been here this morning,' but added, 'because I understand better now how antisemitism can present itself as anti-Zionism, all under the guise of academic scholarship.' A cabal, including at least one Israeli and a well-known scholar from Germany, clapped. The chair restored order.

In the course of my 'defence' I reiterated that it was the displacement of another people that raised the moral problematic for me. I had witnessed the effects of the oppression rather more than even most of the audience. Having been given the last word, I professed that until Israelis acknowledge their having displaced another people, and make some reparation and accommodation there would be no future for the state. In the course of the following day several who had attended expressed their appreciation, albeit in private. A Finnish scholar congratulated me on having raised a vital issue, adding, 'The way you were received added sharpness to your argument.' A distinguished biblical scholar from Germany, who was very distressed by my having raised the question, later pleaded that his people were responsible for killing six million Jews.

The importance of the issue

My study of the Bible in the Land of the Bible brought me face to face with the turbulence of Israel-Palestine and raised questions not only about the link between biblical interpretation and colonial exploitation but about the nature of the biblical narrative itself. An academic interest became a consuming moral imperative. But why should the State of Israel, any more than any other state, be such a challenge to morality? The first reason, I suggest, derives from the general moral question attendant upon the forcible displacement of an indigenous people from its homeland. The second springs from the unique place which the land has in the Sacred Scriptures of both Jews and Christians, and the significance attached to it as the location of the state for Jews. In addition, there is the positive assessment of the State of Israel on the part of the majority of religious Jews of various categories, and in certain Christian ecclesial and theological circles.

So much of my earlier grasp of things had to be changed drastically. I discovered that Israeli propaganda, thanks to one of the most successful disinformation campaigns in modern times, had masked the fact that the creation of the state resulted in the dispossession and dispersion of another people, which was both foreseen and planned virtually from the beginning. The injustice to the Palestinians was passed over in most Western discourse, including biblical and theological scholarship, and in some religious circles was accorded religious legitimation.

The only plausible validation for the displacement of the Palestinians derived from a naive interpretation of the Bible, and biblical literalism swept away any concerns deriving from considerations of morality. However, fidelity to the literary genre of the biblical traditions and respect for the evidence provided mainly by archaeological investigation demand a rejection of such simplistic readings of the biblical narratives of land, and of the prophetic oracles of restoration. To these academic perspectives, one must add one of faith, namely, that God is fundamentally moral, and, for those espousing the

Christian vision, loves all his people, irrespective of race, etc. The Israel-Palestine conflict, then, raises the question of the moral integrity of the Deity.

Gradually I began to situate Zionism within the category of xenophobic imperialism, so characteristic of the major European powers towards the end of the 19th century. I consider the espousal of it by a majority of Jews worldwide to mark the nadir of Jewish morality. Because I trust in a God before whom tyranny ultimately dissolves, and because one learns something from history, I have no doubt that a future generation of diaspora and Israeli Jews will repudiate its presumptions, and repent for the injustices perpetrated on the Palestinians by their fathers and grandfathers.

While I regret the descent of Judaism into the embrace of Zionism, there is little I can do about it. However, the degree to which a thoroughly Zionised Judaism infects the so-called Jewish-Christian dialogue—which I prefer to designate 'a monologue in two voices'—is a matter of grave concern. I am perturbed that concurrence with a Zionist reading of Jewish history—that Jews everywhere, and at all times, wanted to re-establish a nation state in Palestine (with no concern for the indigenous population), etc.—is virtually a component of the credo of the dialogue. In that fabricated scenario, the planned, and systematically executed dislocation of the Palestinian population, far from incurring the wrath of post-colonial liberalism, becomes an object of honour, and even religious significance. While most Jews worldwide—there are notable exceptions—allow themselves to be deluded by such perspectives, I see no reason why Christians should.

Western theological scholarship, while strong in its critique of repressive regimes elsewhere, gives a wide berth to Zionism. Indeed a moral critique of its impact on the Palestinians is ruled out. I try to break the silence in my *The Bible and Colonialism* (1997a) and *Zionism and the State of Israel* (1999a). The former explores the moral question of the impact which colonialist enterprises, fuelled by the biblical paradigm, have had on the indigenous populations in general, while the latter deals with the impact of Zionism on the Palestinians. They are explorations into terrain virtually devoid of enquirers, which attempt to map out some of the contours of that terrain. They subject the land traditions of the Bible to an evaluation which derives from general ethical principles and criteria of human decency, such as are enshrined in conventions of human rights and international law. Such an enterprise is necessary. When people are dispossessed, dispersed and humiliated, not only with alleged divine support, but at the alleged express command of God, one's moral self recoils in horror. Any association of God with the destruction of people must be subjected to an ethical analysis. The obvious contradiction between what some claim to be God's will and ordinary civilised, decent behaviour poses the question as to whether God is a chauvinistic, nationalistic and militaristic xenophobe. It also poses the problem of biblical prophecy finding its fulfilment in what even unbelievers would regard as a form of 'ethnic cleansing'.

I consider that biblical studies and theology should deal with the real conditions of people's lives, and not satisfy themselves with comfortable survival in an academic or ecclesial ghetto. I am concerned about the use of the Bible as a legitimisation for colonialism and its consequences. My academic work addresses aspects of biblical hermeneutics, and informs a wider public on issues which have implications for human well-being, as well as for allegiance to God. While such a venture might be regarded as an instructive academic contribution by any competent scholar, to assume responsibility for doing so is for me, who has witnessed the dispossession, dispersion and humiliation of the Palestinians, of the order of a moral imperative. It is high time that biblical scholars, Church people, and Western intellectuals read the biblical narratives of the promise of land 'with the eyes of the Canaanites'. Such a project is consistent with the vision of Vincent de Paul, whose interpretation of the Scriptures was significantly influenced by his encounter with the marginalised. My study of the Bible in the Land of the Bible introduced me to one such context. Others may not have to go so far.

EDUCATING MYSELF ...
AND OTHERS
Elizabeth Barlow

The formative experience of my life occurred in a small village in the Shuf Mountains of Lebanon in 1955-56, when I was a naive young teacher of English and music. Born in Kalamazoo, Michigan, deep in the Midwest, post-World War II events in other continents had very little meaning to me as I grew up. I attended St Anne's College at Oxford University in England, and in talking with other foreign students began to be much more aware of events in the Middle East. But nothing prepared me for teaching high-school age students, many of whom were Palestinian refugees from a conflict seven years earlier. I considered myself well educated: my family and my college libraries had subscribed to newspapers and popular magazines. I assumed that if I had not heard about events, such as the razing of nearly 450 Palestinian villages and towns, the wholesale theft of Palestinian property, and the refusal of the Israeli government to allow individuals and families to return to their homes, then these events could not have happened.

I decided to keep my ears and eyes open, and my mouth shut, for three months, to see if I could understand the various stories I was hearing from my students and also from fellow teachers, some of whom were Palestinian. I heard about families being forced from their homes at the point of a gun, some leaving for a week 'voluntarily' after news that friends or neighbours were shot, and then not being allowed to return to their homes. Some had heard that their homes, with their furniture and clothes still inside, had been turned over to newly-arrived Jewish immigrants, without the permission of the owners or any compensation. Others had been told that their homes had been ransacked for valuables by Jews and then destroyed to keep the original owners from being able to return and re-establish themselves.

For the first few weeks I thought there must be some mistake. Jews, who had suffered so much in Europe, would not make others suffer. In the name of a 'homeland', they would not render homeless 80 percent of the Palestinian people. They would not rectify one diaspora by creating another. Gradually, as I heard story after story, I realised that these events had indeed taken place. The press, which had covered some parts of the story in 1947-49, was now ignoring it, and the situation clearly was getting much worse.

The class in singing was a real challenge for me. I was teaching several boys whose voices were changing, including one who loved to belt out the songs even though he was tone deaf. My mother, a former music teacher, came to my rescue and sent me some Negro spirituals, which she thought any class would love. So I introduced 'Swing Low, Sweet Chariot'. When we came to the words, 'I looked over Jordan, and what did I see, coming for to carry me home,' I realised that almost the entire class saw a meaning which I had not intended: they were ready to cross the river and march back into Palestine. Until then, I had not realised how many of my students came from a Palestinian background.

During the vacations, I visited Jerusalem and Cairo. In Jerusalem, governed by Jordan at that time, I met a Palestinian who could no longer follow his profession and had taken up being a tour guide. One of his children had been born shortly after the *Nakba* ('catastrophe') in 1948 with a clubfoot. Before the *Nakba*, he could easily have afforded to have the child get the medical care to permit him to run and play with other children. But because of the loss of his home and livelihood in the 1948 war and the Israeli refusal to allow him to return, he and his family were living in penury, and could no longer afford to pay for this fairly straight-forward medical treatment. He had to watch his son growing up handicapped, a living reproach to the father for his inability to provide necessities to his child. When I reached Cairo they were still talking about an Israeli raid into Gaza in February 1955, in which many Egyptians were killed, including a doctor whose family I later met. At the time this seemed as if it must have been a mistake. With hindsight I now recognise these events as a warm up for later atrocities—in this case for the October 1956 invasion of Egypt which was timed just before the US presidential election when the US was presumed to be incapable of action. I now understand that if there had been strong international reaction to the raid and the murders in 1955, the invasion of 1956 might not have happened, nor the war of 1967.

When I returned home, I was puzzled that Americans were not more vocal in trying to rectify what seemed to me to be a very bad situation. I had been brought up to believe that we in the US cared about justice, that we were the ones who always wore the white hats, and that, whatever the odds, you could count on US citizens working to relieve suffering and to restore just relationships. In the more than 43 years since my return from my teaching job in Lebanon, I have been saddened to find that instead of working to rectify a bad situation, our country has in fact made it infinitely worse. It seems to me that usually we have three institutions which, over time, help us to educate ourselves about problems and to galvanise us into action. In the case of the Israeli-Palestinian conflict, I think all three of these institutions—academia, the media, and our churches— have failed us. Let me explain how and why, and what we might do to get them back functioning as they should.

Academia

Since 1982 I have worked as the Outreach Co-ordinator at the Center for Middle Eastern and North African Studies at the University of Michigan. On many issues occurring elsewhere in the world, the US public may be badly informed, but over time courses are offered, books and articles are written, lectures given, and the public becomes knowledgeable about the issue. But in respect to the Israeli-Palestinian issue, it does not work that way. There are many barriers to the free flow of accurate information. The occasion of my hiring gave me my first foretaste of this. I got my job only because a more highly qualified candidate was blackballed by two faculty members who were not even on the selection committee. Unbeknownst to me, a much more highly qualified person had applied. He spoke both Arabic and Hebrew, had lived in Israel and studied there, and would have done an excellent job for the Center. What was the problem with him? In his private life he worked with Arabs, and cogently and resolutely espoused a peace with justice for both communities. Since he was Jewish himself and his family lived in Israel, it was hard to dismiss him as being 'anti-semitic'. Two Jewish faculty members threatened the Center Director that they would resign from the Center faculty if this excellent candidate was appointed. The Center Director was for the first time an Arab-American, and obviously did not want his tenure to be marred by the withdrawal of Jewish faculty.

I was offered the job. Six weeks later, when I found out what had happened, my elation turned to sadness. I felt that they did not want me there as a person who could help educate, but instead believed that I could be controlled, would turn a blind eye to the prejudice and bigotry in our textbooks, and would not challenge the biased information that was being fed to our young people about the Middle East and the US role in it. Soon after I was hired, a highly-qualified colleague at the University of Arizona lost her job in a chain of events which started with orchestrated far-right American Jewish attacks, which faculty at Arizona were not allowed to challenge.[1] Subsequently I saw at close range how an invitation to Noam Chomsky to lecture was withdrawn after protests by Jewish members of the faculty—again with the threat that these faculty members would withdraw from the Center if their demands were not heeded. It was also clear that in the hiring and promotion process it was dangerous to be fair and open on the Israeli-Palestinian issue. In one case, a political science professor, twice recommended for tenure by his department, was rejected by a committee of the college, a rejection for which pro-Zionist people on the faculty later claimed credit. I have since heard of many other occasions when fair-minded

---

[1] The incident is recorded in chapter 8 of Paul Findley's book *They Dared to Speak Out*, 1985: 212-37.

academics on my own and other campuses were either not hired, or were not given promotion or tenure because of fear that they might eventually say something inconvenient. Usually the alleged reasons are not the true ones, and there still are faculty members on our campuses who are sensitive to attempts to squash debate.

On occasion student groups at the university brought in speakers who addressed Arab-Israeli issues forthrightly. Bomb threats were phoned into campus security to pre-empt the possibility of students hearing a non-Zionist view. The university's campus at Flint invited a former missionary in Lebanon and a retired US foreign service officer to speak. Jewish groups objected to both, claiming that the US foreign service officer had to be 'balanced' with an Israeli speaker. The US public was not to be allowed to hear from its own state department without the intervention of a speaker from a foreign government! This occurred at the same time that the University of Michigan, Ann Arbor campus, had invited former Israeli Foreign Minister Abba Eban to speak, obviously a representative of a foreign government, but with no obligation for 'balance'.

Through the 1970s and 80s two Jewish organisations kept separate files on academics and those who were apt to speak at colleges. The note-taking was riddled with errors. The goal was to use this information to block speakers from appearing at campuses. If one of the people on the blacklist was invited, then the local Jewish community would be contacted, and asked to pressure the university to disinvite the speaker. The situation got so bad that in 1984 at its annual meeting, held that year in San Francisco, the Middle East Studies Association voted to condemn the blacklisting practices of both the American-Israeli Public Affairs Committee (AIPAC) and the Anti-Defamation League (ADL), which latter organisation since 1967 seems to have spent more time on Arab defamation than anti-defamation. While the resolution was carried there is no reason to believe that the practice has stopped. Indeed, the ADL was found guilty ten years later in San Francisco of spying on American citizens who were legally working for a wide variety of anti-apartheid, labour and Central American causes. The information gathered in the US by subterfuge was then sent to Israel where it was resent to apartheid South Africa, among other places, for use against American citizens and their relatives in South Africa.

In kindergarten through twelfth grade education (5-18 year olds) the situation is even more troubling. For years American Jewish groups have been monitoring textbooks to make sure that they do not raise awkward questions about Israel and the Arab-Israeli conflict, and do not portray a positive view of Muslims and their culture. On behalf of the Middle East Studies Association and the Middle East Outreach Council for several years I co-ordinated an evaluation of the coverage of the Middle East, North Africa and Islam in US secondary textbooks (Barlow 1994: vi-xii). Our faculty reviewers noticed that when it came to the Arab-Israeli conflict, events suddenly were presented impersonally: 'in 1967 war broke out'; 'after the war, 750,000 Palestinians found themselves to be refugees'; or, 'since Oslo, Palestinian GNP has declined dramatically.' For every other subject, the question of 'Who did what?' was not a problem. The reviewers also found serious distortions in the presentation of Islam (linking the religion with terrorism and the people with violence and fanaticism). Little explanation is given to colonialism and other movements to which Islam may be reacting. The discussion of the Palestinian-Israeli conflict was usually exclusively presented from the Israeli point of view.

One textbook that did an excellent job of portraying Muslim culture and the recent events in the Arab-Israeli conflict had an Arab-American as a senior member of the team. This particular world history text was attacked by Jewish groups. Instead of making their charges directly at the fair and scholarly language used to describe the Arab-Israeli conflict, they had enlisted on their side a Catholic priest, who was induced to complain to the school board (at the hearing on the adoption of this text) because the text, in covering England, pointed out that under Mary Tudor many were charged with religious infractions and put to death, and 'the people called her "Bloody Mary" '. Well, as any historian can testify, the people of that time certainly *did* call her 'Bloody Mary'. Nothing inaccurate in this statement. Yet, using this as the cover, the Jewish group was then able to tell the publisher that if they would be permitted to write the section on Israel and the Arab-Israeli conflict themselves, they would withdraw all objections to the book. Nothing was mentioned at this point about changing the phrase 'Bloody Mary'. Her work had been done. The publisher was about to cave in when the community of San Diego, California, made their views known to the school board, and the text was adopted, without changes, after all. (Personal communication from the senior editor of the text.) This monitoring still continues, although after the Anti-Defamation League was found to be spying on Arab, Muslim and a wide variety of other non-governmental public service groups, Hadassah took over the task. So much money is at stake for publishers that most of them are afraid if a large lobby opposes a book for any reason. And so US textbooks continue to tell only part of the story, often skimming over opportunities missed in US policy, and demonising our supposed 'enemies'. Hardly a good way to teach history.

The media

In the US the media either do not cover issues related to the conflict at all, or else place them in a context which permits the reader to dismiss the story. Let me give two examples of attempts to suppress any discussion. For several years at the University of Michigan I had trouble getting our student paper, *The Michigan Daily,* to cover, or even announce our events. It was hard to get an audience without notice in the paper which students read. Eventually it was discovered that a Jewish student member of the news team felt that it was his contribution to the State of Israel to intercept these press releases and to toss them out before they could be typeset for inclusion in the paper. Thus Israeli apologists would be spared the nuisance of trying to defend the indefensible. He got only a mild rap on the knuckles for his misbehaviour.

The bishop of our church had a weekly human rights commentary on a Detroit station. Once in 1986, when he was gone on vacation, he asked me to say something about the Palestinian situation. I obliged with a four-minute, extremely mild explanation of how land was being alienated from its Palestinian owners, and houses were being demolished. I concluded that what both peoples needed was peace, and that this was not a good way to bring peace about. As a result, I got a death threat, pressure on the University of Michigan to fire me, pressure on my bishop to apologise for having allowed me to speak, and pressure on him to excommunicate me, which fortunately we do not do in the Episcopal Church. I wrote to the Jewish Community Center of Metropolitan Detroit, the group which had complained *about* me, though not *to* me, and provided documentation from Israeli and human rights sources for every point that I had made. They never wrote back. But to the bishop they said that they were deeply offended at having heard these things. I wrote to say that I also was offended to have to hear every day about house demolitions, land confiscations (without compensation, needless to say), arbitrary arrests and practices of torture. I asked if we could not please work together to stop these events, so that nobody would have to hear about them again. But they did not want to stop the events, just to stop hearing about them.

I was never invited to give another commentary on that programme, nor did anyone else touch the subject for more than two years. Without one scintilla of evidence or logic, the Jewish Community Center had managed to silence another venue for human rights discussion at the time when the 'Iron Fist' policy in Israel inevitably led to a full-blown *Intifada*.

Another major problem with the media is the placing of stories in a context which leads to misinterpretation. For years we have heard that Israel is facing resistance in 'its security zone'. When southern Lebanon is termed 'Israel's security zone', it makes it sound as if Israel has a right to be there. But the 'security zone' is an integral part of Lebanon, which is still occupied since 1977 in defiance of international law and UN resolutions. Manifestly Israel has no right to bomb and destroy Lebanese homes, and to maim and kill its people. Nevertheless, news persons announcing an Israeli bombing attack on Lebanon usually slant the story by saying that a certain number of 'terrorists' were killed, which presumably is supposed to make us feel that the bombing was justified. But we all know that even those bombings which are not indiscriminate—and many bombing sorties have been quite indiscriminate—are not precise: a pilot does not know for sure who is in a certain house, and indeed may miss the house altogether and hit another one. Moreover, frequently the victims are children, far too young to have a 'terrorist' label attached to them to excuse their murder. Israelis (and their US supporters) are too apt to label anyone who opposes occupation as a 'terrorist'.

News stories about land confiscation for settlements usually do not mention that the land was formerly Palestinian-owned, and that the new settlements are open only to Jews. Moreover, not infrequently home demolitions are treated as a planning issue, with nothing to inform the reader that Palestinians almost never are given permission to build, and that Jews who build illegally do not face demolition—the land will simply be re-zoned for them.

Media people owe it to our citizens to keep them informed about what is really happening. It is not acceptable to learn only what one side in a conflict is willing to have us know. Americans cannot understand how the US is seen in the world unless we learn the perspectives of all the parties concerned. We will not understand the available policy options unless we have full and correct information on what is in fact happening. It is vital for the press to do its job effectively.

Churches

Most of the major denominations have strong resolutions calling for a two-state solution, return of the refugees, an end to settlements, and the sharing of Jerusalem. But each time most of the denominations met they hosted a Zionist rabbi, whose job it was to work against any resolution not favoured by the Israeli government. Clergy who got out of line were subjected to a smear campaign which might finish their careers.

Local interfaith organisations often found that their coalitions existed only subject to the veto of the Jewish partner (this is what Marc Ellis has termed the 'ecumenical deal'). In Toledo, one coalition's newsletter was printing a report from a member who had just returned from Jerusalem. The local rabbi waylaid the editor on the way to the printer, and took the copy from her. This local coalition member was not to be allowed to tell her own story about what she had seen! A coalition in Ann Arbor decided several years ago to speak up on the question of the many new Jews-only settlements on Palestinian land. But voices in the coalition, hoping for harmonious relations with the local rabbis, asked that first a letter be sent to one of the local rabbis explaining why we were thinking of working on this question. There was no direct response to the Christian clergyman who had signed the letter. Instead, some days later in an address on one of the High Holy Days, the local rabbi told his congregation that he had been subjected to a 'blood libel' by his Christian colleague. Never mind that there was no blood libel whatsoever involved. Never mind that if he misread the letter and was angry, he could have answered privately. What was intended was to stop any possibility of discussion or action. And indeed, his ploy was successful; discussion of settlements did stop for several months.

Most Americans after the *Shoah* are ready to take into consideration Jewish concerns. However, we make a mistake when allowing these concerns always to be defined by an Israeli government that does not seem to have any vision for peace in the Middle East, or even a vision of Jewish steadfastness for justice. Most young Jews that I have met at my university recoil from the violence and racism stemming from extremist Israeli groups. Indeed, uncritical support of Israel has been placed at the centre of the Jewish faith. One almost feels that it has become the object of worship, as a result of which many such young idealists find it hard to embrace Judaism and its historic ethics. Regrettably, a significant number of them are abandoning the faith of their fathers.

Those of us who have the interests of the Jewish people at heart might feel that it is time to abandon uncritical support of anything and everything Israel does. Friends do not let friends drive drunk. The policies pursued by recent Israeli governments, and their all too submissive partner the US, cannot lead to a long-term peace within Israel, or between Israel and its neighbours. We need to challenge ourselves and our friends on all sides of the conflict to envision what peace might look like, and to talk about the steps needed to get to that peace.

My response, and what we can do together

In the realm of *academia*, it is important for every young student to get a full view of history, as accurate as we can make it, without ethnocentrism or Eurocentrism. Ideally students should recognise the long periods of pluralism practised under Muslim governments in Andalusian Spain and in the Middle East. Indeed, Jews considered the life in Muslim Spain to be their 'Golden Age'. Also, a more rounded understanding of the anti-colonial struggle around the world might help our students understand the sensitivity of other cultures to our efforts to control them or their resources. The US has on many occasions made policy decisions which foreclosed better options. We sometimes are our own worst enemies. US history needs to be taught with an examination of the possible options and their probable consequences, to compare with the policy chosen and its results. Only in this way will students, and the community, learn to hold accountable those who control US policy.

Because textbooks can do so much damage, we need to make sure they are reviewed by experts in the field, and that these evaluations are widely circulated to educators. Families need to check the texts used by their young people. There are many special interest groups already operating in this field. What is needed is for experts to participate in the process of producing textbooks, either by writing them, consulting with publishers during the process, or by reviewing them after they are published.

What to do about the *media* is a question many of us have struggled with for a long time. Many of us are tired of having the realities of life in the Middle East ignored, or placed in a self-serving context. Both non-coverage and biased coverage need to be challenged. One of the people who has had a remarkable impact is Ali Abunimah from Chicago, who listens to NPR, reads papers, and watches television. He offers advice to news editors on what was left out of their coverage in a friendly but professional way. He also has a list of friends who get copies of his letters, so that with little or no research, they can add their views to the same recipients. If you want to help, contact him at <ahabunim@midway.uchicago.edu>. Most news writers and editors want to appear to be professional. If you explain to them that they have written only one side of an interesting and complicated story, and give them suggestions about how they can get more information about the story, they may listen and may actually appreciate your help. SEARCH, a media watchdog located in Framingham, MA, also co-ordinates appropriate responses to inaccurate stories or out-of-focus editorials.

The advent of the web and email has given us a certain amount of independence. No longer can a few papers control the dissemination of news. There are other ways to find out what is going on in Jerusalem or Hebron. We need to use email and web sites to connect with church bulletins, the religious press, and human rights organisations. Now pictures can be transmitted electronically. We can show Christians around the world what a home demolition really looks like. We can show pictures of sick people unable to reach hospitals because of Israeli-imposed closures. We can show the long lines waiting for permits to drive two miles to visit relatives or to do business. As I recall, the image of Bull Connor fire-hosing freedom fighters in the American South during the Civil Rights movement radically changed the way America thought about Civil Rights. The photo of a young Vietnamese girl being napalmed by a US plane raised fundamental questions about the purpose and conduct of the Vietnam

War. We can disseminate the images from Jerusalem to our fellow citizens who have been hitherto oblivious of what is happening.

Above all, we should not give up on the media. Many have tried to write letters or articles before, and when they are not published, they abandon hope. We need everyone to work hard, at least for the next year, to explain to others what is happening. A major time investment is not required. One can simply forward to one's email group messages that come from Jerusalem. One can also forward these messages to the local and religious press.

Church groups are already at work. The key is to connect with those who are working for justice, which can lead to peace, rather than those that are part of the problem. The group I am working with is 'Friends of *Sabeel*—North America', working in support of *Sabeel* in Jerusalem, the Palestinian Christian Ecumenical Center for Liberation Theology. Other 'Friends' support groups exist in the UK, Sweden, and Australia. In North America we have a chapter in Canada as well, and several regional groups around the United States. We try in the US to educate church people about the existence of their fellow Christians in the Holy Land, and about the serious injustices which both Christians and Muslims face under the Israeli occupation. As a partner with *Sabeel* in Jerusalem and based on our biblical understanding, we work for that justice which alone can bring about the fullness of peace for which we all long: a justice which allows each man to live under his own fig tree, and for families to live in the homes they have built, and to reap what they have planted. We inform our fellow Christians through books, exhibits, visiting lecturers, films, communications with the media and through conferences in North America alternating with conferences in Jerusalem. We try to develop close relationships with our Senators and Representatives in Congress so that our concerns will be constantly in front of them.

We also work with other religious and human rights groups in the struggle. The Christian Peacemaker Teams (CPT) have for some time placed themselves between Israeli bulldozers and Palestinian homes targeted for destruction. They work in conjunction with Israeli groups such as the Israeli Coalition against House Destruction

(ICAHD). It is heartening to see groups in action that cross religious and ethnic lines to work for justice. The American Friends Service Committee has sponsored joint tours to the United States of Israelis and Palestinians who, in joint appearances, describe how they work to oppose home destruction. Churches could sponsor these talks, or could work in partnership with CPT or ICAHD.

There are some American churches that have formed partnerships with churches in Jerusalem or the West Bank. They visit each other, write to each other and learn from each other. Youth groups visit each other. Sometimes youth groups here help with work in a place such as Father Elias Chacour's Prophet Elias School in Ibillin. Sometimes the US partner will advocate with our State Department or with the Israeli government on issues of human rights. Sometimes the Holy Land partner will help educate the American partner on the history of the area.

Churches for Middle East Peace, a consortium of fourteen Christian denominations, prepares statements for the President and Congress on issues important to peace, like the sharing of Jerusalem, or the necessity to give all refugees the choice to return if they wish, and to compensate all who lost property, whether or not they wish to return. Individual churches can use their work in advocacy, or host conferences or conduct study groups. *Sabeel* has published several books which could be the basis of a Christian education series. Some churches sell the needlework that Palestinian women make as a way of supporting their families. There are good examples of partnering work all around us.

On the other hand, there are so-called 'Christian' groups that are doing a great deal of damage to the work for peace and to the image of Christianity. I refer to the Christian Zionists such as Pat Robertson and Jerry Falwell who by their actions are working to uproot the native Christians in the area, expand the Jewish state and advance the day of Armageddon, when all of humanity and the whole of God's created order will be destroyed.

What is at stake

It seems to me that a great deal is at stake in this issue, both as US citizens and, in my case, as a member of the Christian faith. The US, when first established more than 200 years ago, called for government by the consent of the governed. What a shame that our recent foreign policy has mimicked all the mistakes of the Western colonial powers. What a shame that we are now seen, not as the friends of freedom and democracy, but as the friends of the oppressors. In the name of our own ideals, we need to reclaim our foreign policy and to submit it to close and continuing scrutiny, holding responsible those who violate our goals.

But for US Christians in particular there is a great deal at stake. For one thing, the continued existence of the Jerusalem Christian community, the earliest Christian community, hangs in the balance. It seems amazing to me that Christians can work so hard to transplant Christianity into other continents, and not be concerned that our own policies are uprooting it in the place where it started. But even beyond this question is the nature of the faith itself. Does Christianity endorse the massive and continued subjugation of one people by another? Does it endorse ethnic cleansing? This was much discussed in relation to the Nazi era, Black slavery and then second-class citizenship in the US, and apartheid South Africa. Most Christians believe that the God we worship is the God of the whole creation, and that God loves his creation. To accept subjugation, apartheid or ethnic cleansing as God's way is a serious misreading of the Scripture, which Christians understand from the life and message of Jesus Christ. If US Christians accept without challenge the serious harm being done to fellow Christians (and also our brothers and sisters, the Muslims) in the Holy Land, we will be seriously redefining our concept of Christianity to be a religion in which the touchstone is power, not justice. God then becomes a tribal totem, not the universal deity. This is not the religion taught by Jesus, nor will it be a religion that our children, or anybody's children, will want to embrace.

Some forty-five years later it is with chagrin and embarrassment that I recall my ignorance and misconceptions about the Middle East when I first travelled there. But I think it has helped me understand the mindset of many of my fellow citizens. I have also learned that behind the determined Zionist propaganda campaign lies a deep fear of being homeless and vulnerable again. Only when we cross religious and ethnic lines to work for justice and safety for everyone can we bring about the peaceable kingdom.

THE PREMISED LAND:
PALESTINE AND ISRAEL
Stephen R Sizer

The predestined land:
the Arab-Israeli conflict
through Zionist eyes

As a young Christian at Sussex University in the mid-1970s I was strongly influenced by dispensational and Christian Zionist leaders such as David Pawson, Tim LaHaye and Hal Lindsey. Devouring Hal Lindsey's best-selling book, *The Late Great Planet Earth* (Lindsey 1970), and hearing in person his lectures on eschatology and the Book of Revelation (Lindsey 1983), it seemed as if the Bible was literally coming true in this generation.

The Jews, the chosen people, had been brought back to their promised land in 1948. Apparently, the prophetic clock was now ticking. God had miraculously delivered them again in 1967, giving victory over their Arab enemies. Jerusalem, their eternal capital, was now once again, under Jewish sovereignty. The Temple would soon be rebuilt. The prophetic signs were being fulfilled on the front pages of our newspapers. The world seemed to be rushing toward a cataclysmic end in the great battle of Armageddon. The threat of nuclear war, the fear of world domination by atheistic communism, as well as Palestinian terrorism were futile attempts to annihilate the Jewish people and destroy the State of Israel. The moral responsibility of evangelical, Bible-believing Christians was clear—stand with God's 'chosen' people, because God was on the side of those who 'blessed' Israel.

The perplexing land: how my attitudes began to change

Alongside these Zionist convictions there was also a strong desire to visit the Holy Land, to see for myself where Jesus walked. It never occurred to me that there might be an indigenous Church, except for the small but growing assemblies of Messianic believers spoken of in revered but hushed tones.

My first pilgrimage: misinformation

Friends associated with the Garden Tomb and the Churches Ministry Among Jewish People (CMJ) helped me plan my first pilgrimage to the Holy Land in 1990. On their advice a Messianic guide called Zvi was engaged to lead our group. With the *Intifada* at its height it did not appear strange that he was unwilling to meet us at our hotel in Arab East Jerusalem. Instead we picked him up near the Jaffa Gate in West Jerusalem. The sight of heavily armed Israeli soldiers, encounters with occasional stone-throwing Palestinian children, and Zvi's opinion that some of the archaeological sites on the West Bank were 'unsafe' for tourists fuelled my latent prejudice against Palestinians.

Our memorable tour began with a visit to Yad Vashem, the *Shoah* museum. This helped explain the Israeli preoccupation with security. They could not rely on the West any more than they had done in the 1930s. During the week Zvi enthusiastically showed us how the new State of Israel was turning a barren and deserted wilderness into a land flowing with milk and honey. We visited the kibbutz at En Gev in the Golan with its armour-plated tractors, and Masada to remember the heroic last stand of the Zealots against the Roman invaders.

My 'conversion' came in two parts. The first came on the *Via Dolorosa*, at the *Lithostrotos*, the Roman pavement below street level at the Sisters of Sion convent. A member of the party asked Zvi an innocuous question about the Palestinians. He responded by giving us all a piece of paper with the heading 'Who are the Palestinians?' Ignoring the significance of the archaeological site before us, he proceeded to 'prove' that there was no such thing as a Palestinian. They had no unique history, culture or language. They were Arabs who had entered Israel in the early 20th century to threaten the embryonic State of Israel. Zvi was adamant, the Arabs should return to Arabia. The Jews had a divine right to *Eretz Yisrael* which extended from the Nile to the Euphrates.

The second part of my change of mind came in a meeting later that week with Riah Abu El Assal, then Archdeacon of Nazareth. In a simple presentation he explained how he was a Christian Arab Palestinian Israeli. He spoke of the historic presence of an indigenous Church in Palestine long before the founding of the State of Israel. He shared with us his joy at having just received back his Israeli passport. He had been banned from travel abroad for four years without explanation, or charges ever having been made. At the end of his presentation Riah warmly shook hands with Zvi, and we left Nazareth. But my bubble had burst. We had met a real live Christian Palestinian. They did exist. And so began the stream of questions that would not go away.

Back in Britain the search began to make sense of the historical and theological issues behind the Arab-Israeli conflict. Among the most helpful guides were Kenneth Cragg (1982; 1992), Colin Chapman (1983), Gary Burge (1993), and Dan O'Neill and Don Wagner (1993). There were also biographies of several Palestinian Christians. 1990 was a significant year, seeing the publication of three important books by Naim Ateek, Elias Chacour and Audeh Rantisi.

West Bank tour with Garth Hewitt: radicalisation

In the 1980s Garth Hewitt and I found ourselves on the same ministry team at St Saviour's, Guildford. Discovering our common interest in

Palestine, Garth invited me to join him on a concert tour of Jerusalem and West Bank churches in early 1991. Garth had written a series of songs about the plight of Palestinians and the issues of justice and peace in the Middle East. He has a rare talent for empathising with people in such a way to express in song their pain and suffering, their faith and hope. It was a most moving experience to hear him sing about Palestine to a wide range of Palestinian audiences, both Christian and Muslim. Someone understood them and had the courage to voice it, unafraid to sing about Palestine.

Conditions for travel were difficult, with tensions high, due to the *Intifada* and draconian Israeli security measures. The tour included concerts in East Jerusalem, Bethlehem, Ramallah, Zababida, Nazareth, as well as Amman and Salt in Jordan. In East Jerusalem, for example, a concert was arranged at the Hakawati Theatre, a Palestinian cultural centre. The theatre was packed and the reception Garth received from the audience, almost exclusively Muslim, was incredible. The noise from their clapping and cheering was deafening, and I feared he had started a riot. As if to confirm my suspicions, as we left the theatre, we were confronted with a blazing yellow-plated Israeli car left in the wrong place and now a 'legitimate' target. Trying to get close to take photographs I was dragged back into our car as the Israeli military jeeps arrived to investigate.

Later, the Anglican Bishop in Jerusalem, Samir Kafity, wanted us to experience life in a Palestinian village under occupation, so he arranged for us to stay overnight with families in Zababida, following a concert in the little Anglican chapel there. Driving through the West Bank required the use of a couple of brightly coloured *keffiyeh* strategically placed on the dashboard to avoid our being mistaken for Jewish settlers. We found ourselves experiencing the harsh conditions faced by Palestinians every day under military occupation, hidden from the touristic gaze of pilgrims travelling just a few miles away in the Jordan Valley.

The day we arrived in Zababida, the Israeli authorities had cut off the water supply and electricity as a collective punishment because the village had refused to pay a fine. Each family had to

147

carry water from the ancient well, while a limited supply of electricity was provided by a communal generator the village had bought to become self-sufficient. It was not powerful enough, however, to provide for the whole village at the same time, so each house was rationed to a couple of hours of electricity per night. Even in the church we had a choice between Garth's amplifier and the electric fans. As guests of the community we found ourselves being hosted by different families, taken from house to house, following the supply of electricity around the community as the evening wore on. The following morning after enjoying typical Palestinian hospitality, we heard that the village was now under a closed military curfew. As Garth had a concert in Jerusalem that evening a brave soul agreed to run the gauntlet and drive us out of the village back to Jerusalem. Even Bishop Samir Kafity and his driver were not exempt. Wishing to attend the concert in Zababida the night before, Bishop Samir was threatened at gunpoint at a roadblock by Israeli soldiers who tried to prevent his journey. 'Come this way again and we will shoot you,' he was warned.

In Ramallah, Garth's concert was one of the first public gatherings permitted by the Israeli military authorities after months of arrests, intimidation and nightly curfews. Audeh Rantisi was our host, a gracious and warm pastor who, with his wife, Patricia founded the Evangelical Home for Boys. Audeh spoke powerfully of his conviction that peace would never come to Israel until there was justice for the Palestinian as well. He insisted there were two ways to spell 'peace'. 'If the Zionists insist on spelling it "piece" they will never find security with their Arab neighbours.' Having read his book, *Blessed are the Peacemakers* (Rantisi 1990) before the tour, it was a delight to be asked by his publisher to take photos of the boys from the Home for the front cover of the UK edition. Unfortunately, the provocative graffiti on the walls behind the boys in my photos somehow disappeared in the process of publication.

On this and subsequent tours my convictions were further shaped by deepening friendships with Naim Ateek of *Sabeel*, Jonathan Kuttab, a human rights lawyer, Edmund Shehadeh, of the Arab

Bethlehem Centre for Rehabilitation in nearby Beit Jala, Zoughbi Zoughbi of Wi'am, a conflict resolution centre in Bethlehem, Bishara Awad of Bethlehem Bible College, Salim Munayer of Musalaha, a reconciliation project in Bethlehem, Cedar Duyabis of the YWCA, East Jerusalem, and Tom Getman of World Vision. Though a small and diminishing presence in the Holy Land, the Palestinian Church has been blessed by God with some courageous and outspoken leaders.

Zahi Nassir: identification

In 1992, at the request of Bishop Samir, a three-month visit to our Diocese of Guildford (UK) was arranged for the Revd Zahi Nassir from Nazareth. Newly ordained, the intention was to broaden Zahi's experience of the Anglican Communion. During his stay in our home, three notable events stand out which helped me understand what it felt like to be a Palestinian.

At a clergy gathering Zahi had the opportunity to meet the Mayor of Guildford. In her gesture of welcoming, the mayor explained that she had 'once met your Prime Minister, Golda Meir'. Zahi politely informed her that Golda Meir was not his Prime Minister. 'She had been a good Prime Minister to her own people but not for the Palestinians.' There was incomprehension in the mayor's face and an embarrassing silence ensued until someone moved the conversation on to less controversial matters.

At another event intended to give Zahi an opportunity to speak about Palestine to Christians in Guildford, a senior member of a large evangelical church stood up and asked if Zahi could answer a basic question, 'What is a Palestinian?' Zahi handled the insult with dignity, inviting the questioner to answer it himself. Nevertheless the public embarrassment of having to justify the existence of his own people cast a shadow over Zahi's stay. Kenneth Cragg's assessment that Zionists seek to perpetuate the myth of 'the political non-existence of Palestinians' (1992: 241) was borne out during his visit.

On another occasion Zahi travelled to Wales by train and borrowed a book of mine to read on the way. He chose *Israel, An Apartheid State* by Uri Davis (1987). Nervous at being seen reading the book, he made a brown paper dust cover to hide the title. It had never occurred to me that reading a book on a train in England might be perceived as a threat to the security of Israel, and therefore be a hazardous pursuit for a Palestinian.

On what were, by now, becoming regular visits to Israel-Palestine, my affinity for Palestinians grew as I had to endure intrusive and rigorous interrogations from Israeli security staff at Ben Gurion airport, but also sadly at Heathrow and Gatwick airports, presumably with the connivance of the British authorities. Elias Chacour's description of the degrading treatment he and other Palestinians endure when travelling, solely because of their race, and its similarity to the way Nazis treated Jews less than forty years earlier is most poignant (Chacour 1990: 1-5).

At the end of a visit to participate in Zahi's priesting, we debated whether he should come with me into the airport terminal at Ben Gurion, or whether we should say goodbye in the car park. He had been embarrassed on a flight to Cyprus when a group of expatriate clergy had disassociated themselves from him and fellow Palestinian clergy in order to obtain more lenient treatment going through airport security. We decided not to be intimidated. Two Israeli security staff approached us and asked me, 'Is he with you?' When I replied that Zahi was a friend of mine, they wanted to know his name and address. It was surreal. They dealt with him through me as if he were a child, or an adult who could not speak for himself. They disappeared to check his name on their database. 'Was he on your list?' I asked. 'No,' they replied. 'Did you check my name?' I added. 'Should we?' they queried. 'You never know,' I responded with a smile.

On the pretext of 'airline security' often detailed and personal questions are asked about friendships, contacts and places visited that go well beyond the legitimate needs of aircraft safety. This form of interrogation, unique to Israel, appears more to do with intimidation and intelligence gathering than airline safety. My worst encounter occurred in 1992 on a trip to Israel and Jordan for a concert tour with Garth Hewitt. Having travelled alone back from Amman that morning via the Allenby Bridge to Tel Aviv I was interrogated for nearly three hours, and enjoyed the delights of a body search, as well as the inspection of the entire contents of my luggage. The Israeli security staff threatened to withhold my cameras, and would not believe that I was an Anglican vicar. They accused me of spying, a life-long but sadly unrealised ambition, and they eventually escorted me to the waiting plane. I was even forbidden to carry my cameras in my hand luggage. Guilty of many things, it is nevertheless a disturbing 'Orwellian' experience to find yourself unable to convince people that you are who you say you are.

The Premised Land: my response
Pilgrimage research: investigation

Between 1993 and 1997, growing interest in pilgrimages gave me the impetus for post-graduate research into the impact of pilgrimages on the Palestinians. I interviewed over one hundred pilgrims and Palestinian Christians, and surveyed twenty-five British tour operators. The results revealed deep-seated prejudices and stereotypical caricatures of Palestinians, and an absence of contact between pilgrims and the indigenous Christians. One operator explained why, in common with all other tour companies, they did not refer to the land as Palestine.

> We never use the word 'Israel' in our brochures and I've always stuck with that ... We always use the word 'Holy Land'. 'Palestine' is equally emotive. Our people are not going there for political reasons, they're going to the holy places. The place has always been called the Holy Land and we try to keep to that (Sizer 1994: 79).

A survey among pilgrims of their associations or connotations of words like 'Jew', 'Arab' and 'Palestinian' showed the term 'Palestinian' to be the least positive, the least neutral and the most negative image of the three (Sizer 1994).

While the presence of tens of thousands of Western Christian tourists and pilgrims in the Holy Land at any one time has great potential for good, ironically, for the most part, it does great harm. That is because most Christians visiting the Holy Land follow an itinerary purposely designed or encouraged by the Israeli government Ministry of Tourism to bring them into contact only with Jewish Israel, perpetuating the myth of the Zionist dream being fulfilled. Like my own first tour, typically itineraries include visiting the Knesset, Yad Vashem, Masada, the Dead Sea, a kibbutz, and an Israeli cultural evening, all under the watchful influence of a Jewish guide. Contact with Palestinians and visits within the Occupied Territories are avoided as much as possible. Even the tourist maps, available free from the government agency, no longer show the international borders of the West Bank, or Syrian Golan Heights. My research found that 95 percent of pilgrims make no contact with the indigenous Palestinian Church. Most tour groups are oblivious of the fact that they will be passing into illegally held 'Occupied Territories' on the West Bank, in order to visit places such as the Old City of Jerusalem, Bethlehem and Jericho.

My analysis of pilgrimage tour operators revealed four categories. For secular operators the presence of an indigenous Church is irrelevant. Christian operators are largely ignorant of it, and Zionist operators are antagonistic. Only the comparatively few who identify with the name 'Living Stones' offer any dialogue between pilgrims and Palestinian Christians.

The vast majority of UK operators appear ignorant of the ethical issues implicit in their business. They fail to recognise how they are manipulated by the Israeli authorities and how detrimental their business is to the indigenous Christian community. Based on this evidence it is not surprising that so few pilgrimage groups ever meet Palestinians.

Kenneth Cragg observes,

> Sharp moral issues are easily submerged by outsiders
> in archaeology or tourism, while the local Christianity
> is relegated to sentiment and the museum (Cragg 1992:
> 235).

It is not pleasant for Palestinian Christians to watch air-conditioned coaches full of Christians from around the world driving past their church and impoverished community every day, to visit yet another holy site, fearful of any contact with 'terrorists'. My many interviews with Palestinian Christians assure me that radical changes are needed in the practice of pilgrimages if we are not to perpetuate or exacerbate the gradual haemorrhaging of the Palestinian Church.

The continuing presence of the indigenous Christian community is the primary ethical issue facing pilgrimage operators and tour leaders in the immediate future. It should constitute the agenda for responsible tourism to the Holy Land. Elias Chacour echoed the feelings of many Palestinian Christian leaders:

> Your visit to Ibillin was not just a courtesy visit but an
> act of solidarity with your brothers and sisters in Christ.
> We need to know that you care and we are not
> forgotten. We have been deprived for 50 years (Sizer
> 1994: 107).

Kenneth Cragg summarises the issue the Palestinian Church faces daily.

> Local Christians are caught in a degree of
> museumisation. They are aware of tourists who come
> in great volume from the West to savour holy places

but who are, for the most part, blithely disinterested in the people who indwell them. The pain of the indifference is not eased insofar as the same tourism is subtly manipulated to make the case for the entire legitimacy of the statehood that regulates it (Cragg 1992:28).

The ethical issues and decisions encountered in promoting responsible tourism to the Holy Land are therefore considerable and complex. Those over which Western Christians have some influence include the choice of British or Israeli airline; Jewish or Palestinian land agents, guides, and bus companies; whether to accept subsidies or promotional material from the Israeli government Ministry of Tourism; and the level of payment made for services provided in the country. For example, Israeli guides invariably earn significantly more than Palestinian guides.

A number of specific and practical recommendations for pilgrimage tour operators, leaders and guides followed as a result of this research. For example, tour operators and leaders are urged to ensure that within itineraries adequate time is given for meetings with Palestinian Christians, especially those in the Occupied Territories, and that long-term reciprocal relations are nurtured between their churches.

Travel on Sundays should be avoided and time taken to worship with the local Christian communities, under their own leadership. Formal liturgical worship in hotels or locations without the participation of indigenous Christians should also be avoided. Itineraries should include visits to Christian charitable and humanitarian projects such as hospitals and schools.

Wherever possible Christian agencies, buses, hostels, hospices and guides should be used that will bring revenue to the indigenous Palestinian economy, in preference to those agencies of a purely tourist nature which are under Israeli control.

The initial research led to the award of an MTh with distinction from Oxford University (Sizer 1994). Further research undertaken between 1994-1997, which amplified and enhanced the initial findings, resulted in the award of a DPhil from International Management Centres (Sizer 1997d).

Pilgrims and peacemakers: illumination

In 1995 Garth Hewitt and I made a second concert tour of churches in Israel and the Occupied Territories. This also provided the inspiration for his book *Pilgrims and Peacemakers*, based on interviews we had with Jewish and Palestinian peacemakers (Hewitt 1995). One episode in the book highlights an unusual application of the parable of the Good Samaritan. After a rather tense visit to Gaza when I had naively accepted a lift in a yellow-plated Israeli car into the heart of Gaza City to speak at an Anglican service, we decided a short break would be good, and I offered to show Garth the beautiful scenery of northern Galilee. It was February, and by mid-afternoon the light was fading as I drove a borrowed minibus up the winding road past Mount Hermon, and into the snowy slopes of the occupied Syrian Golan Heights.

Above the snow line we encountered a group of young Israeli army conscripts. They were cold, wet and tired, and wanted a lift. We nervously ignored them and carried on driving up into the darkness. With hopes of showing Garth the isolated UN post at Quneitira fading we turned round and headed home. As we turned a corner our headlights caught the shape of one of the young soldiers lying in the road, his companions attempting to revive him. Wet and cold he appeared to have hypothermia. Garth helped them lift the semi-conscious soldier into the mini-bus, and we continued to descend before being met by an army vehicle that took the unknown soldier to hospital.

Despite my anger at the arrogant Israeli settlers and soldiers I had encountered in Gaza the day before, I realised that these young conscripts, just seventeen-years old, were as vulnerable, needy and human as my Palestinian friends. It reminded me of Abuna Elias Chacour's profound statement that we are not born Jews, Arabs or

British. First of all God makes us all babies. The encounter made me
more determined than ever to,

> Pray not for Arab or Jew,
> for Palestinian or Israeli
> But pray rather for ourselves
> That we might not divide them in our prayers
> But keep them both together in our hearts
>
> (Hewitt 1995: 149).

Responsible tourism: solidarity

With the assistance of Highway Journeys, and in partnership with
Amos Trust, a series of 'Living Stones' pilgrimages was arranged
from 1994-1997. The specific purpose was to bring together British
pilgrims and Palestinian Christians. The intention was to experience
something of the ancient spirituality of the Holy Land, as well as
learn from this suffering Church how they witness to the Christian
faith in terms of justice, peacemaking and interfaith dialogue. The
accommodation, agents and guide were chosen specifically in order
to bring maximum benefit to the local Christian Church and Palestinian
tourist economy.

    While most Protestant tour groups treat Sundays as just
another day for visiting sites, or hold private Communion Services in
their hotels or at places like the Garden Tomb with expatriates, we
insisted that our group worship with the local Christian communities,
in their own language, singing their hymns and following their liturgies.
The fellowship at St George's in Jerusalem and Christ Church in
Nazareth, for example, is always warm, appreciated and unforgettable.
Rather than fill each day with visits to archaeological sites we mapped
out itineraries that included visits to refugee camps, reconciliation
projects, demolished homes, hospitals and schools. Despite repeated
closures we have managed to get into Gaza with our groups on each
occasion. Whilst evangelicals may be critical of the liberal agenda of

the World Council of Churches, it is heartening to find that on one of the most densely populated pieces of land on earth, the Near East Council of Churches and other Christian bodies are putting the Gospel into action, offering vital educational and vocational training to refugees irrespective of their ethnic or religious background.

The impact of taking a large tour group into Gaza was very significant, attracting in 1994, quite unintentionally, the interest of international journalists and film crews, recording reactions to the signing of the Peace Accord at the border. According to our Palestinian guide, it was the first visit of its kind by such a large group in five years or more. Moreover, feedback from the participants on each occasion was immensely encouraging.

In Jericho, while we watched tour buses hurtle past to photograph a two-hundred-year-old sycamore tree that Zaccheus most certainly did not climb, we discovered a community of Christians. In what looks like a deserted refugee camp from the wars of 1948 and 1967, the YMCA, World Vision and Christian Aid are investing in the future of Palestine, giving young men and women the chance to learn vocational skills, such as in car mechanics, carpentry and computers. It was embarrassing to discover on our first visit that we were the only British group ever to visit the camp.

The cumulative effect of what has increasingly become known as *Living Stones* visits has been much more constructive in its impact on both pilgrims and Palestinian Christians, leading to long-term relationships and mission partnerships. Highway Journeys, for example, have subsequently formed a Highway Projects team which has taken a number of teams of young people from Britain to assist with Palestinian youth camps in Ibillin, and restoration projects, such as at the Four Homes of Mercy in Bethany and the Princess Basma hospital on the Mount of Olives.

Eyewitness testimony: publication

Beginning in 1995, I was invited to write a series of articles for *Evangelicals Now*, based on interviews with Palestinian Christian leaders about the political and theological issues surrounding the peace process.[1] The flak received from Zionist readers, hostile to a pro-Palestinian perspective, gave some indication of the depth of feeling within British evangelicalism on the Arab-Israeli issue. Despite further criticism and even the occasional anonymous threat, the articles began to flow, and, more importantly, were published. These included 'Where to Find Christ in the Holy Land' (Sizer 1996); 'The Mountain of the Wall, the Battle for Jerusalem' (Sizer 1997a); and 'Barak and the Bulldozers' (Sizer 1999d).

With the political situation deteriorating, in part, due to the provocative decision to continue with the building of an exclusive Jewish Settlement on confiscated land overlooking the popular pilgrimage site of the Shepherds' Fields outside Bethlehem, the *Church Times* carried an article on the controversy surrounding the Har Homa settlement (1998b). It highlighted the political strategy and economic incentive behind the settlement which has profound and disturbing ramifications for the indigenous Christian community.

It effectively 'lays siege' to the Christian Palestinian communities of Beit Sahour and Bethlehem. It eliminates their land reserves, isolates them from Jerusalem and cuts them off from the rest of the West Bank to the north. It threatens the very existence of these ancient Christian communities. This settlement is also part of an ambitious plan to build a new tourist city on the northern entrance to Bethlehem called, 'Bethlehem, Israel'. This tourist centre will inevitably further suffocate family-owned Christian businesses in Bethlehem and Beit Sahour, and deprive the already flagging Palestinian economy of badly needed revenue. According to Afif Safieh, the Palestinian General Delegate to the UK, and a Christian, 'The economic repercussion of the Jabal Abu Ghoneim-Har Homa settlement will inevitably result in driving the Christian community into exile' (Sizer 1998b:7). Clearly the intentions of the Israeli Government to create a 'Disney-style' Bethlehem in time for the millennium celebrations and

---

[1] All the articles mentioned in this paper, as well as others relating to Holy Land pilgrimage research and Christian Zionism are available from my church web-site: www.virginiawater.co.uk/christchurch/articles.html.

the large number of additional visitors raised serious ethical issues which tour operators and pilgrimage tour leaders cannot avoid.

Further research: recognition

Following interest in my research (see Ateek 1997: 130; Wills 1997: 18; Prior 1997: 325), I received an invitation to speak at the 3rd International *Sabeel* Conference in Bethlehem in 1998 on Christian Zionism from a British Perspective (see Sizer 1999a). Similar invitations came from the Centre for Jewish Studies in the School of Oriental and African Studies, London University; Wycliffe Hall, Oxford; Bethlehem Bible College; together with Bristol, Wells and Chester Cathedrals. In the same year the opportunity arose to convene a global internet conference on 'ethics in tourism' for MCB University Press, the world's largest publisher of management journals. This brought together academics and practitioners from around the world, leading to my guest editing of a double edition of the *International Journal of Contemporary Hospitality Management* (Sizer 1999b). Tearfund, the largest evangelical relief agency in Britain, has subsequently begun to address the issue of 'ethical tourism', helped by the conference and subsequent meetings (Gordon 1999).

The Promised Land: confronting the issues

Meeting the Living Stones, the indigenous Christians of Israel-Palestine, listening to their story, and reading of the Bible through their eyes, has shattered my previously held naïve Zionist views. They have encouraged me not only to think my way through the issues, but motivated me to carry our first-hand research, so that my views are based on facts rather than prejudice.

My research has highlighted how the Palestinian Christian community has suffered isolation, discrimination and persecution akin to 'ethnic cleansing', and a form of apartheid. The plight of Palestinian

Christians is exacerbated by Christian fundamentalism infatuated with Zionism, which in the words of Don Wagner, is 'Anxious for Armageddon' (Wagner 1995). Christian Zionism is a complex, controversial and extremely influential theological movement that pervades Western evangelicalism and Pentecostalism. Its impact on the indigenous Church of the Holy Land has been entirely negative.

For instance, many fundamentalists believe that the Judaeo-Christian Scriptures endorse a Zionist agenda, giving the contemporary State of Israel a divine mandate to rule Eretz Yisrael, with Jerusalem her sovereign capital, centred on a rebuilt Jewish temple. Until now there has been little critical research into its theological origins or its variant forms (but see Prior 1999; Wagner 1995). Further doctoral research currently in process is examining these assumptions and will provide a definitive critical rebuttal of the movement.

In 1971, Archbishop George Khodr of Beruit made this prediction.

> According to our knowledge, after four more decades of the rhythm of evacuation, no Christians will be left in Jerusalem. The result will be that the Holy Places will remain without the presence of the people. It will be an assemblage of churches ... viewed in that land as a pre-Israeli relic ... It will be like visiting Baalbec when you see the Temples of Bacchus and Jupiter and then without any emotion except the aesthetic emotion ... Some religious influences will be left, some nuns ... and highly qualified professors of theology, and archaeologists from the Protestant world who will serve as natural guides for tourists (in Cragg 1982:110).

Kenneth Cragg argues that Western Christians should not leave the responsibility of rectifying such a situation to the Israeli authorities, since they are only concerned with maintaining access to shrines, exploiting Western Christian tourism and bringing in 'lucrative foreign exchange'. The absence of Palestinian Christians simply makes the realisation of this objective less complicated.

If Christian minorities suffer ... it is no more than
unfortunate. The Christian museum will be in safe hands
(Cragg 1982: 111).

In the light of my research, travels and encounters with the
indigenous Christians of the Holy Land, I am now determined to
work to ensure that they do have a future, and that, in the words of
Archbishop George Carey, we do not aid the creation of 'an empty
Christian Disney World' by default.

That the majority of Western Christians continue to ignore,
and in some cases malign the indigenous Palestinian Church in such
a troubled situation is not only deeply offensive to them, but is a
contradiction of our faith, and is ultimately sinful. It reminds one of
the behaviour of the priest and the Levite in the Parable of the Good
Samaritan who walked by on the other side.

HOLY LAND—MY ALTERNATIVE PILGRIMAGE
Janet Davies

May more eyes see
More ears hear
More lips speak

Thus read the poster on a wall in a back street room in the Gaza Strip in March 1982.

'It's your fault' (meaning Britain) gesticulated the old man, wagging his finger at me. 'It was you who promised us freedom and independence, and then walked out on us in 1948 leaving us to be shot, murdered and dispossessed of our homes, our land, our livelihood, our human rights—everything!' Like so many Palestinian men and women, this old man, now living in one of the eight refugee camps in the Gaza Strip, still held the key to his house, wearing it like a necklace on a piece of string round his neck, with the dream that he and they would one day, return to their villages and take up possession of their homes, and their olive trees, which had been so violently stolen. With the words of the poster imprinted in my mind and on my heart, and with the angry accusation levelled at me by the old man, began the introduction of an erstwhile innocent to what we at the turn of the millennium still dare to call 'The Holy Land'.

I shall focus here on three questions: How did I come to be in the Holy Land? What effect did my growing awareness of history and events there have on me? Why, in conclusion, having seen and heard, do I believe it is important to speak out for peace with justice for two nations, Israel and Palestine, and three faiths, Christian, Jewish and Muslim?

Coming to the Holy Land

I have always called my story the 'Alternative Pilgrimage' because pilgrims from the US and Europe, including Britain, for the most part, never meet with the indigenous people, be they Christian, Jew or Muslim, and are frequently amazed both to learn, and occasionally discover, that there are 'living stones' with much to share.

I had lost my husband, Alan, from cancer in September 1981, and the important fact for me about this particular journey, was that Alan knew I might well go to the Lebanon, Egypt and Israel/Palestine, as part of my work as a staff member of Christian Aid. So when Christian Aid asked me whether I still wanted to make the journey in these circumstances, I said 'Yes'. The experience, although very often traumatic in what I was both seeing and hearing, was to unfold, not as a single journey, but as the pilgrimage of a life-time, giving me, not only a personal restorative contribution in my own bereavement healing, but, I dare to say, an empathy with people who had been deeply wounded. I remain indebted to the Revd Dr Carlisle Patterson, Head of Christian Aid's Overseas Aid Department in 1982, who accompanied me, and got me so firmly hooked into Middle East issues. I was, in fact, the first Christian Aid Area Co-ordinator to visit Israel/Palestine, Egypt and the Lebanon. I have since returned many times to Israel/Palestine.

My own story and experience started in the Lebanon in February 1982, prior to the devastating June war of that year, which included the Sabra and Chatila massacres, and where I was to see some of the 400,000 Palestinian refugees. These were people who had fled from Palestine in 1947-48, when the State of Israel was declared, and who fast became a neglected, forgotten people, whose existence can be likened to a life-support machine, where the oxygen is rapidly running out. My first night in Beirut, at the then famous Mayfair Hotel, was not only my introduction to the sound of nightly gunfire across the city, but the beginning of my journey into the seeing and hearing of a dispossessed Palestinian people, and the incredibly committed work of the Near East Council of Churches, one of Christian Aid's major partners at that time.

Until 1982, Palestine—the Holy Land—had been but a series of names of places and associations through biblical stories and events which had taken place in Bethlehem, Jerusalem, the Mount of Olives, Emmaus, Jericho, Nazareth, to name but a few. I had little understanding or knowledge of what had happened to the Palestinian people as a result of the declaration of the State of Israel in 1948, and the subsequent June 1967 war, when Israel conquered the West Bank, the Gaza Strip and the Golan Heights, from which, in breach of international law and several United Nations resolution (especially Resolution 242) she has resolutely failed to withdraw.

As I sat on a wall on the Mount of Olives, overlooking a scene stretching from the Kidron Valley to the walled Old City of Jerusalem, and the series of high modern cranes, as the Israeli Government continued apace to extend the Israeli settlements, I was reminded of how frequently I had spoken to groups on behalf of Christian Aid in Liverpool, about poverty and all its attendant miseries and implications, without ever having experienced what that meant until I arrived in the Bustees of Calcutta and smelt the poverty of the people. As I continued to look across the Kidron Valley, with the cry of the people ringing in my ears, I pictured in my mind's eye, Christ weeping over the City, a place where undoubtedly, He still weeps. For Jerusalem is a microcosm of the world today, where 'Justice is nailed to the Cross daily', in the words of Naim Ateek (Director of *Sabeel*, the Ecumenical Palestinian Liberation Theology Centre in Jerusalem), which he spoke to our group during a Bible Study on 26 March 1999.

Back at the YMCA (the Capitalino Hotel), on Nablus Road, East Jerusalem, which over the years has become home for me and many Christian Aid staff members, I first witnessed with my own eyes the bullet holes in the lift, put there by Israeli soldiers on one of their many raids, wreaking havoc and fear on an innocent community. Until it was recently replaced with a modern unit, that lift remained a constant reminder, as it traversed between the basement and the fifth floor, of justice being nailed to the Cross. On the fifth floor of the 'Y' are the restaurant and balcony with their commanding views over East and West Jerusalem. One can also see St George's Cathedral, the Garden of Gethsemane, the Mount of Olives and many other features. Yet, it is from that very balcony where one longs to say, 'How beautiful the view', that, over the years, I have watched the now total encirclement of Jerusalem through the erection of the settlements occupying high ground, often referred to as 'watch towers'. The lands on which the settlements have been built have been confiscated from Palestinian families, often on the pretext of 'security' needs. Hence the inability to comment on the beautiful view, for it is tragically, a constant Gethsemane.

The effects of a growing awareness

The YMCA is always a hive of activity—a meeting point for so much of Palestinian life and culture, creating as much normality as possible. For visitors like myself, there is always a welcome. *Ahlan wa Sahlan.* The Arabic 'welcome' is constantly on the lips of everyone, and nothing is too much trouble. But what is life really like for those gentle, hospitable people whose daily lives are surrounded by so many violations of the United Nations Declaration of Human Rights? I was both to see and hear that daily story.

Most of us, in the West, take for granted the choices freedom offers us, such as getting into our cars and driving to work each day. Observing their daily routines, I quickly became aware that with the constant closures of borders, Palestinians find it extremely difficult, and sometimes impossible, to make even quite short journeys to work. For the same reason they often cannot access medical treatment, attend school, meet friends or attend worship. In fact, it has even been reported in the British Press that Palestinian women have lost babies in childbirth through being prevented from passing through checkpoints to reach hospital. Families are unable to plan a family outing to Jerusalem, because they do not have the necessary travel documents. The young people at the YMCA will often say to me, 'Janet it is lovely to see you, but you, as a visitor, have the freedom to visit where you like, whilst we, in our own country, do not have that right or privilege'. May more eyes see, more ears hear, more lips speak.

Everywhere I travelled in the West Bank and the Gaza Strip, the situations I saw and the stories I heard were deeply disturbing. Four generations of families in some of the refugee camps have known no other life. The original tent camps have become, over the decades, sprawling concrete and tin-roofed masses, with little or no regular electricity, water supply, or other basic facilities. Israel holds the power over the water supply and the land, which it continues to confiscate, which means it can, and does, turn off the water supply to the Palestinians whenever it chooses. In the Gaza Strip, I have seen entire orange groves decimated by the heat of the sun, due to the Israeli authorities turning off the water supply. Yet, on the immediately adjacent settlements, the lawn sprinklers dance their cooling spray. One compares such disparity with the former 'apartheid' regime in South Africa.

The Palestinian Agricultural Relief Committee (PARC), a major partner of Christian Aid, often experiences serious difficulties in obtaining licences to dig wells for irrigation purposes, and even when successful, is frequently limited with regard to the depth it is permitted to drill the earth. As a consequence, PARC hastens to bring all its land under cultivation, as by doing this, it is less likely to be confiscated. Likewise, olive trees, which are so important to the Palestinian people and a major part of their livelihood, are frequently uprooted and destroyed by Israeli soldiers. In the light of that I recall being incensed on receiving a leaflet through *The Tablet*, from a UK Israeli Foundation, inviting people to buy a tree, or a glade of trees, or even a forest of trees in the Holy Land.

During my visits, in 1982 and 1984, I was made particularly aware that not only was there a military ground force operating, but a major psychological warfare game operating above the ground. Jet planes roared across the sky swooping in low over the Palestinian villages, whereupon, everyone, including myself, froze to the spot, white with fear, not knowing what might be ejected from their gun holders. I recall reflecting that inflicting such fear on a daily basis not only grossly violates people's human rights but flies in the face of anything to do with Judaism. The same principle applies to the question of torture which, until recently, Israel alone of the nations incorporated into its legal system. I felt mentally and physically 'wiped out', sitting with those who shared their experiences of profound suffering.

The distinguished Jewish theologian, Professor Marc Ellis, of Baylor University, Texas, poses the question of whether the Covenant can be in operation while Israelis are hooding and torturing Palestinian people (Ellis 1999). It is an awful irony that people and nations, which themselves have experienced barbaric treatment, can, in turn, inflict genocide and ethnic cleansing on others, sometimes in the name of religion. As we move into the next decade, this will be a conundrum confronting all of us. I know from my discussions with many Palestinians over the years as to what it means to be human, that they are the first to acknowledge the barbarous treatment meted out to the Jews through the Holocaust. However, they insist that the Holocaust had nothing to do with them as a people, and question why they now should have to pay for that evil through 'The Catastrophe' *(al-Nakba)* of 1948.

I consider that the time is overdue for the lead nations, especially the United States and Europe (including Britain with its historical involvement), to address seriously this question at international level. Many times in discussions leading up to the year 2000, Palestinians have questioned me as to what my country, Britain, is doing to enable Palestinians achieve nationhood. 'All of you who visit us and spend time with us, which we value, also intimately know what is happening to us. Can you not influence your government—and why is your Church so silent?' With an ever-increasing young generation of Palestinian people, such questions are real and urgent. How long will they allow themselves to remain disinherited?

Young Palestinians have had particular problems. The situation with respect to university students is especially troubling. Frequently over the years, students at the Universities of Bethlehem and Bir Zeit have been prevented either from going home for vacations, or from returning to university from their homes, whether in the Gaza Strip or on the West Bank. Indeed, the Israeli authorities have closed Palestinian universities for months at a time, with all the dire consequences for their academic advancement. One readily understands why the 1987 *Intifada* happened: the Palestinians lived in a permanent prison, with the world failing to intervene.

The demolition of family homes is particularly distressing. Try to imagine what it is like to wake up in the morning to find a bulldozer at your front door, with Israeli soldiers pushing you around and demanding that you get out 'now' as the house is to be demolished. Frequently, families are prohibited from taking more than a few possessions with them. In 1984, I observed such a scene from a hilltop in Galilee; in that case, the family was not allowed to take anything with them. Homes are demolished regularly on the grounds of not having a building permit. Palestinians, however, have great difficulty getting building permits. Owning the land, and needing to extend their present house is no advantage. Often, in utter frustration, they build without a permit, and often have to pay the consequences, demolition.

From 1948-1996, the process of trying to keep alive the glory of Palestinian life and culture was enormously difficult, for Israel set the educational curricula for Arab schools and teachers. Sitting with Palestinian teachers in their homes, listening to their frustrations, their anger and their deep pain, was heart-rending, as no aspect of their life and culture could be spoken of. 'What kind of geography and history can we teach, when Palestine is no longer a place on the map? We have been completely annihilated—wiped out as a nation of people.' How, I asked myself, would any of us respond to such iniquity? An equally moving experience for me was spending time in the Gaza Strip in 1982, with women who had founded 'The Union of Palestinian Women', which worked to offer mutual support, and to keep the Palestinian culture and identity alive, particularly in the home.

The women presented me with a gift of a dress-length of material, exquisitely embroidered with cross-stitch in red and green, on the black background, depicting the colours of the Palestinian flag. It was not lost on me that, prior to 1996, flying those colours could lead to imprisonment.

The moment of truth finally came for me through two experiences in February 1998 following the *Sabeel* International Conference in Bethlehem where a thousand delegates, Christian, Jew and Muslim, from all over the world had gathered.

Firstly I wanted to fill a gap in my own developing awareness. I and my Christian Aid colleague, Tony Graham, took the opportunity to visit Ein Karem, traditionally the setting for the *Magnificat*, and Yad Vashem, the Jewish memorial to the Holocaust victims. Ein Karem is also traditionally the home of Elizabeth and Zechariah. It is where Elizabeth, pregnant with John, ran to greet Mary, who had just discovered her own pregnancy. The *Magnificat*, also known as Mary's Song of Justice for all people, is displayed on tablets in every language around the courtyard of the 'Church of the Visitation'. Ein Karem is now an Israeli village, the Arab population having been driven out in 1948. Tony and I then moved on to Yad Vashem. We visited the Children's Memorial, set in total darkness, where one holds onto a rail for guidance, relieved only by tiny lights which depict the names of the children who died in the *Shoah*. As we emerged, stumbling slightly, from the darkness into sharp sunlight, Tony quietly said, 'And there, Jan, across the valley, is Deir Yassin.'

I already knew that, on the night of 9 April 1948, Menachem Begin's troops had attacked the village of Deir Yassin and killed 254 children, women and men. The men were killed after they had been paraded round the city. Their bodies were thrown down the village well. The next day, soldiers went to Ein Karem and warned the people what would happen to them if they did not immediately leave their homes. The parish priest of that largely Christian village led his people over the hill towards Bethlehem, and into permanent exile. (In 1948 some 418 Palestinian villages were destroyed by Israel.) This profoundly moving set of experiences prepared me for Marc Ellis' subsequent call, at the Christian Resources Exhibition (Sandown Park, Esher, England in 1999), for an International Pilgrimage of Peace, inviting Jews, Muslims and Christians to start from Yad Vashem and Deir Yassin, finally converging together on the City of Jerusalem.

I was to stay on in Jerusalem for a further ten days. Throughout the time of the conference, there had been the growing threat of a war with Iraq. My friends and colleagues were more than anxious about my staying on when they had all left for home. In fact, I did enquire about the possibility of getting an earlier flight to the UK, but due to the mass exit of people from Israel, this did not prove possible. I was advised to register with the British Consulate in Jerusalem, which I did. I was also informed by them that if a missile attack happened, I would be provided with a gas-mask. 'Fine,' I said, 'but what about my Palestinian friends here at the YMCA, with whom I am staying?', to which the response was silence! As I replaced the telephone receiver in my bedroom, I realised that I had been afforded a protection which would not be granted them—that, in effect, their lives were being placed at a much lower value than mine. It was a point at which I began to understand the obligations which freedom places on those of us fortunate enough to have it.

Speaking out for peace with justice

The gas-mask episode was the culmination of a long process of growing awareness that the decision to live or not to live for the Palestinian people, even in the period of the 'peace accords', remains the continuing stark choice. As I began to realise the human cost of the establishment of the State of Israel, I came to realise that the extent of the Palestinian 'Catastrophe' (*al-Nakba*) had been concealed from most Westerners, including myself. Few are aware of the dispossession of the Palestinian people. Tragically, too, the Church in Britain has maintained what Marc Ellis describes as 'the ecumenical dialogue of silence'. Time and again, Christians in the Holy Land say they feel deeply let down by the Western Church, and particularly by

Britain and America, each of which has historical and contemporary responsibilities for the present situation.

I am often reminded of the words of Maya Angelou, 'History despite its wrenching pain cannot be unlived but, if faced with courage, need not be lived again' (Angelou 1994: 272). Thankfully, there is a growing number of individuals and groups from across the religious and cultural divides in Israel/Palestine, who are trying to realise this possibility by standing with the people, searching for peace with justice. I think immediately of the Christian Peacemaker teams in Hebron, with their red hats. They are made up of Mennonites, Brethren, Quakers and a Catholic nun, largely from North America, and stand, bravely, between the Israeli army and the local Palestinian people, trying to defend them and their human rights. On the mantelpiece in my Liverpool home stand two pieces of stone from Palestinian homes which have been demolished by Israeli soldiers in Hebron, but whose occupants, in their hour of need, were supported by the Christian Peacemaker teams. This is a lasting memory from my 1999 visit to Hebron, accompanying Garth Hewitt from Christian Aid, in which we spent time with the Christian Peacemakers, hearing their stories, which Garth, in turn, so beautifully gathered up in prayer and song.

For the last ten years, a group known as the 'Women in Black', mostly Jewish women, who are sometimes joined by Muslim and Christian women, have been meeting at 1.00 p.m. on a Friday, round a square in West Jerusalem. They stand in silence for an hour, holding their banners and signs, as an act of peaceful protest. I have stood with them and witnessed the yells and insults hurled at them, but their continuing silent presence is a powerful witness to the message that there is another way. Again, it was a privilege to accompany Garth Hewitt who took me and another Christian Aid colleague, Tony Graham, to meet Rabbi Jeremy Milgrom who co-ordinates the Rabbis for Human Rights. They, too, constantly stand with Palestinians and Bedouins, whose homes have been demolished, and also support the Christian Peacemaker teams in Hebron.

In Jerusalem, I have spent time with LAW—the Palestinian Society for the Protection of Human Rights and the Environment, a non-governmental organisation dedicated to advancing human rights through legal advocacy. LAW is affiliated to the International Commission of Jurists and the Paris-based International Federation of Human Rights Leagues with the World Organisation Against Torture (OMCT), and is a member of the Euro-Mediterranean Human Rights Network. LAW is a Christian Aid Partner, and is a constant advocate of Human Rights. Sadly, on most days, despite the current peace process negotiations, an e-mail message from LAW gives details of yet another Israeli violation of Palestinian human rights.

My alternative pilgrimage has taught me to stand alongside such groups who are working for an alternative way of living for the peoples of two nations and three faiths. Archbishop Emeritus Desmond Tutu, speaking recently about freedom on BBC Radio Four, had this to say: 'Yes, we got rid of apartheid in South Africa, and gained freedom, but we then discovered that freedom has obligations, and the demands of freedom are very, very irksome.' 'Freedom has obligations'—I dare to suggest that those words are addressed to each of us without exception, and lead me into the conclusion of this piece.

It has been an enormous privilege, in the course of my working life, to have been given the opportunity to visit several countries, including South Africa, Namibia and Zimbabwe. Without exception, whenever I have asked the people in the host country, what they would like me to tell the people back home in Britain about their story, the response has always been, 'Please tell your people what is happening to us, and please pray for us as we pray for you.' Such a mandate has, I believe, put me under permanent obligation with no escape, and Israel-Palestine is no exception. As a consequence, I am reminded of a second phrase often spoken by Naim Ateek—'The door to peace lies through the door to justice.' For all of us, as Maya Angelou's words quoted earlier display, it takes courage not to live in wrenching pain again, and, in Naim Ateek's words, it takes courage to begin to push open the door. Yet, if Jew, Muslim, and Christian are facing it together, peace with justice can become a reality. Since my own induction to Israel-

Palestine in 1982, I have sought to hold fast to the people's cry encapsulated in the words of the poster on the Gaza office wall with which I opened this chapter.

I have been greatly supported in this process by Christian Aid, which not only enabled me to make the initial visit in 1982, but stood with me in all its continuing implications, and also by the United Reformed Church and its Commitment for Life Programme. The 1996 *Sabeel* International Conference, held in Jerusalem at the YMCA, was not only a keystone event for me and my colleagues, but was also a watershed for the Palestinian people. Immediately prior to the conference, many of us had stood amongst the excited Palestinian crowds in East Jerusalem, as they filed into the polling stations to record their votes for the first time, for their President and the Palestinian National Authority. Throughout, however, they were being closely watched from every vantage point by Israeli troops, from the turrets of the walls of the Old City to the polling stations themselves. There were many signs of hope and optimism. However, on our visit to Bethlehem in 1998, we saw the beginnings of the destruction of the afforested Jabal Abu Ghneim, a beautiful Palestinian-owned hillside beside Bethlehem, now denuded of its forest of trees, with swathes of concrete roads providing the infrastructure for a new Jewish settlement, renamed Har Homa.

My personal watershed took on firm shape when, following the 1996 *Sabeel* Conference, I accepted Naim Ateek's invitation to co-ordinate a Friends of *Sabeel* UK (FOS-UK). This has proved to be a major focus for sharing the Israel-Palestine story over the last three years in the UK and Ireland. Just three years old, FOS-UK works both with the ecumenical network of Churches, and the recently established 'Rediscovering Palestine' network of organisations committed to peace with justice. It aims to encourage international support of this commitment as well as offering challenge in respect of largely ignored issues such as the 'Right of Return' for Palestinian refugees under UN Resolution 194. This issue recently formed the subject of a major lobby of the UK Parliament (24 November 1999) which led to an Early Day Motion Debate (30 November 1999). FOS-

UK also contributes to the international support which is urgently required as talks about the final status of Jerusalem take place between Israel and Palestine.

In 1998, FOS-UK organised a major lecture tour which gave opportunity for hundreds of people throughout the UK to engage in a challenging debate with Professor Marc Ellis, Professor Yasir Suleiman, a Muslim and the Director of Advanced Middle East Studies at the University of Edinburgh, and Revd Dr Naim Ateek. As our three guests shared a platform together, we were afforded a vision of how it can be when Jew, Muslim and Christian stand side by side to share their story, and their hopes and longings for resolution. 'Tell the people what is happening to us.' Such is the continuing cry of the people and the continuing mandate, not just to me, but to all those people who know something of the real story, to enable more eyes to see, more ears to hear, and more lips to speak for peace with justice for two nations and three faiths.

LAND RIGHTS
IN ISRAEL-PALESTINE:
AN AUSTRALIAN PERSPECTIVE
Ray Barraclough

From one land to another

I came to Jerusalem from a country where the issue of ownership of land is yet to be resolved. This need for resolution spans a period of more than two hundred years. Recent decisions in the High Court of my country have addressed this contentious issue and have set new landmarks, both legal and political, that acknowledge indigenous people's ownership of land. From our Australian experience we knew that disputes over ownership of land stir deep passions. We were to discover at first hand that disputes over land ownership are not remote from Jerusalem also.

In the European conquest of Australia the land, though occupied by people, was considered in the legal code to be unoccupied. The short-hand term for this imperial assessment was *terra nullius* ('land belonging to nobody'). The original inhabitants were regarded as having no rights of ownership. The land was supposedly empty of any society save that recognised by a selective interpretation of international law (Reynolds 1992: 31-54, 65-76). With the term *terra nullius* we are not far removed from 'A land with no people for a people with no land', a key slogan made famous by Zionist ideologues.

But this is to jump ahead of myself. Before coming to Jerusalem my wife, Dorothy, and I had been involved in struggles alongside Australian Aboriginal peoples for land rights for their people. This had involved street marches, demonstrations, vigils, and a short stint spent in the police watchhouse until released on bail.

It also required that one become much more familiar with the history of British conquest and occupation of the land eventually called Australia. It had meant encouraging conservative Australians, who could see no reason for changing land ownership patterns, to be prepared to read Australian history through the eyes of its Aboriginal inhabitants. It meant re-visiting that history.

For some it led to a revising of history so that the romantic, heroic and propaganda tales of white pioneers bravely carving out farms in the bush and wilderness gave way to a more realistic estimate of the tragedies as well as the triumphs involved. It meant that dispossession needed to be faced as well as possession. It meant accepting that 'there are no exits from history'—a telling phrase that I encountered in reading Jewish reflections on the *Shoah* (Holocaust). The past shapes the present.

This re-learning had meant for me, as an Anglican priest in Australia, an effort to integrate three areas of life that I am drawn to: theology, history and politics. To seek to do this in Australia was a life-changing challenge. To seek to do it in Jerusalem meant, first of all, to begin on a steep learning curve.

In Jerusalem is encapsulated layer upon layer of religion, history and politics. Therein, in large measure, lies the mix that draws so many people (and media representatives) to be perpetually fascinated by this city.

Dorothy and I arrived in Jerusalem without having done much homework. This was not completely by accident, or due to hasty packing after the decision was made to journey from Australia to take up a staff appointment at St George's College, Jerusalem. We felt our learning about the Middle East would best be done living in the landscape, sensing the present dimensions, and meeting a range of its peoples. We who had had to learn so much about the layers of our own country needed now to spend time being pupils in a new and ancient classroom. We consider that we have never matriculated from that course. There is still so much more for us to learn. But a preliminary essay, such as this one, can be attempted.

The Israel-Palestine question barely registered in our experience before we came to Jerusalem. It was remote in regard to its location and pertinence to our lives, and was devoid of any personal connection for us. Indeed, we knew no one from that part of the world.

As with all Christians we brought theological luggage with us to start with. I use the term 'luggage' rather than 'baggage'. The latter has too pejorative a ring. The luggage that keeps us together in our life's journey is a mixture of one's childhood and all its multi-faceted relationships and experiences, of one's education both formal and pragmatic, of socio-economic and class factors, of political impulses, of personality types, and an articulated as well as a gut-level theology.

As regards the last mentioned both Dorothy and I, in late adolescence, had journeyed into conservative evangelicalism. In our thirties we journeyed out of evangelicalism. I was drawn more to the journey for which liberation theology provides maps, while Dorothy was drawn to blending her natural mystical feel for religion with her growing experience of the women's movement. The strong patriarchal shape of both Palestinian and Israeli societies gave little room for that latter aspect. We also came consciously owning the egalitarian aspirations by which the great majority of our fellow Australians profess to live.

Even in our most ardent evangelical days Christian Zionism had never been part of our luggage. Thus, while we could appreciate the strength of Zionism's appeal to both secular and religious Jews (for we too were nationalists), it had never been part of the clothing packed into our theological suitcases.

We realised that our awareness of the sad history of Christian anti-Jewishness down the centuries had to be expanded and extended. Jews' experience of history includes not only efforts at assimilation into European life, but also (especially from eastern Europe) recurring patterns of harassment and pogroms. As a backdrop to their existence in gentile-ruled Europe was the centuries-old, and readily tapped, stream of anti-Jewishness. Awareness of this is relevant even today, with the emergence of far-right parties in recent elections in Austria, Switzerland, France and Denmark. Such awareness of the past and the present is indispensable in order to gain insights into the present aspirations, commitment and drive of Israel's Jewish citizens.

As a lecturer in New Testament in the Brisbane College of Theology I was becoming more aware of the international discussion concerning anti-Jewish aspects contained in the New Testament writings and in the centuries beyond (Rubenstein and Roth 1987). I was conscious of Gregory Baum's critique of those New Testament writings in which he discerned the seeds of social pathology expressed in anti-Jewish polemics. For example, he considered that 'The author of the fourth gospel transforms Jesus' preaching against ideological religion into a polemic against Jews, against the entire Jewish people.' He cited as illustrations John 5.37 ('You have never heard God's voice'), 5.42 ('You do not have the love of God within you'), amongst other texts (Baum 1975: 79).

As regards awareness of the life experience of Palestinians—we were woefully ignorant. At least we did not have to unlearn much. But we certainly needed to learn Palestinian history right to the present day. Here the focus was on what the Palestinians had experienced in the 20th century, for that has been the crucial century for their present condition.

As well, we doubtless carried impressions drawn from Western stereotypes of Palestinians. At the personal level, experience was different from expectation. For example, Dorothy, having only a few phrases in Arabic in her vocabulary, was wary of simple shopping expeditions in East Jerusalem. In practice the experience was the opposite of her anxiety. As she shopped in East Jerusalem time and time again she was welcomed with generous and genuine Palestinian hospitality. Repeatedly she was invited to meet the family, and to share a cup of mint-flavoured tea with the relatives whose welcome was unmistakable.

Past and present religious maps of the Middle East had not been traced in any detail on the walls of our minds. The fact that the majority of Christians in Jerusalem, in Israel and the West Bank were Palestinians—that was something we had to discover when we reached Jerusalem.

We were not so much innocent as ignorant. Being Westerners by culture, we had been exposed to the stereotypical images that were associated with Jews and Arabs in Western films, literature, theatre, and humour. Only after living in the Middle East is one alerted to how stereotyped such images are. And negative rather than positive colouring still shades those images in Western circles.

A key ingredient in our growing awareness of the Israel-Palestine question came through the courses conducted by St George's College, Jerusalem. Each course included an address on the contemporary situation by three speakers. One was an Israeli Jewish citizen, well versed in the past and present dimensions of Israel's existence, a second, a Palestinian well versed in the past and present dimensions of Palestinian existence, and, a third, either a Western press correspondent, or a speaker drawn from a Western embassy or consulate. The range of views certainly opened up many aspects of the contemporary Middle Eastern scene.

History, theology and politics are my three points of reference for reading the Israel-Palestine paradigm. As we sought to chart a map of understanding through the complex political landscape of Israel and the Occupied Territories, we needed time simply to build bridges in our understanding. History is essentially people's stories becoming bridges for linking the past with the present. There are many bridges into Jerusalem because there are many stories that have to be heard. And we confess that have heard only a minority of the stories.

A patchwork of stories

There are categories of stories that can hold a people together. When Archbishop Desmond Tutu was in Jerusalem in 1990, at a dinner hosted by Palestinian Christians he asked his hosts what were the humorous stories arising during the *Intifada* that was then surging. It took a little time for his hosts to respond, but two stories that I remember were told.

A Western tourist sat down in a Palestinian cafe in East Jerusalem. Unsure of the vocabulary, yet wanting to order a local dish, he sought to order some *hummus*. But being a little confused he asked the waiter for a dish of Hamas. To which the waiter replied: 'Hamas, no. But how about a good serving of PLO?' The second story came from Gaza. A group of Palestinian youngsters was throwing stones at Israeli soldiers. Anxious Palestinian women watched from inside their doorways. As the soldiers moved threateningly towards them the children ran away. But a little four-year-old, unaware of the others' flight, remained with stones in hand. As the soldiers neared the child four or more women rushed out shouting: 'It is my son! Let him be!'. According to the Palestinian storyteller the leading soldier stopped and was heard to remark: 'I have heard of a woman having many children but I have not heard of a child having four mothers!'

Israelis also have a heritage of humour. Jewish jokes are proverbial. One that reflects the tendency of Israeli Jews to hold views strongly is posed in a question: If a Jewish man is marooned on an island how many synagogues does he build? Answer: Two. So that he can have one synagogue that he refuses to attend.

But the stories we heard from both Palestinians and Jews in the main were stories of pathos, of hope, of anguish, of fear, of desire for vindication. It will take many years for the stories to be told and retold because many of the stories spring from trauma. And the trauma does not have to be directly experienced. The trauma of the *Shoah* colours a nation's story, as well as those of old and young Israeli Jews. The stories of the forced removal of Palestinian families in that region's wars in the last fifty-two years echo not only through refugee camps (still existing to this day) but in the generations born since those armed conflicts. The trauma experienced by thousands of Palestinian families who lost a relative during the *Intifada* is still to be worked out. The trauma that accompanies every cruel attack on a school, or bus, or mall in Israel is still to be worked out.

Those involved in grief counselling recognise the recurring phrase: 'If only …' As it is for individual situations of grief and loss, so also it is compounded when communities and nations take action that in hindsight could have been so much better 'if only …' If only the two-state proposal promulgated by the United Nations in 1947 had been tried. If only the Mufti of Jerusalem had not sided with fascist forces during the Second World War. If only the Israeli military occupation of the West Bank had been short-lived. If only one Arab state could set a striking example of just and participatory rule.

Many people, reliant only on television pictures think that the Middle East has always been a place of tension. Such has not been the case. Speaking very generally, for centuries Muslims, Jews and Christians have lived together in the Middle East, not with equal power, but yet with sufficient peaceful order to guarantee the steady continuation of their communities' life. For example, when Jews were expelled from Spain in 1492 they found that space was given them in the largely Muslim Middle East that was denied them in many regions of the largely Christian Europe. Moreover, Palestinian Muslims and Palestinian Christians, for centuries, have lived peaceably together with respect for clan and regional customs a feature of everyday life.

Some key points in history

In trying to understand the Middle East one cannot say that at this point, or at that point, 'it all started'. Modern European nationalism, of which Zionism is a part, has various births. Nor is the debate resolved over whether Palestinian nationalism grew in imitation of Zionism, or as a separate national vision for a Palestinian state that ideally could transcend clan rivalry. The Israel-Palestine issues have many strands leading back into many eras.

What one can say is that the carving up of the Ottoman Empire at the end of the First World War was a crucial period. Representatives of the British and French empires sparred over the divisions of power and patronage in the Middle East. Both the Arabs and the Jews believed that they had been given promises by Britain— promises that could not be jointly realised (Fromkin 1989: 173-87, 276-83). Thus were planted seeds of conflict that still are being harvested in the present Middle East.

The latter years of the First World War saw aspirations of Christian triumphalism being backed up by armed force on the part of the victors.

Consider two examples. After the French commander, General Gourard, took Damascus from the Turks he delivered a speech to an invited crowd by the grave of Saladin. As Gourard stood by the grave, he is reported to have said: 'My presence here consecrates the victory of the cross over the crescent'. Across the Channel, British Prime Minister Lloyd George declared in 1917 that General Allenby, in taking Jerusalem, 'had fought and won the last and most triumphant of the Crusades'. A local anecdote that we were told colours that episode. Allenby was advised by his Jerusalem hosts, the Spafforth family, not to ride through the Jaffa Gate (as the Kaiser had done in 1898) but rather to walk, so as to reduce the sense of triumphalist conquest (Vester 1988: 278-79).

More powerful stories

Other stories, too, need to be considered. When politics and religion are mixed, as often is the case even in secular states but much more so in Jerusalem, there is a desire on the part of those holding power and those seeking power to gain the high moral ground. Here Israeli and Palestinian stories abound. But the stories are not lined up equally on either side. A powerful story from one side does not necessarily silence a corresponding story from the other side.

Consider the most powerful and tragic story that Israeli Jews tell and retell—the account of the *Shoah*. This story is embedded in the psyche of Israeli Jews. It stands among the most powerful and frightening experience any people has had to recount over the centuries. Massacres chill the blood of those who learn of them. The killing of a million Armenians in 1915, the 'killing fields' of Kampuchea in the 1970s, the slaughter in Rwanda in the 1990s, and the massacre of Palestinians in the refugee camps of Sabra and Shatila in 1982—these are tales of horror and cruelty.

In drama, in novels, in family remembrance, the stories of the *Shoah* are told and retold. No more powerfully so for me than in the children's memorial at Yad Vashem. As a leader of groups, that came for courses at St George's College, I visited that centre some thirty times. With its simple multiplied vista of candles and the roll call of Jewish children's names, it never lost its capacity to move me deeply.

In response Palestinians could not deny the enormity of the *Shoah*. But, as they rightly point out, this horror was inflicted by Europeans, not by Arabs. The tragedy occurred in the heartlands of Europe, not in Palestine. This cruelty was done by European, not by Palestinian hands. Yet in reparation, they assert, European powers have paid not with their own land but with Palestinian land. While the State of Israel became a refuge for Jews who escaped the devastation of the *Shoah*, Palestinians were made into refugees. Palestinians see themselves as being required to pay the price in terms of their own homeland for Western guilt. Westerners who have to face the roots of anti-Jewishness in European culture (it is present even in such distant places as Australia as well) also have to face this dimension of Palestinian complaint.

A second batch of stories contains the loaded word 'terrorism'. Before reaching Jerusalem we were alert to the 'rubbery' use of this term. Did not our neighbour Indonesia brand as 'terrorist' the Fretilin fighters struggling for East Timorese independence. Was not Nelson Mandela imprisoned by the South African government for leading a 'terrorist' organisation? On one occasion I recall listening to the English news in Jerusalem and hearing on the same bulletin reference to activities by 'terrorists' in the Middle East and by 'armed militants' in Northern Ireland. One is reminded of Australian media coverage of the 'militia' in recent events in East Timor. That members of 'the militia' terrorised the population through bashings, rapes and murders never seemed enough for news broadcasters to describe them as 'terrorists'.

That being said, terrorism is a savage barbarity. I see no defence for it. It has been perpetrated by small groups, I repeat small groups, of Palestinians and Israeli Jews. The loss of life and the shattering of families that are cruelly produced by bombs planted in Israeli schools and Israeli buses have no defence. So, too, the cold-blooded violence of Baruch Goldstein in murdering worshipers in a mosque in Hebron chills the blood. That both groups of terrorists have devoted supporters amongst Palestinians and Jews respectively is a sign of a barbarous sickness, not of a story that merits any support.

One heard moving stories from both the Jewish and the Palestinian experience. With grief we heard of an assault upon a caring woman who was a baby-sitter for our Jewish friends Yehezkel and Dahlia Landau. The woman was killed by a Palestinian attacker as she was on her way home in West Jerusalem. The shock at such killings reverberated through families, friends, through city and nation. This act of violence gained no positive purpose but simply reinforced set views throughout the country.

We heard a story of a Christian Palestinian lad named Joseph who lived in Beit Sahur, near Bethlehem. The *Intifada* was in progress in this part of the Occupied Territories. The town had been placed under total curfew by the Israeli military. Poor families had meagre stocks of food. Joseph knew such families. At great risk to himself he would defy the curfew to take food to those in need. On one such errand Joseph set off, but he did not return home. He was killed by the security forces. His uncle, who recounted this story, had tears in his eyes. 'We are Christians. Jesus committed himself to gentleness. My nephew Joseph—we will never forget him. His life will soften the world.'

One's attitude to the Israel-Palestine question is shaped at the heart level by tragic stories such as these. At head level one reads both of past and contemporary events to gain some understanding of the multi-faceted dimensions of the question. At the gut level various responses can readily be resorted to, especially by those whose lives are irrevocably affected by the Israel-Palestine dynamic. The responses of revenge, of depression, of reinforcing stereotypes, as well as responses of determination to keep working for a peaceful way forward despite the tragedies, all attract their respective respondents.

Friends shaping our perceptions

Our attitudes to the Palestine-Israel question are shaped also by the people we meet. We are indebted to many people for their contribution to our lives and to our understanding of the Israel-Palestine situation. In naming but a few we wish to see them as representative of many of their compatriots who live in Jerusalem.

The first persons to name are our neighbours in Jerusalem, Naim and Maha Ateek. Naim is well known through his writings as a Palestinian theologian, especially in his articulation of a Palestinian liberation theology. As an eleven-year-old child, Naim experienced the sudden uprooting that came to his family and their Palestinian neighbours in Beisan on the 12 May 1948 (Ateek 1989: 8-10). Given but a few hours to leave their family home, Naim carries with him the outer and inner experience of being dispossessed of both home and homeland. Naim and Maha both seek for a peaceful and just resolution of the Israel-Palestine issues. Their faith as Christians indelibly moulds that hope. Their commitment to justice not only for their fellow Palestinians but also for a just relationship between Palestine and Israel shapes their lives and ministry.

Another home in Jerusalem and another family—Naomi and Eli Rockowitz. Soon after our arrival in Jerusalem I met Naomi who was our professional guide around the ruins of the Temple Mount. Naomi grew up in Melbourne in a secure Jewish home. But her commitment to modern Israel prompted her to make *aliyah*, to become an Israeli citizen, and to work in Jerusalem. Naomi and Eli (who came to Israel from New York) expressed for us the desire of a younger generation of Israelis to have peace, but for such peace to be anchored in security for their children. Every attack that threatened the lives of Jewish children sent a tremor through their aspirations.

From Jerusalem to the West Bank. There we were welcomed

by Cedar Duaybis. Cedar's husband was a Palestinian Anglican priest. As a family they had known the eroding stresses of living under Israeli military occupation. Their son, as a boy, had suffered a nervous breakdown in response to the early morning raids on their home by the military. As a Palestinian woman Cedar also voiced a lament that transcends national borders:

> Whenever there is injustice, the heaviest burden almost inevitably falls on the shoulders of women. Palestinian women have had to keep the family together and to bear the burden of its survival … As a Palestinian Christian woman the conflict rages not only around me but also inside me, a conflict between myself the Palestinian, myself the Christian, and myself the woman.

The immediate pressure of military occupation has receded from Cedar's world. She now seeks to build for reconciliation and security for her children.

The fourth personal influence came through Yehezkel and Dahlia Landau. They are Orthodox Jews who are committed to working in the long term for rapprochement between the Jewish and Palestinian peoples. Dahlia came as a girl to Israel from Central Europe soon after the end of the Second World War. In her adult years she discovered that her family home in Israel had belonged to a Palestinian family who had fled during the 1948 conflict. Several male members of that same family, in subsequent years, had joined the struggle against Israel. As peacemakers Dahlia and Yehezkel made contact with the family and in co-operation have established a house where Jewish and Palestinian children can learn together.

Our own personal experiences also shape our views. On one Friday morning Dorothy stood on a traffic island in a busy intersection in West Jerusalem with the 'Women in Black', a group of Jewish women who were protesting against their nation's policy of occupying the West Bank. Each woman held a red rose which a supporting florist donated to their cause each Friday. After the vigil

Dorothy entered a shop for a drink. There she was accosted by a gun-toting settler from a Jewish settlement in the West Bank. If he wanted to make a convert that day he failed miserably. She was shaken by the rage and the armed presence of this man.

Recent developments and the future

Changes have come since we were last in Jerusalem. Most notable, of course, have been the Israeli-Palestinian negotiations that were initiated through the Oslo Accords. The tragic assassination of Yitzhak Rabin, the affect of Benjamin Netanyahu's rule, and now the era of Ehud Barak are each marked by varied stages in those negotiations. Moreover, there is growing acceptance within Israel of the inevitability of a Palestinian state.

An important challenge, among many, facing the emerging Palestinian Authority under Arafat's leadership is respect for human rights. A key reason for the widespread support for the PLO amongst Palestinian Christians was their desire to establish a democratic, secular state of which respect for human rights would be an integral part. The alternatives amongst the varied states in the region—absolutist rule (Iraq, Syria) or an Islamic state (Iran)—held no attraction for them. Noted Palestinian Christians, such as Hanan Ashrawi, have sought to keep respect for human rights high on the Palestinian agenda.

This issue is pertinent to ongoing relations between Israel and Palestine. Israel is a democracy. It seems to this observer that democracies offer the best political framework within which human rights can be respected. There is no perfect system. Witness the tragedy of deaths of black prisoners in the jails of democratic Australia. But our Jewish and Palestinian friends share a common desire in their yearning for peaceful and accountable relations within and between Israel and Palestine.

To live in Jerusalem is to live in a city with subliminal tension. Both peoples claim Jerusalem as the capital for their state. Israeli Jews speak in terms of Jerusalem being the 'eternal capital'. I was struck by the words of Meron Benvenisti, an Israeli well-experienced both in the dynamics and administration of Jerusalem. He observed that one can have Jerusalem or one can have peace. But one cannot have both (in Elon 1991: 247).

It is still too early to tell what will be a long-lasting resolution for Jerusalem. Some may dream of Jerusalem as an internationally administered city. But more hard-headed decisions by those holding power in the immediate region are likely to prevail. What will emerge in the long term? Who can tell? I am reminded of an anecdote emanating out of China. It was the early 1950s and on a boat for America were passengers fleeing from the emergence of Mao's China. Among them was an American missionary and a Chinese Christian. When the latter asserted that 'Christianity will again have a place in China', the missionary replied with fervour: 'How can you see that? Mao Tse Tung and his party will ensure that they rule China for the next twenty years or even for several generations!' The Chinese Christian replied: 'Oh, I was thinking about the next 100 or 200 years'.

From one land to another

Although we lived in Jerusalem, we were yet outsiders. We held Australian passports. Thus the anguish, the grief, the yearning, the hopes—these we could know only in small part. Yet it has been our aim, since returning to Australia, to share with our fellow Australians some of the dimensions of anguish and hope, peacemaking and despair, yearnings and frustration, that are the experiences of Israelis and Palestinians. We seek to share such dimensions with our fellow Christians, and in particular with our fellow Anglicans. We have received varied responses. And it is impossible in a brief meeting to take one's listeners to any depth through the labyrinth of factors shaping the Palestine-Israel question.

Australians are not good at debriefing those who return from lands and experiences beyond the local landscape. As well, one has to deal with stereotypes built into our culture of Palestinians and

Israelis, of Arabs and Jews, that are repeatedly encountered in informal conversations, in newspaper cartoons, in ethnic jokes.

And the twist fundamentalist Christianity adds with its apocalyptic (I would say diseased) visions of End Times in the Middle East is best noted but not enlarged upon. It flowered in the era of the Gulf War. As regards building positive relations between Israelis and Palestinians that theology, in the best of times, is a waste of time. In the worst of times it is an abomination.

The Israelis and Palestinians are negotiating. Such negotiations have involved and will involve large steps as well as small ones. For Israeli political leaders, whether Labour or Likud, to shake the hand of Yasser Arafat, was a world-width stretch across a negotiating table. For Palestinian leadership to acknowledge the *de jure* as well as the *de facto* existence of Israel was a large step that had to be taken in their psyche as well as on their political map.

We live a small life within the compass of history. One, therefore, can contribute in small ways. This chapter is a part of that contribution.

AS THE PRICKLY PEAR
Kathy Bergen

In September 1982, I went to Jerusalem for four months, and stayed nine years. I lived and worked in the Palestinian community throughout the period from just after the Israeli invasion of Lebanon until after the Gulf War. During those nine years, I experienced the aftermath of the Israeli invasion of Lebanon, the pre-*Intifada* years, the *Intifada*, the months leading up to the Gulf War, the Gulf War and its effects on the Palestinians, particularly those living in the West Bank and Gaza Strip. The time I spent living in Jerusalem and working in the Palestinian community has become the centre of my being, a turning point in my life, and the focus of my work since that time. I look at my studies and my work experience prior to going to Jerusalem as preparing me to be there, and everything I have done since as a result of my having studied, lived, and worked there. The nine years I lived and worked in the Palestinian community was truly a life-changing experience for me.

Growing up in a Russian Mennonite family in Coaldale, a small prairie town in southern Alberta, did not prepare me for my adult experience in Jerusalem. It did, however, create in me a curiosity that pushed me beyond the borders of that small town and beyond the covers of the Sunday school lesson books. I have fond memories of Sunday school. The pictures in our Sunday school lesson books were of biblical scenes and personalities drawn or painted by artists from the 12th and 13th centuries. However interesting these pictorial portrayals of the Old and New Testament stories were, they did not bring me closer to understanding the everyday life of Jesus. The pictures for me, growing up in that small, closed, and in many ways isolated town of 2,000 persons, thirteen churches, and a Buddhist Temple, portrayed to me a distant culture. Those Sunday school lesson books with their pictures and Bible stories represented a world far away and alien to mine, a world that was hard to build a bridge to from my own. So, in many ways the Bible stories remained stories for me, even throughout the many years of biblical and theological studies I engaged in, until I lived in Jerusalem. It was not until I discovered the 'living stones', as Father Elias Chacour has said, that the biblical realities became my realities. To live in the place that Jesus lived, taught, and died because of the life he lived, made the biblical stories come alive for me. The Palestinian people have preserved many aspects of the culture from the time of Jesus. As I became immersed in that culture, learned more about the history of the region, and experienced the geography of the land, the biblical accounts took on a new meaning for me and for the way I lived my life.

A relationship with God has always been central to my life. The quest for a closer relationship with God, and the desire to learn how that relationship might be manifested in my daily life, took me through some of the Mennonite institutions—Bethel Bible School in Abbotsford, British Columbia, the Canadian Mennonite Bible College (CMBC) in Winnipeg, Manitoba, and the Mennonite Biblical Seminary in Elkhart, Indiana. The public post-secondary institutions I attended—Mount Royal College in Calgary, Alberta; the University of Lethbridge in Lethbridge, Alberta; and the University of Manitoba in Winnipeg, Manitoba—helped me to bridge the sacred and secular worlds, and allow those two worlds to become one within me.

During the four years of seminary I was challenged by the writings and lectures of liberation and feminist theologians. I became aware of my own oppression as a woman, and the implications of having grown up female in a working-class immigrant family. I learned how the interpretations of the Bible from a male perspective and how the development leadership models by men had made an impact on my life. I came to understand how patriarchy permeated all levels of the Church and the society I found myself in. In spite of that, I felt called to ministry, and was encouraged by my professors and colleagues to become open to pastoral ministry.

Growing up as a female in a poor immigrant family, I experienced discrimination—as a foreigner, as someone from a working-class background, as a female. By discovering my Anabaptist Mennonite roots, while at CMBC, I became aware of my Church's teachings concerning our responsibilities in the face of injustice. I knew that my life's calling had to include not only pastoral work on the personal, interpersonal, and communal level, but also working for a more just society—justice and peace for all—in my Church, in my community, in my country, and around the world.

I decided to join a group of seminary students and professors, led by Millard Lind, Professor of Old Testament at the Associated Mennonite Biblical Seminaries in Elkhart, Indiana. It was a decision that changed my life. For four months I studied archaeology, biblical geography and biblical geology with Jim Fleming, at the Jerusalem Centre for Biblical Studies, in the Old City of Jerusalem. Millard Lind arranged for us to take a course on modern Israel at the Hebrew University, and a course on modern Palestine organised by Harry Huebner of the Mennonite Central Committee (MCC, West Bank), based in East Jerusalem. A few weeks after we arrived in Jerusalem, the Sabra and Shatila massacres were carried out against the Palestinians in those two refugee camps in Lebanon. It was this atrocity and the unravelling of it in the months to come that began my journey towards discovering modern Israel and modern Palestine.

My semester of studies in Jerusalem changed my life forever. As I learned about the situation of the Palestinians in the Occupied Palestinian Territories, and came to see the horrors of military occupation as the Palestinians experienced it, I knew there was a role for me in that part of the world. The conflict was not only between the Palestinians and Israelis. I came to see that the injustices towards the Palestinians would continue because the United States was giving political and financial support to Israel, so that it could meet its goals. How could I ever apply the principles I wanted to live by to the Middle East?

The situation in the Middle East seemed to be so complex, and the more I learned about the realities in the West Bank and Gaza

Strip, the more complicated things appeared to be. However, one day in one of the classes I took at Hebrew University, I was able to connect what was happening to Palestinians to what I experienced as a woman in Church and society—oppression. All the principles of oppression were present in the conflict between Palestinians and Israelis—the power imbalance, the internalised oppression, the feelings of powerlessness—were present in my life as a woman who grew up in a patriarchal society. This insight was so basic and simple, but it gave me a new perspective in which to see, evaluate and analyse the situation between Palestinians and Israelis.

I began to see the Palestinian-Israeli conflict from a different perspective. I saw with my own eyes what was happening to the Palestinians—things that I had not heard or read about in the North American media. Phrases like 'the security needs of Israel' took on a new meaning, because I could see that confiscating Palestinian land, demolishing Palestinian homes, destroying Palestinian trees, placing Palestinians under administrative detention, and building Israeli settlements on confiscated land were not done because of 'Israel's security needs' but were steps to achieve Israel's political goals.

Some Israelis I talked to spoke of Israel as 'a light unto the nations'. For me Israel did not have a special or privileged place in the community of nations. Israel is not a 'light unto the nations'. Rather, it is a country, like any other country, that needs to defend its interests, and is not exempt from its behaviour. Jews who have chosen to become Israelis have become part of this reality in helping to maintain Israel's power. In fact, Israel's oppression of the Palestinians pointed to its desire to expand its territory *de facto*. I saw the Israeli political leadership as no different than the politicians of any other country—doing what they had to do in order to maintain the power they had achieved.

It was during that semester in Jerusalem that I began to see and to feel what life was like for Palestinians living under Israeli military occupation in the West Bank, including East Jerusalem, and the Gaza Strip. As we travelled around the Occupied Palestinian Territories, I witnessed the confiscation of Palestinian land and the building of illegal settlements on it for exclusive Jewish use. I saw the destruction of olive trees, fruit trees, and vineyards by the Israeli army, leaving Palestinians without a source of livelihood. I heard about the destruction of Palestinian homes for the purposes of collective punishment. Many people we met had been in Israeli prisons under administrative detention, a form of punishment without trial. We heard of the many people who had been deported because of their political beliefs and activities.

I remember vividly the first time the vehicle we were travelling in was waved through an Israeli checkpoint along with the vehicles of settlers living in the Occupied Territories because we all had yellow licensed cars, whereas the Palestinian cars had blue licence plates. The long line of Palestinian vehicles were being searched by the Israeli soldiers and the people thoroughly questioned. At that moment, for the first time, I realised that there was an apartheid system being developed in the West Bank and Gaza, only to learn at a later point that Palestinians living in Israel, who had Israeli passports, were third-class citizens, with no opportunity to work their way out of that class due to the fact that Israel is a Jewish state. I also discovered that Israel had never declared its borders and did not have a constitution. Many things did not make sense to me. Why did Israel allow the Palestinian and international NGOs (non-governmental organisations) to operate, and then destroy so much of the work that had been done?

We met some of the Palestinian and international NGOs that were helping to build the Palestinian economy and infrastructure in the West Bank and Gaza Strip, while being harassed and deterred by the Israeli army. None of this seemed to make sense to me, and it all seemed so very complex and complicated. However, I began to see that Israel's control of the Palestinians in the Occupied Territories was not for security reasons only, as we were often led to believe, but was a way of humiliating, demoralising, and destroying a people and their political and national aspirations. I remember the moment when I was able to make some connections between what was happening in the West Bank and Gaza and the oppression I had experienced as a woman in both Church and society. I was witnessing one people, the Israelis, oppressing another, the Palestinians. This was the side of the Israeli-Palestinian conflict we had heard very little about in Canada and in the US. Certainly, the mainstream media did not report the kinds of things I saw and heard while talking with Palestinians in the West Bank and Gaza.

I had come to Jerusalem to learn more about biblical archaeology, geography, and geology in order to interpret better the biblical texts in sermon preparation, biblical teaching, and in understanding better the environment in which Jesus lived, worked, and taught. After all, it was the life and teachings of Jesus that provided a spiritual basis and an ethical framework for my life and work. I assumed that to understand better the culture and environment of Jesus would help me to appreciate more his mission, his words and his teachings, for my mission in life. Following the semester of studies in Jerusalem, I planned to return to Canada and enter pastoral ministry in the Mennonite Church. I did not. I was never ordained, nor have I ever entered the ordained pastoral ministry. However, I consider the work I have done since graduating from seminary in 1982 as justice and peace ministry, and I continue to do my work from a biblical, Christian, Anabaptist perspective.

The geography, geology, and archaeology I studied contributed to my acquiring a better understanding of the world of Jesus and therefore of the messages of the biblical accounts. However, I did not realise how politicised archaeology was until I studied in Jerusalem. For most Israeli archaeologists, the discovery of new *tells* (archaeological sites) and the analysis of the layers of the *tells*, is a way of confirming a Jewish presence in that part of the world. As one professor at Hebrew University put it: if we can substantiate the biblical accounts through our archaeological discoveries, we can prove our existence in this land and prove that it was ours and still belongs to us (Jews worldwide). He also indicated that he and many other Israelis saw the Old Testament/ Hebrew Bible as giving the Israelis a mandate to claim 'The Land' and 'possess it'. It was the first time I was confronted with applying that part of the scriptures to modern-day life. It sent me on a quest to find ways of interpreting that part of the Old Testament in ways that were consistent with the rest of the scriptures and the events unfolding before me in the Middle East. As I continued my studies that semester, it became more and more difficult for me to read Joshua, Judges, I and II Kings, and many of the Psalms. It was too painful. Many passages I read in the Bible were echoed in the daily lives of the Palestinians. The similarities between some of the biblical accounts and some of the present-day accounts were striking. History repeats itself? Was I witnessing a replay?

The Bible came alive for me in new and different ways that I had never expected. It also set me on a quest to understand better the biblical concept of 'The Land' and 'Chosenness' as articulated in the Old Testament. How could this land belong to one people and not to another? Why was one people occupying another? What would be some of the long-range consequences of this military occupation for Palestinians and for Israelis? Why did the Palestinians have to pay the price for anti-Jewishness in the West? Why was the Bible used as a document to justify the right of one nation to live in this land and oppress and control another nation?

I remember driving around the Sea of Galilee, with our professor reading the biblical story of Jesus and the sower. I looked around me and saw the types of soil the author was talking about in the parable. Around me I saw fertile soil, rocky soil, and soil with huge thistles and other 'weeds'. I understood in a new way the images the author used. In Jerusalem we stood on the original steps leading up to the temple of Jesus' time. I could hear the words of Jesus, 'Be not as white sepulchres …', as he looked across the Kidron Valley at the Jewish cemetery that is still in use today.

I remember the first time I saw a tour bus with 'Nazareth Transport' written on it. Nazareth, Bethlehem, Jerusalem, and other places in 'the Holy Land' entered the 20th century for me, and Israelis and Palestinians became 20th-century people who now inhabit that land.

Following my semester of study in Jerusalem, I began to work with MCC in the West Bank and Gaza, and later with the Canadian

Organisation for Solidarity and Development (OCSD, Quebec).

While my life and work during the nine years I lived in Jerusalem consisted of a variety of tasks, I saw it all as justice and peace ministry:

1. The most important part of my work was peace education and information work. I provided opportunities for any foreigners who came to the Holy Land to learn about the situation in the West Bank and Gaza. It was a way of 'being a voice for the voiceless'. Not that the Palestinians could not speak for themselves, but when they did they were harassed and often put in prison by the Israeli authorities. The tours I organised gave people the opportunity to have their eyes opened to the realities of the Palestinians, and their hearts opened to doing something about the situation. This work took many different forms. One effective way of educating people who came to visit or study was to take them on settlement tours. This allowed them to see for themselves how Israeli settlement policy was affecting the Palestinian people, and how that policy was contributing to the further dispossession of the Palestinian people.

2. Another reason for being in Jerusalem was to support the local Christian community. Among the many ways I concretised this were teaching at the Bethlehem Bible College, participating in interfaith dialogue meetings, supporting the work of a Palestinian Theology Group by fund-raising for and organising the first international Liberation Theology Conference in Palestine.

3. A third reason for working in Jerusalem was to support the Israeli peace and protest movement. This support took many forms, including attending rallies, sit-ins, and actions organised by these groups, helping to establish the local chapter of the Fellowship of Reconciliation, and, during the earlier years, acting as a liaison between some Israeli groups and individuals and some Palestinian groups and individuals. I often found myself introducing Palestinians and Israelis to each other and being a bridge between the two peoples in so many ways.

I came to see that the conflict between Palestinians and Israelis was being fuelled by the United States by its policies in the Middle East. This reality provides the primary focus of my current work with the American Friends Service Committee. As staff working on Middle East issues in the US, we work to educate the US public and policy makers about the situation in the Middle East. We work to build public support for a just US policy in the Middle East, and in support of self-determination for all peoples of that region. An unjust and unbalanced US Middle East policy is the main obstacle to a just and comprehensive peace in the Middle East, including that between Palestinians and Israelis.

My peace and justice ministry has brought me into solidarity with the Palestinian people, whom I have come to know, love, and respect. Their struggles have become my struggles, and their hopes and dreams have become my hopes and dreams. Since 1982, I have continued to work for justice for the Palestinian people and for a just solution to the Middle East conflicts. I continue to draw strength from many of my Palestinian friends and colleagues who continue to work for justice and liberation of their people, and from Israelis who work in solidarity with Palestinians in order to create a more just and peaceful Middle East for all. The hope is in the struggle. As Palestinians continue to struggle, in what seems to be a hopeless situation at times, and I continue to work in solidarity with them, I am reminded of the words of John Howard Yoder, that it is not our effectiveness, but our faithfulness to our beliefs and the causes we work for, that is important. The prickly pear cactus has become an important symbol representing the Palestinian people. This plant is found all over Israel and Palestine. It is almost impossible to uproot or destroy. In spite of the decades of suffering, the Palestinian people continue to struggle and will not be destroyed.

FROM ZION TO PALESTINE:
A JOURNEY FROM CHRISTIAN ZIONISM TO JUSTICE IN THE HOLY LAND
Don Wagner

His biographer Christopher Sykes describes why Britain's Prime Minister, David Lloyd-George's advisors were so frustrated when he was about to enter negotiations for the post-World War I treaties concerning Palestine. Apparently, Lloyd-George was either uninterested, or could not grasp several critical political issues because, as Sykes notes, he could not consider the Holy Land except through the concepts honed during his fundamentalist Christian upbringing. On the eve of intense negotiations, Lloyd-George chose to sit and recite from memory the biblical geography he had learned in Sunday school, rather than review the extensive briefing papers and maps with his advisors.

David Lloyd-George received his biblical education from a maternal uncle, Richard George, who was a lay preacher in a fundamentalist Bible Church in Wales. The Prime Minister would later state: 'I was brought up in a school where there was taught far more about the history of the Jews than the history of my own land.' The political orientation of Lloyd-George, like his colleague Lord Arthur Balfour and the philanthropist Lord Shaftesbury before him, was influenced more by his particular interpretation of the Bible than by political science, historical facts, geopolitical realities, or the expert advice of the British Foreign Office. I came from a similar background.

Christian Zionism

My initial consciousness of the Holy Land probably began when I was four or five years of age. I would join my grandparents for their evening study of the Bible after a hard day's work on the farm in rural western New York, where I was brought up while my father fought in World War II. We used the Scofield Reference Bible, which was popular in fundamentalist churches throughout North America and Europe since it publication in 1909. The Scofield Bible contains interpretative keys and notes written by Cyrus I Scofield, a fundamentalist preacher, who superimposed these notations on the biblical text. The Scofield Bible influenced several generations of North Americans and many Europeans to adopt a type of theology that became popular in the late 19th century, called 'futurist premillennial dispensationalism'. In brief, this theology interprets biblical passages in a literal manner and believes that many texts will have a future prophetic fulfilment. As a result of this theology, I, like many others, developed a world-view that was decidedly influenced by certain 'prophetic signs of the times' and the sense that we were living in the 'last days'. The key event that confirmed this latter-day countdown was the establishment of Israel in 1948, which was interpreted by our pastors and evangelists as a fulfilment of the ancient biblical prophecies.

Once Israel was established, we anticipated the fulfilment of several events that the Scofield notes predicted, such as the takeover of Jerusalem by the 'revived' Jewish state, the rebuilding of the Temple, the rise of the Anti-Christ, the Battle of Armageddon, and the Return of Jesus Christ. Considerable speculation by preachers, evangelists, and writers would seek to offer predictions as to the identity of the Anti-Christ and the date of Jesus' Return. However, the comforting features of this highly pessimistic view of history was a teaching called the 'rapture,' which stated that Jesus would return to remove the true believers from history before they went through the final battle at Armageddon. In other words, 'we' would not need to go through the horrifying events at the end of history, called the 'Tribulation', because we were among 'God's elect'. The contemporary movement called 'Christian Zionism' is rooted in this school of biblical interpretation.

By high school I began to question the end-time theology, and certainly by my college years it had been left behind. During the late 1960s and early 1970s I underwent a radical political and spiritual transformation that came in two stages. One of the issues that captured my attention in my theological studies and my initial parish assignment was the Holocaust, and the courageous stance of a minority of Christians in Germany called the Confessing Church. They chose to resist Hitler and to fight his regime as a religious duty. During those years my brand of Christian Zionism shifted from the fundamentalist-apocalyptic type to the more liberal version. While I was not active in Zionist political activities, I was certainly a Zionist and did what I could to oppose anti-Jewish antisemitism. I was a supporter of the State of Israel and hoped to have the opportunity to visit the Holy Land.

During the late 1960s and 1970s I was involved in several progressive causes: working in the anti-war movement during the Vietnam era, struggling against racism in the United States, opposing apartheid and being arrested at the South African Embassy in Washington, DC, and resisting the full payment of my federal income taxes (approximately 25 percent) due to the military spending by my government.

Following seminary, I accepted a pastorate with an African-American congregation in the inner city. After the riots in nearby Newark, New Jersey, in the late 1960s, our church decided to work on the severe antisemitism that divided the Jewish and African-American communities. In my second pastorate I was able to continue this work in a wealthy suburb of New York City as a youth pastor. Among our major programmes were two summer educational trips for high school and university students, where we studied the Holocaust and the Reformation, and then visited related sites in East and West Germany, Czechoslovakia, and Poland. The visits to Auschwitz, Dachau, Terezin, and the memorial to the Jewish ghetto in Warsaw are still etched in my memory. My commitment to Israel and Zionism had been reinvigorated, underscored by what I had learned concerning the Holocaust, in many ways a more powerful political and theological orientation than my millenarian upbringing. I continued to maintain my commitment to the Jewish people and the struggle against antisemitism, but the liberal Zionism that I had adopted would soon be challenged.

The process of change

In late 1973, I accepted a position on the staff of a large and influential Presbyterian church in Evanston, Illinois, just north of Chicago. I recall driving to Chicago during the 1973 War, and being troubled by the losses that Israel endured during the initial days of that October (Yom Kippur) War. Upon arriving at the church, my initial committee assignment was to chair the Adult Education Committee and plan activities that would bring new life to a relatively dormant body. By early 1974, North Americans were in long lines for fuel due to the Arab boycott. People were angry about this inconvenience, so our committee thought it might be a useful educational moment.

One of the committee members proposed that we might consider organising a series of classes on the Middle East conflict. The proposal came from a lay-member of the committee who had been involved in the settlement of Palestinian refugees during the early 1950s. He seemed to be quite critical of Israel, and this disturbed me greatly. I immediately went on the offensive and wanted to be certain that the Israeli position was well-represented. We agreed that the series would be 'balanced', alternating the Israeli perspective with the Palestinian. To open the series, I was able secure the Israeli Consul General for the Midwest, who gave a passionate defence of Israel. One of our committee members brought in the second speaker, Professor Ibrahim Abu-Lughod, Chair of Political Science at Northwestern University.

By this point the meeting room was filled with curious participants as interest in the subject had spread. Professor Abu-Lughod's presentation provided the first occasion on which I heard a well-reasoned, intellectual analysis of the Palestinian case. It was also the first time that I actually met a Palestinian. The session stopped me in my tracks as it challenged all of my perceptions about the

Palestinians, Israel, and the Zionist movement. It defied everything I had heard for years in the popular media about Palestinian terrorism. I had accepted the Israeli position uncritically and never thought twice about it.

However, a few days after the Abu-Lughod presentation, I received an intimidating telephone call. The caller identified himself as a Holocaust survivor from nearby Skokie, Illinois, who said: 'We are offended that you would dignify the position of the PLO by having a terrorist like Abu-Lughod in your church. If this seminar is not stopped, your church will be picketed on Sunday.' I was not aware that the professor was a member of the PLO's National Council (the Palestinian Parliament in exile). I told my boss about the call and he looked concerned, but offered a nervous joke: 'Wagner, you've only been here a month and you have set back Christian-Jewish relations several decades.' That Sunday morning, we headed for worship with a backup plan in the event that we would be picketed, but it was an idle threat.

The series continued with the President of the Chicago Anti-Defamation League of Bnai-B'rith, followed by another Arab leader, upon which I received another anonymous call. This time the caller said: 'If you do not end this seminar immediately something will happen to you.' This call made me angry. I had been committed to free speech and, during the turbulent 1960s, I had experienced the Church as a central democratic institution where opposing views could be aired. My commitment to the Church had been renewed during the anti-war movement and the pivotal role that Christian and Jewish leaders had played in opposing US policy during the Vietnam War. In the black community, I brought Black Panthers, Marxists, and conservative Republicans together for heated debates on vital urban issues. I had never been threatened for arranging such forums in the past. The tactic represented pure intimidation and it had the opposite effect on me.

Once I got over my anger, I became intensely curious about the Palestinian issue. I met with Professor Abu-Lughod and other Palestinian intellectuals in Chicago and began a period of study, listening, and questioning my Zionist assumptions. I felt considerable guilt whenever I would share new insights, and friends would respond: 'You are becoming antisemitic.' While I was beginning to gain a significant political education, the missing piece for me was the theological dimension. How would I deal with issues of the 'land', the 'Covenant with Israel', and Israel as God's Chosen People, and the promises to Israel in the Bible? I had no answers.

The opportunity arose to join a group of clergy and faculty who organised a study group after returning from a 'Traveling Seminar on the Eastern Orthodox Church in the Middle East' with Professor Bruce Rigdon of McCormick Seminary. Here the theological issues began to surface in new ways and within a year the study group became the Middle East Task Force of the Presbytery of Chicago, giving us official standing within a sanctioned church body. We decided to expand our horizons and, thanks to a grant from our national church (Presbyterian Church USA), our committee brought four Christian leaders from the Middle East: two Coptic Orthodox theologians (Dr George Bebawi and Bishop Samuel of Cairo); a Palestinian theologian (Dr Paul Tarazi of St Vladimir's Orthodox Seminary); and Gabriel Habib, soon to be the first General Secretary of the Middle East Council of Churches.

The presentations by these Middle Eastern Orthodox theologians introduced me to a new world of Christian thought. My seminary studies had not adequately prepared me concerning the continuity of Christianity in the Middle East, from Pentecost to the Reformation. Like most of my seminary colleagues, I had concentrated on Biblical Studies and the Early Church, and, like most Protestants, my study of Church History moved from the New Testament and Early Church history to the Reformation. I had only a vague knowledge of what had occurred between the 4th-century Church Councils and the 16th-century Reformation, and certainly had no idea that there were fourteen million Christians in the Middle East today. It never occurred to me that there were Palestinian Christians who were suffering under Israeli occupation, let alone eight million Coptic Christians in Egypt, plus a Christian majority in

Lebanon. The presentations by these Orthodox theologians put together the issues of historic continuity of the Church, and challenged me concerning the survival of Christianity in the Middle East today. Further, the injustices imposed on the Middle East as a result of my government's unconditional support of Israel and control of the oil rich Arab Gulf region raised significant moral questions that engaged my passion about justice.

Gabi Habib and Dr George Bebawi encouraged me to visit the Middle East and see the situation first hand. I saved my money and vacation time, taking my first trip alone during a lull in the Lebanese Civil War, landing in Beirut in September 1977. Most of my American colleagues thought I was crazy to waste my time and money visiting Beirut, which had become a euphemism for terrorism and anarchy. My two new Middle Eastern friends took me under their wing, introducing me to the spectrum of Lebanese politics. I had the opportunity to meet with right-wing Christian Phalangists at the Maronite Kasleek University, followed by the Antiochian Orthodox theologian, Bishop George Khodr, whose quarters had been recently bombed by Phalangist militias due to his public opposition to their political viewpoint. I was introduced to top PLO officials, some of whom, to my surprise, were Christians. I spent significant time in Sabra and Shatila Refugee Camps in southern Beirut's 'belt of misery', where residents in these impoverished tiny homes showed me the keys to homes they were forced to leave in Haifa, or in villages in northern Galilee. One morning, Fr George and I slipped behind Syrian military positions and walked across the devastated mounds of rubble that once was Tel al-Zataar Refugee Camp, where up to 16,000 refugees had been killed during fifty-two days of Syrian and Lebanese Phalangist bombardment.

After a week of intense activities throughout Lebanon, I made my way to Jerusalem, and saw the Holy Land for the first time. On my first night, I stayed up the entire night talking to the Palestinian staff at the YMCA in East Jerusalem. They all had stories, and although they were guarded with the American stranger, what they shared was an incredible eye-opener for me.

I returned to Chicago as a changed person. I wrestled with what I could do as a volunteer and joined several Arab-American organisations, but felt that the question of Palestine needed to become an issue that was acceptable to mainstream Americans, as was the Anti-Apartheid movement. As clergyman, I believed the Churches of North America represented a specific challenge and an important arena for my involvement. Many were now willing to discuss the Palestine question, but advocacy on behalf of the Palestinian cause was still viewed as either supporting terrorism or being antisemitic. I tried to test the idea of full-time advocacy work on behalf of the Palestinian cause and met with Presbyterian national staff in New York City. I was told bluntly: 'We agree that there have been injustices done to the Palestinians, but if you get involved in advocacy for the Palestinian cause, you can forget ever getting a job in a church again. The opposition in the United States is too great.' They were correct on one level, but I had undergone such a deep theological and political transformation, that I could not heed their advice.

Having exhausted other options, I left the pastorate in 1980 and became the National Director of the Palestine Human Rights Campaign, where my real education began. While PHRC was a secular organisation that had grown out of an Arab American network, I embarked upon the effort as a religious and political calling in response to the injustices that I had seen. I served as Director for nearly ten years, and, while we had few victories, we gave ourselves to the cause of Palestinian rights and justice on a daily basis. We were able to assemble a Board of Directors that included Palestinian intellectuals such as Edward Said, Ibrahim Abu-Lughod, and Ghada Talhami. Soon a handful of Christian peace leaders and theologians such as the philosopher Nicholas Wolterstorff of Yale University, Jim Wallis and Wes Granberg-Michaelson of Sojourners, the Christian feminist theologian Rosemary Radford Ruether, and the Catholic activist Daniel Berrigan. Jewish activist, Noam Chomsky of MIT, and Israeli activists, like Felicia Langer and Holocaust survivor Dr Israel Shahak, were regular speakers at our conferences. Fr Elias Chacour, Jonathan Kuttab, Revd Riah Abu al-Assal, Canon Naim Ateek, Nora Kort, Dr Hanna and Tanya Nasser, and many other Palestinian Christians educated us and articulated the case for a secular democratic state in Palestine.

It was also the Palestinian Muslims who introduced me to Islam and gave me a burning desire to work on improved Christian, Muslim, Jewish co-operation. I will never forget the power of a beautiful young Muslim woman in Beirut while we were in the basement of a hotel near Israeli bombardment that began the invasion of Lebanon on 4 July 1982. While our group was frightened and I was getting my soul ready to die, I caught a glance of a young Palestinian mother, comforting her child as F-16s screamed overhead and dropped blockbuster bombs a few blocks from us. She had a prayer on her lips and rocked her infant in a 'Madonna and Child'-like scene that brought comfort to me. I thought that her faith as a Muslim put me to shame, and I realised that there was a great deal about our common beliefs that we could share in common, and learn from one another.

Looking back

Having been raised and initially influenced by Protestant Evangelicalism, I can honestly state that I have returned to many of the central theological principles of the Calvinist Evangelical tradition, but with marked differences. As for Christian Zionism and political Zionism, I would echo the words of Dr John Stott, noted British Evangelical leader, who once told me: 'I have come to the conviction that I find Zionism and Christian Zionism to be Biblically anathema.' Personally, I would go further, as noted in my book *Anxious for Armageddon* (1995), that I find that form of Christian Zionism that is rooted in dispensational Christianity to be a form of heresy. There are a number of reasons for this conviction:

1.   The Church (ecclesiology) is replaced by modern Israel as the instrument of God's mission in history.

2.   Christian Zionism adopts modern political Zionism as an ideal political programme, which reduces the Christian message to a racist, particularistic, programme that overrides the Gospel of universal love for all people.

3.   Christian Zionism has no compassion for the suffering of, and human rights, and political justice for the Palestinian people. As a result, Christian Zionists are generally hostile to the needs and aspirations of Palestinian Christians, who find themselves in rapid numerical decline, and in need of international support and advocacy.

4.   Christian Zionists adopt a Zionist practice of elevating the Zionist possession and sovereignty over the land of Palestine, which subverts the biblical message of God's ownership of the land, and the command that humans are to be just stewards of the land, even the land called 'holy'.

5.   Finally, it seems that one of the major mistakes of Zionism (and of Christian Zionism) is the reduction of the Christian message and the mission of the Church (universal) to a 19th-century form of Germanic nationalism called Zionism. By its nature, these types of nationalism are based on the elevation of a particular people (group) as having certain rights and privileges over other people. In South Africa, this type of nationalism led to the imposition of Apartheid and severe racist practices that now have been recognised as an evil form of racism. In the case of Zionism, the Jewish

state is moving in a similar direction, that of imposing an apartheid system on the Palestinian people in East Jerusalem, the Gaza Strip, and the West Bank, but labelling it 'the peace process'.

W H Auden once said: 'What can I do but seek to expose the unfolded lie.' Such has been the direction of my life with regard to the peoples of Israel and Palestine, as ineffective and modest as these efforts may have been. One is sobered by the long road toward justice that lies ahead, but one lives in the hope of having been faithful to the people and the march of truth in this particular cause, which has been unmistakably laid at my doorstep.

'LORD, WHO MAY DWELL IN YOUR SANCTUARY? WHO MAY LIVE ON YOUR HOLY HILL?' A PALESTINIAN PILGRIMAGE

Ruth V and Thomas C Hummel

Our first encounter with Palestinians was in the summer of 1969. We had just graduated from university with minors in archaeology, and the culminating experience for that programme was a three month tour of Middle Eastern antiquities and a six-week archaeological dig on one of the supposedly bronze age towers (which we discovered to be Roman) surrounding the city of Amman in Jordan. Centred in the American Schools of Oriental Research (ASOR) house near the third circle we were a quick walk from the site. But as we began our survey we quickly learned that our governmental permission was not enough. Because our site bordered on a Fatah hospital we also needed Palestinian permission if we were to proceed. Some delicate negotiations and many cups of tea soon convinced the Palestinians that we were not a threat. As the excavation progressed we soon developed a relationship with both the Palestinians and the guards of the nearby Queen Mother's Palace. They would take turns inviting us to tea and it was on those occasions that we first began to glimpse the tensions existing between the Palestinians and their Jordanian hosts.

One of the most significant insights into the Palestinian plight came when we were invited to visit one of the refugee camps with a doctor from the Lutheran World Federation. There we saw the misery of people recently displaced, as well as the more long-term agony of those who had lost their homes in 1948. The camps were both squalid and dignified; squalid because they were overcrowded and lacked the necessary infrastructure of a fully-fledged town, and dignified because they were kept neat and the people within them had worked at making them home, even if they thought it would, or should be a temporary home. Discussing with the leaders of the camp produced a long explanation of the Palestinian tragedy, illustrated with ancient maps on the walls showing the locations of villages, their villages, which had disappeared from modern maps because the Israelis had destroyed them, or changed their names.

One could not live for any length of time in Jordan in the summer of 1969 without being aware of the effects of the recent war (1967) on Jordan. The West Bank had been lost and Jordan was flooded with refugees who held Jordanian passports. The question which loomed was whether Jordan would become a *de facto* Palestinian state. The events of Black September, when the Jordanian Government suppressed the increasingly volatile large Palestinian community within the state, answered that question for the immediate future, but the future of Palestine and the Palestinians had become for us a concern which would continue to haunt us even when we returned that fall to the United States to begin graduate school.

One experience we had while in Jordan that summer was particularly symbolic for us. We climbed Mount Nebo, the mountain climbed by Moses before his death, to survey the Promised Land which he could not enter. We, like Moses, could glance over the rift valley into Palestine, but, again like Moses, could not enter. The pain of being so close to the sacred sites of Christianity, but being unable to visit them was intense. This exile continued until the summer of 1986, because we chose to return time and again to the Arab Middle East, and, therefore, could not easily visit Israel, a country with which the Arab world was still officially at war.

When we returned from that summer in Jordan we quickly became aware that our view of the Palestinian situation differed from that of most of our compatriots, and especially that of the American government and media. But as opposition grew to the war in Vietnam being in fundamental disagreement with American foreign policy was itself becoming normal. So for years we lived with a personal knowledge about and concern for the Palestinians, but were largely unsuccessful at opening the eyes of people to an awareness that there was another reality—that of the Palestinian people.

When our academic work took us to Bethlehem, Pennsylvania we became involved with people who were struggling with the significance of the *Shoah*, and, as historians and theologians, we also became engaged in that issue. Teaching students about the Holocaust and working with survivors meant the situation in Palestine took on a more convoluted complexion. In 1986, Ruth was given a fellowship to study the Holocaust for six weeks in the summer in Israel by an organisation sponsored by the American survivors, while Thom was awarded a summer Fulbright Fellowship to Israel. Because this was our first trip to Israel, and, as far as we knew, our last, we decided to go two weeks early and tour the country with four days in the north (Haifa, Acre and the Galilee) and the rest of the time in Jerusalem and its environs.

Our first few days' hotel accommodations in West Jerusalem came with the ticket, but, once we had the opportunity, we moved into Casa Nova in the Old City and became immersed in the life of Christian pilgrims. Every evening people from around the world would gather at long common tables, and eat Italian food and drink wine, and talk about what had brought them to the Holy Land. For the most part it was to see the sights as Western Christians, not to know modern Israel or the Palestinians. Our self-imposed pilgrim/tourist itinerary was full, so we were not particularly interested in adding any more commitments, but we had promised friends to contact George Hintlian, Secretary of the Armenian Patriarchate, and a noted historian of the Christian communities of Jerusalem. We composed a note to drop off at the Armenian Convent, explaining that we knew how busy he was and that we just wanted to bring greetings from a common friend. Thinking that we had sufficiently fulfilled our obligation we went to visit the beautiful medieval church of St James. Within five minutes George appeared, and began an animated tour of the church, followed by an extended conversation over tea.

The next day we invited George to accompany us to Jericho, and slowly a relationship began which altered our lives. Over the next week, George began to introduce us to the other Jerusalem, the Jerusalem of indigenous Christians and Muslims. When we went off to our respective programmes we were presented with the Israeli view of who they were, why they were in Palestine, and how they saw Israel's importance as a partial redemption of the pain of the Holocaust. The Palestinians were for the most part invisible in this Israeli world-view. During our breaks, however, we would get together with George, and he would open our eyes to the political, social, religious and ethnic complexities. Rarely would he preach. His method was not to dismiss the Israeli perspective, but, rather, to supplement it with the viewpoints of the other inhabitants of the land. By the end of that summer, we had come to know Israelis, Palestinians (both Christian and Muslims), as well as many of the Armenians, Greeks, Copts, Syrians and Ethiopians who are permanent residents of the city. It was truly a post-modern experience, since the narratives told by these different groups were not merely different, but frequently in substantial disagreement with each other. We left confused, but intrigued, and decided to return again next summer to continue our education, and to help George on a number of academic projects he had planned.

During the following summer of 1987, most of the time was spent visiting small villages, collecting the reminiscences of people who had lived in Palestine during World War I. Armed with a recorder and informed by word of mouth who were likely candidates we would visit these elderly people, evoking memories sometimes humorous, sometimes painful, under the watchful eyes of concerned relatives. The responsibilities were divided, with George and Ruth asking the questions and recording the responses, while Thom, with his limited Arabic, was expected to maintain eye contact and respond with the appropriate facial gesture, smile, frown, shaking of the head in sympathy, and disgust at some ancient wrong. The stories which arose out of these interviews are fascinating, and are providing much of the material for a volume on 'Daily Life in Palestine During World War I', currently being completed by George and Ruth. In fact, it was some preliminary observations about these interviews and the situation in Palestine at that time which was the subject matter of the first lecture delivered at the Swedish Christian Study Centre by Ruth in March of 1991.

By the end of that second summer we had become committed to working on helping to interpret and preserve the importance of indigenous Christians and Christianity in the Holy Land. This was not just an academic interest, but a response to the emigration of large numbers of Christians from Palestine as their educational and job prospects shrank under Israeli occupation. The policy of Israel had become one of absorbing all of Jerusalem and much of the West Bank. For those of us living in Jerusalem the most obvious manifestation of this was the growth of settlements around the city, encircling Arab East Jerusalem, and cutting it off from the rest of the West Bank. The frustration among the Arab residents was obvious, and by the time Ruth returned in March of 1988 the *Intifada* had begun. The most visible result of the uprising was the segregation of the city. It became rare to see Jews in the Old City, outside of the Jewish quarter, and East Jerusalem became more like a small Arab city. Those of us with friends in both sections of the city would travel around freely, but our Jewish and Palestinian friends would not venture into the 'hostile quadrant'. As the *Intifada* grew the situation became less disciplined, and it was not uncommon to be stoned while visiting East Jerusalem if one looked Western, or drove through in a car with Israeli plates. One taxi we were in was hit with a huge stone thrown from the top of building in Salah al-Din Street, although no further action was taken after getting out and speaking Arabic, but the car behind us was completely burned because it was hired from an Israeli firm.

Because of the *Intifada* the spirit of the Old City began to change tone. The repeated closures meant that the *suq* was frequently empty and the shopkeepers desperate for business when open. There were few parties, and wedding celebrations were kept low-key and private. The mood of defiance also grew during this time and the Palestinians became more united. The Christians and the Muslims came together in a common cause and the leaders of the frequently contending Christian communities began to issue joint communiqués, expressing their frustration with the prolonged Israeli occupation and its effect upon the Palestinians and their institutions. The extent of this sense of common cause uniting those under the occupation was symbolised for Ruth during a visit in August 1991 when neighbours ushered her into the Armenian convent at night where the body of a boy killed by the Israeli authorities during a demonstration was being prepared for burial, after being snatched from a government hospital. The Armenian community gathered in grief, but also in pride, in having produced a martyr. But it was all done at night, away from the prying eyes of the authorities from whom the body had been stolen before an autopsy could be performed. Despite an Israeli ban on mass gatherings, thousands turned out for the funeral, in solidarity with the dead teenager.

Another significant symbol of the pain of the occupation and the *Intifada* was the icon of the Virgin located in the 'prison of Christ' within the Holy Sepulchre. The local Christians began praying to the icon, almost obscured by years of soot from the candles of pilgrims, for succour, and believed that sometimes her eyes would be open and sometimes shut, and there were even sightings of the Virgin crying. Farida, an Orthodox Palestinian, would tell us these stories with a real excitement because they were signs that God had not deserted the Christians of his homeland. Taking a small devotional candle we frequently would stick it in through the iron grating in front of the icon to illuminate dimly her face. Just as Farida said, sometimes her eyes would appear open and sometimes closed.

The times were politically charged, and it was virtually impossible not to be dragged along since neutrality was seen as treacherous. The fiery rhetoric and provocative actions charged the atmosphere and it was during this time that the Jewish Quarter became increasingly 'religious' and nationalistic. Every meal at the home of Israeli and Palestinian friends was accompanied by stories of how the *Intifada* was affecting both societies. It became harder to maintain good relations on both sides of the political, religious divide, and friends from the time of the Fulbright exchange started to show hostility to us on account of our commitment to the Christian Palestinian community.

This was also the time when a good friend, Nora Kort, who was co-ordinator of social services for Orthodox and Catholic charities, was invited to attend a meeting at the Zionist Confederation House. While there she was asked to express some of her own observations on the Israeli-Palestinian situation. With greatly suppressed emotions she explained how the house they were in had been her family home, confiscated in 1948, and that the piano still there had been her mother's. For decades afterwards her father still kept the key to the house in his pocket. This episode points both to the depth of the problem, but also demonstrates the beginnings of a willingness to enter into dialogue, even when it hurts.

These were also times when the spirit of messianic expectation reached an even higher pitch. In the courtyard of our own apartment charismatic Christians from Christ Church would appear for a few weeks of fervent spiritual activity. One group spoke in tongues in the middle of the night. Another lady living below us with her cats would have periodic fasts, which she forced upon the cats who would then howl in protest, which melted our hearts, although not that of their owner. A couple from England with two teenage children would gather for two weeks on the roof across from our balcony on even numbered days from 11 a.m. to 12 noon waiting for the rapture. The Gulf War brought this expectation of the end days to fever pitch and a friend who was stuck in the Scottish hostel during the Scud attacks tells of how a couple from Los Angeles arrived in high spirits, with seven suitcases each. When questioned by our friend one night in the shelter they explained that they had flown in to be present for the rapture of the righteous, and had brought a suitcase full of tracksuits for each year they would be spending in heaven with Jesus, and that they had received a great discount on these tracksuits during a K-Mart blue light special.

If the Gulf War did not bring the last days it did usher in a new phase in the geo-political situation of the region, after which the prospect for peace began to emerge with the Madrid Conference, and then the Oslo Accords. Through contacts at Bir Zeit University, especially Albert Aghazarian, we were able to be at many of the conferences and discussions that arose, analysing the meaning and appropriateness of the agreements, and what future there would be for Palestine. The settlements, the replacement of Palestinian workers with foreigners, the economic consequences of the *Intifada* all made some agreement necessary if Palestinians were not going to be driven from their land by economic necessity. Emigration was a growing problem, and continued to drain away the most educated and resourceful people. It became obvious that if this exodus did not stop the ability of Palestine to become a viable state would be severely crippled. But the agreements made by Arafat and Rabin were for many who had stood up to Israel in the *Intifada* a bitter pill. It was also a bitter pill for the Jewish nationalists who wanted to keep ancient Samaria and Judaea.

It was against this backdrop of the *Intifada* and its aftermath that George began to help the Free Churches of Sweden to create the Swedish Christian Study Centre just inside Jaffa Gate. The purpose of the centre was to expose visiting Swedes to the social and religious realities in the Holy Land. It was also a place where Christians could meet to discuss common concerns, and where conferences could be held which would bring together Western and indigenous Christians to speak about the history of Christianity in the Holy Land and its future. In fact, Ruth gave the first lecture at the centre, drawing upon the work she did with George interviewing survivors of World War I in Palestine. During Holy Week of 1994 Thom was asked to give a lecture at the Swedish Centre which was prepared while on sabbatical as acting chaplain at Peterhouse College, Cambridge. This lecture was later expanded, with illustrations chosen by Ruth, based on her work on early photography in the Middle East, and was published in 1995 as *The Patterns of the Sacred: Russian Orthodox and English Protestant Pilgrims of the Nineteenth Century*. As Ruth says in the introduction, the book is an attempt to explain to the Christians of the West the nature of pilgrimage and the sacred sites as understood by the Eastern Church, and to explain to the Eastern

Christians how the Protestant pilgrims understand their journey, and why they react to the sites the way they do.

It was at this lecture that we met Fr Michael Prior who invited Thom, who was returning to England, to attend a conference on Christians in the Holy Land, sponsored by the World of Islam Festival Trust at Cumberland Lodge in Windsor Great Park (for the papers, see Prior and Taylor 1994). This was an opportunity to meet a number of religious leaders and scholars with similar interests in the Palestinian Christian cause. Out of that meeting friendships were begun with Hugh Wybrew, former dean of the Anglican Cathedral in Jerusalem, Naim Ateek, director of *Sabeel*, and Anthony O'Mahony of London University's School of Oriental and African Studies (SOAS).

George, with the assistance of the Swedish Christian Study Centre and its various directors, worked to put together the First International Conference on the Holy Land in July 1994. We worked with them on this endeavour and presented papers, which later were published in a volume *The Christian Heritage in The Holy Land*, edited by Anthony O'Mahony, with Göran Gunner and Kevork (George) Hintlian (1995). The second international conference was held in 1996, and later published in *Patterns of the Past, Prospects for the Future*, edited by Thomas Hummel and George Hintlian (1999). By this time, George had become the Director of the Christian Heritage Research Institute, which together with the Swedish Centre holds conferences and publishes the proceedings, sponsors scores of lectures on a multiplicity of topics, and fosters the writing of books on Christians and Christianity in Palestine. While Naim Ateek and *Sabeel* focused on the issues of social justice for Palestine and the theological problem of the Promised Land and its implications for the dispossessed the International Conferences organised by George tried to remind the Christian world of its place in the history of Palestine. In the process we came to see each group complementing the work of the other.

Since we first journeyed to Palestine in 1986 and became acquainted with George Hintlian we have spent six weeks or more each year in Jerusalem working on the various projects mentioned above, and others still gestating. But mostly we have come to have a second home, and to know people in a way that is only possible if one is involved with them through good times and bad over a long period of time. The 'Palestinian issue', or the 'problem of Christian emigration', or the 'future of Jerusalem and the Church in that city' are all topics which we discuss in a number of forums in Oxford and Washington, as well as in Jerusalem, but they are more than abstractions for us because these issues concern our friends and our colleagues in the faith.

As peace begins to unfold in Palestine the question arises, What is the future of Christianity in the Holy Land? Will the Christian shrines become a Disneyland-like theme-park in a Jewish and Muslim world, or will there be a place and a purpose for the indigenous Christian communities? We have suggested that the Christians of Palestine are uniquely placed to be the welcoming hosts to the diversity of Christians who come to the place of Christ's earthly life and ministry. The Holy Land can and should be a place where Christians of all denominations can come together and learn about each other. Local churches should work together to enhance this critical role. There is also an evangelical role to be played by the local Christians, not by preaching on street-corners and trying to convert their neighbours, but by providing a House of Christian Heritage, a place where visitors can go not only to be oriented to the Christian sites, but to have the Christian message in its moral simplicity and its historical complexity presented to a public increasingly ignorant of Christian beliefs.

We began thinking and writing about Christians in the Holy Land because we found the visiting Western Christians ignorant of their Eastern brothers and sisters. In a world ruled by secularism and consumerism Christians need to embrace each other if we are to reach out to a world which needs to hear the Gospel. Where better to begin this process than in Jerusalem? There Jesus gave his final address to his disciples:

> Thus it is written, that the Messiah is to suffer and to rise from the dead on the third day, and that repentance and forgiveness of sins is to be proclaimed in his name

to all nations, beginning from Jerusalem. You are witnesses of these things. And see, I am sending upon you what my Father promised; so stay here in the city until you have been clothed with power from on high (Luke 24.46-48).

Then he led them out as far as Bethany, and while he was blessing them, he withdrew from them and was carried up into heaven.

CHANGED BY MEETING THE INVISIBLE PEOPLE OF THE HOLY LAND
Garth Hewitt

A personal journey of discovery

I remember sitting watching television as the PLO was being thrown out of Beirut, and it was one of those moments when your eyes suddenly open. I said to myself 'who are these people, and where should they be going—where is the land of Palestine?' The next day I was having a meeting in an advertising agency with a Christian organisation, and I told them I was thinking of writing a song called *Where is the land of Palestine?* They looked at me appalled, nobody said a word, and I realised I was touching on something that should not be spoken about. Consequently, I began to do some reading. I had only a very vague view of what was going on in Israel-Palestine.

As a teenager, I had been given the view that the Israelites were promised the land by God, and therefore the return of Jews to the land of Palestine was a fulfilment of prophecy. When I arrived at theological college, my lecturers challenged me on this view, and I came to recognise that much as I might be delighted that now the Jews had a land, it was not to do with the fulfilment of Scripture. In the Six-Day War I remember being enormously encouraged that this tiny little country had managed to punish its big bullying neighbours. This, I think, was my view up to the early 1980s, and I was hardly aware that there were any Arabs in the Holy Land. It seemed as if I simply had ignored who the Palestinians might be that had done the hijackings in the 1970s, and why. I had made no connection at all, but in the early 1980s the scales fell from my eyes. I sat up in front of the television set, and remembered that the first film I had ever seen as a little child, in an old church hall, was about the land of Palestine, but then it seemed to disappear, and was no longer on maps. And so my search began.

After reading many books, I finished my song *Where is the land of Palestine?* and started to put it into concerts. It met with bewilderment. At that time, people would still protest when I was singing songs against apartheid in South Africa. Christians would come up and complain that I was giving only one side of the picture, and that I had been duped by Archbishop Desmond Tutu, who was of course a 'gun-toting Communist'. Strangely enough, these people seem to have all disappeared now. They were all against apartheid, apparently.

At Heathrow Airport I picked up a book called *Blood Brothers* by Elias Chacour. This focused my journey of discovery. I could not believe it. I was introduced for the first time to one of the 'living stones'. As one of the organisers of the Greenbelt Festival (a Christian arts and music festival held over the August bank-holiday weekend), I contacted him through his publisher, and we invited him to come and speak at Greenbelt. Somehow the messages all went astray during the first year, and it was only in the second year that he arrived, and even then he was left in his hotel room instead of being brought onto the site for his first seminar. Eventually he got there, and overwhelmed the Greenbelt audience, who had never heard his story, and were delighted by this man of faith from Galilee. In the Sunday morning Eucharist, when the Peace was exchanged by over 20,000 people, Abuna Elias came up to me and said 'Let's do this in Galilee.' I agreed. Now I was to go and see for myself.

Not long afterwards, Bob Wilkes, who worked with the Church Mission Society (CMS, a mission organisation of the Anglican Church with strong links with the Diocese of Jerusalem), heard my song *Where is the land of Palestine?* and asked if I would like to go there. Now the first tour was beginning to take shape. We talked with the then Anglican Bishop of Jerusalem, Samir Kafity, and he agreed to host my visit and organise a variety of concerts. As I told people that I was about to go, a strange thing happened. Worried Evangelicals came up to me and told me that I was going to meet the wrong people. 'What's wrong with them?' I asked. The implication was that, somehow, they were not quite where they should be spiritually. I was to discover later that this was not what they meant at all. It was that, politically and theologically, they disagreed with them. In fact, the people that I was to meet were of enormous and deep faith, whose understanding of God, history and the Bible was to challenge and deepen my own faith.

In 1989, in the middle of the *Intifada*, along with friend Tony Neeves, who had been with me to many places of poverty and struggle, and with Richard Handforth from CMS we headed off for the first time to the Holy Land. We were welcomed everywhere. It was a time when the Palestinian spirit was very high. To sing *Where is the land of Palestine?* in the West Bank during the *Intifada* was exhilarating. Concerts were attended by Christians and Muslims alike, and also by Jewish peacemakers, and I began to make friendships which have stayed with me ever since.

One night as I sang at Ibillin in Galilee with Elias Chacour, I saw a priest in the audience wearing a *keffiyeh* giving me the familiar peace sign. It was Riah Abu El-Assal. I was to meet him properly the next morning. He was then Vicar of Christ Church, Nazareth, soon to become the Archdeacon, and now he is the Anglican Bishop of Jerusalem. I was not well the next morning, and as I staggered up the steps to Christ Church, Nazareth, we were running nearly an hour late, but the children had waited to sing for us, and the enthusiasm of their singing moved me to tears. When I sang *Where is the land of Palestine?* Riah presented me with a cross and a *keffiyeh*. Later I met with Canon Naim Ateek, now the Director of the *Sabeel* Liberation Theology Centre, and Jewish peacemakers, such as Rabbi Jeremy Milgrom, and Yehezkel and Dalia Landau.

Perhaps most significant of all, we heard the stories of ordinary people. I will never forget being in Ramallah as Israeli armoured vehicles moved round the houses we were in, and we heard the stories of two families where the husbands were in prison, and where young children had been arrested. We heard the painful story of what it meant to be under this brutal occupation. In Gaza I interviewed Miriam, who later featured in a song of mine *(Song for Miriam)*, who was shot in the leg by the Israeli soldiers when she ran out to try to find her brother and take him to safety during a shooting incident. For me, it was a clear-cut human rights issue. It was strange—only a few years earlier I had stood in Auschwitz-Birkenau in the height of a Polish winter, and felt the eerie silence and the horror of knowing what had occurred in that place. It was another situation where I had been ignorant of the history of how much persecution Christians had done to Jews during the centuries. I committed myself afresh in Auschwitz to stand against human rights abuse. I was startled to discover that it was not only Jews, but also gypsies and homosexuals who had suffered. It seemed to me that anyone who had been to that place had to have a commitment to speak up for the forgotten wherever they might be, so that it should never happen again to anyone else.

Since I first went to the Holy Land, I have been back every year at least twice, sometimes taking groups, sometimes going to renew friendships or make new ones, often marvelling at how tourist groups can rush through the land, treating it like a theme park, having their own pious moments, but failing to see the pain of the people of the land. When the local people say 'Don't just look at the old stones, meet the living stones,' this is the only thing that helps the journeys make sense. It seems to me that if the Gospel we cherish works, then it must work here, in the very land where Jesus walked, in one of the hardest and most painful situations. Here, two wounded communities are shoulder to shoulder, and one has appropriated the land of the other in what may come to be looked upon as the last great colonial venture. It made me do my own theological exploration, and to recognise that the dispensationalism that raised its head in Britain during the 19th century was eventually to influence even the Balfour Declaration.

I remember on my first trip asking Naim Ateek what he thought of the views of the people who say that this land belongs to the Jews, and, therefore, that the Palestinians must get out because of what God promised in the Bible. He pointed out that this was a very primitive view of God, a very tribal view. Our understanding of the New Testament blows such a view apart, and we meet an inclusive God. Since then I have also heard my Jewish friends draw this conclusion, as they speak of the character of God as reflected particularly in Second Isaiah, and of the return of the Jews in the post-Exilic period, where they did not come back with invasion and the driving out of 'the other'.

I have also come to realise that for all religions and communities there are 'myths of origin': we have mega-stories that can inspire and give identity, but if we take them as in some sense literally and historically true, we can create a cruel and exclusive God, rather than a generous and inclusive one. So the God of the Exodus, who takes compassion on the children of Israel, and is to send them to a land flowing with milk and honey, is also the God who seems to order the invasion of the land of 'the Canaanites, the Hittites, the Amorites, the Perizzites, the Hivites and the Jebusites' (Exodus 3.7-8). A theology for a new millennium, surely, has to be one that takes us beyond such a tribal and vindictive God. At the end of the day, it is a challenge to all the faith communities, particularly the three that have roots in this part of the world. One thousand years ago, the enthusiasm at the time of the millennium ended up in the horror of the Crusades. Could it be that now, as we are beginning the new millennium, there could be a new faith, a new theology, that says good-bye once and for all to the tribal God?

Saying good-bye to the tribal God

This was particularly brought home to me after spending some time with Jeff Halper, who is Co-ordinator of the Israeli Campaign Against Home Demolitions. He is a warm-hearted, balding, bearded anthropologist, a secular Jew with a twinkle in his eye. His group sits in front of bulldozers to try to stop the home demolitions that are happening in the Palestinian community. If the family is willing, they also start to rebuild some of the houses as a way of confronting the occupation. He explains to me how this sort of action has opened the eyes of the peace movement, because this time they actually have to go into the West Bank and meet with families and get to know them. He says, 'The West Bank is further from Israel than Thailand. People haven't been to Thailand, but they find it exotic, and would like to go there, whereas with the West Bank they haven't been there—and they travel in a bubble on bypass roads, never having to see the reality of it.'

His comments confirmed my own view while I was there recently that somehow I was in a Star Wars movie, or maybe even a Mad Max movie; huge settlements are being built, like fortresses— they are complete in themselves, and you need never venture outside except to the bypass roads that take you to your work in Jerusalem. Do people ever walk outside and actually touch the soil that means so much to the local Palestinian community who would like to farm it? Jeff, as 'an Israeli in Palestine', has stepped through the 'invisible membrane', as he describes it, to make contact with this other world. This is unusual. 'Israel has created such an insulated bubble,' he says. 'Palestinians are outside the debate—nobody is asking the Palestinians, they're not even in the conversation.'

Having gone through the membrane, though, he has discovered another people, another language, another cuisine, another tradition, another history, a real place. He is an academic who gives tours around all the neighbourhoods of Jerusalem, yet he did not know that the Palestinian neighbourhoods of Jerusalem even existed until a couple of years ago. They were places he had never heard about. They are only on the other side of the hill, but it is the Third World, where there are no sewage systems, or streetlights. The university where he lectures in Jerusalem overlooks one of these neighbourhoods, known as Issawiya. He acknowledges that until the demolition protests started he had never been there. To the students and faculty it is invisible, and even though there have been forty demolition orders in this neighbourhood, and it is part of their daily view, no one has been there.

A little while ago a man was shot in a demonstration against demolitions in Issawiya, and the incident was in all the papers. After this Jeff asked the students and the faculty how many had heard of Issawiya. Ninety-eight percent had no idea where it was, nor that they could see it from the window. This is all part of the ability to close out 'the other'. For me, it was a reminder of visiting Johannesburg in apartheid times. I had just come out of Soweto, and I was explaining what I had seen to students at Witwatersrand University. 'But we've never seen it,' they replied. Even though it was only twenty minutes down the road, they had never been there.

Meanwhile, Ardie Geldman up at Efrat Settlement says, 'We have no obligation to the Palestinians—they are not Israeli citizens.' He maintains that God has given the whole of the land of Israel-Palestine to the Jewish people. To him, the West Bank is Judea and Samaria, and Jerusalem cannot be negotiated. His tribal God says, 'It's yours, so grab it,' whereas Jeff Halper, a secular Jew, refuses to let the forgotten people be forgotten, and espouses humanitarian and moral values that reflect the worth of every human being. There is a special challenge to religious people: are we still going to worship a tribal God who excludes and ignores the others? Or is there some other kind of God, perhaps closer to the one that Jeff does not acknowledge, yet appears to bear witness to: the God who includes all equally? Could we not say good-bye to the tribal God in this new millennium and say 'All are chosen, or none'? We are all in this together, and loving our neighbour as ourselves can unite us all.

If religion is to have a credibility in the new millennium, then it is time that religious leaders of all faiths spoke up against the horror of what is happening to the Palestinians in a land some like to call Holy. As Christians, Muslims and Jews we can be liberated from our tribalism. Perhaps it is only right that one who does not acknowledge God can nevertheless show us the way. Jeff Halper, a secular Jew, has walked through the invisible membrane and found another world, a world that he loves, a people that he loves, a humanity that he loves. Maybe he can give us clues for a morality, a dignity and even a theology for a new millennium.

Politics, human rights and faith

Faith itself is challenged by the politics, the morality and the human rights issues that are highlighted so strongly in Palestine-Israel. Events of brutality and human rights abuse can challenge and help us to have a deeper understanding of the character of God. I remember on a radio programme on the BBC in Britain called *Desert Island Discs*, Holocaust survivor, the late Rabbi Hugo Gryn being asked about whether God was there in Auschwitz. He replied 'God was present, but powerless.' This made me do a lot of thinking afterwards, because if you were to suggest that God was not powerless, it would indicate a cruel or an uncaring God. As I have travelled around in Palestine-Israel, I have had to ask similar questions. Perhaps this is where a Christian understanding of the Body of Christ can be helpful—that we are called to be the community that brings hope. In other words, God has no hands, no feet but ours, and where good people are silent over small things eventually holocausts happen, whether it is to Jew, Palestinian, Armenian, in the Balkans, Cambodia or Rwanda.

If we take a different view, we somehow end up with a less than moral God, who for inscrutable reasons decides that one group can be arbitrarily favoured and another group cannot. So, if we recognise that politics itself was affected by the bad theology of the last century, with its primitive view of God, then, surely, faith communities now can have a view of God that reflects the presence of God in the community, of a just and compassionate God who endorses human rights for all, and equality for all. When Archbishop Desmond Tutu says he was 'puzzled about which Bible people are reading when they suggest religion and politics don't mix' he is proved right again and again. But what is the character of this God? Is this a God who oppresses, or one who liberates? The God of empire, or the God of community? The God who lords it over others, or the God who serves?

My journey of discovery has led me to this point, where I have to walk away from a tribal God. When Jesus spoke in the synagogue at Nazareth, at first what he said, as he quoted from Isaiah, was very acceptable, but when he suggested that it was inclusive, and for all people, they wanted to throw him over the cliff. If this is the lesson we learn from our pilgrimage to the Holy Land we have learnt a lesson that is relevant to every community. We have learnt a lesson about speaking up against injustice wherever it occurs, about racism wherever it occurs, about human rights abuse wherever they occur. Then the Gospel really comes alive, and the words of Jesus, quoted from Isaiah in Luke 4 about bringing 'good news to the poor' and 'setting free the oppressed', become a tangible reality.

A personal response to what I have seen

The first thing I did when I came back from my first visit to the Holy Land was to do a 'Chain of Love' tour in conjunction with the Church Mission Society in Britain. We went round the churches of Britain, having a Palestinian guest, singing the songs that I had written, and it was subtitled 'The Palestinian search for peace with justice'. For the largest part of the tour, the special guest with me was Riah Abu El-Assal, who at that time was the Archdeacon of Nazareth. He won the hearts of people, and with the songs and the stories, the response to the presentations was quite extraordinary. In surprisingly many cases, people had simply not heard this side of the story. I gradually recorded songs on several CDs which reflected lessons I had learnt in that part of the world, culminating in putting them together on the album *Journeys—the Holy Land*, subtitled *Pray for the Peace*. Songs like *Ten Measures of Beauty*, with its chorus *Pray for the peace of Jerusalem*, have been picked up in many different places in the world, not least in Jerusalem itself.

I followed this up with a Lent book, *Pilgrims and Peacemakers. A Journey through Lent towards Jerusalem* (1996), which in daily readings helped people to explore Lent, Holy Week and Easter in the context of learning from the local Palestinian Christian community and from Jewish peacemakers, and introducing them to the 'living stones'. This book has been picked up by many groups, and while out in the Holy Land I have seen groups reading from the book at different stages of their pilgrimage.

More recently I have fulfilled an ambition to do a second book, *A Candle of Hope* (1999), which is a journey through Advent, Christmas and the New Year to Bethlehem, featuring the three Christmases that are celebrated in the Holy Land: the 'Western' (25 December), the Orthodox (7 January) and the Armenian (19 January). This book is to take people into the New Year, having gone through the Advent period, and once again to be guided by the local Christian community, and by Muslim and Jewish peacemakers. The pain of the Palestinian community, for whom the situation since Oslo has been so much worse, is reflected in this book.

Through the Amos Trust, we have helped to co-ordinate regular visits to meet the 'living stones' of the Holy Land first hand, and help to set up a network in Britain of organisations that have a concern for justice for the Palestinian community. 'Rediscovering Palestine' was first featured at the 1998 Christian Resources Exhibition, an exhibition held annually in Esher, England. This venture has fascinated people, particularly at an event in which the largest exhibitor is the Israeli Tourist Board. Many people have been delighted to see that the Palestinian voice also is there to be heard.

One of the joys of our experience in all of this is that we are now linked to an international work, that in some way tells the story of the invisible community which is gradually reappearing. I am grateful for the Palestinians. They are invisible people to millions of pilgrims, and yet they have shown me something of faith, shown me lessons from history. I would like to clasp hands with Christians, Muslims and Jews, and walk forward with all the community, in which no one group has to dominate another, and where the character of God is inclusive, compassionate, just and loving. I say, 'Thank you' to the invisible people of the Holy Land. 'You have shown me the way forward.'

NEVER JUDGE A COUNTRY
BY ITS POSTCARDS
Peter J Miano

I never could have imagined how a one-month study leave from parish ministry would change my approach to biblical studies, and, indeed, alter the path of my life. I never intended to do either. Indeed, I never intended to visit the Holy Land at all. Throughout my seminary training, my graduate studies in New Testament, and the early part of my experience in parish ministry, I viewed the thought of travel to the Holy Land with distinct suspicion and even disdain. After all, I had studied with some of the world's best biblical scholars at some of the world's best institutions. I had absorbed the most recent and best texts in the field. How on earth would a junket to the Holy Land contribute?

Even the words of Jesus spoken to the woman at the well in Samaria seemed to invalidate the very idea of sacred place and pilgrimage: 'The hour is coming when neither on this mountain nor in Jerusalem will you worship the Father' (John 4.21). Like many others, I took these to mean that journeying to a specific place for one's spiritual enrichment was unnecessary. In the field of biblical studies, geographical place is almost completely ignored by scholars. Biblical scholars focus on texts, i.e., biblical literature, rather than on geographical contexts.[1] The largest and single most powerful guild of biblical scholars bears the telling name, 'The Society for Biblical *Literature*' (emphasis mine). My experience in the countries of the Near East has caused me to realize that this state of affairs is symptomatic of a defect in biblical scholarship. The antidote is contextual study of the Bible which is another name for *authentic* pilgrimage.

---

[1] This simple reality contrasts sharply with the point of departure in the field of Near Eastern Studies, in which geography is understood to be hugely determinative (cf. Roux 1992: 1).

I first came to the Holy Land as a rather reluctant and sceptical participant in what I realize now was a fairly standard tour. It was a ten-day package which I expanded by including self-directed travel through Jordan and Egypt, in addition to Israel and the Occupied Palestinian Territories. Prior to my departure, the tour company prepared me for everything the tour would encompass, but this did not include the realities I would encounter, in spite of a carefully scripted itinerary.

In a nutshell, most Western Christians experience the Holy Land through the medium of commercial tourism which treats the Holy Land as if it were Disneyland, a religious destination resort, a biblical theme park. For the typical American tourist, who is usually a first-time traveller and often leaving the United States for the first time, 'pilgrimage' is a walk through the corridors of a faith museum. It is an historical nostalgia-experience, but not a journey with a living Lord. In the years since my first visit to Israel and Palestine, I have come to realize that what passes for pilgrimage is nothing more than commercial tourism.

The prevailing paradigm for pilgrimage to the Holy Land resembles the dominant approach to biblical studies in that both ignore important realities. Both, by and large, are disembodied from actual living realities and social contexts. The dominant academic guild of biblical scholars is so preoccupied with arcane minutiae that it is not even accessible to intelligent lay people and clergy. This is not due to any sinister plot to exclude anyone, but rather it is due simply to the increasingly high level of specialization which the guild expects of scholars.

For me, travel and work in the Holy Land itself has been a pilgrimage, a journey into a deeper relationship with God. It has been life-changing. It has been a spiritual experience of the deepest and highest order, as it can and should be for everyone. But I wonder from time to time if I would have ever left home if I had known in advance what I was about to learn, and how my life would change. Images are almost always more pleasant than realities.

Christian travel to the Holy Land is dominated by commercial tourism, and Christians arrive in the Holy Land with cherished images instilled by tour company promotional material. More than a few travellers have arrived in modern-day Israel hoping for a life-changing spiritual experience in 'The Land of the Bible',[2] only to learn that there is a huge gulf between the images they start with and the facts on the ground. Indeed, high-volume tourism is designed to enable the traveller to avoid challenging realities. Tours are carefully choreographed to avoid contact with indigenous people other than the licensed guide and the bus driver.

I first visited the Middle East in February 1988. The *Intifada* had been raging for two months, but when I arrived in Palestine via the Allenby Bridge, I had no idea what an *Intifada* was. There was no mention of it in the tour company's promotional material. Of course, I was aware through various media that the Palestinians were causing disturbances again, but I considered this par for the Middle Eastern course. I noticed the closed shops of Jericho and the proliferation of graffiti on walls, doors and buildings, but I did not yet realize that these were symptoms of the *Intifada*. Jericho struck me as being rather like an inner-city ghetto in the United States. I quickly inferred that even 'Israel'[3] had its slums.

My first great awakening occurred when I arrived in Bethlehem, within twenty-four hours of stepping foot in the Holy Land. As in Jericho, the shops were closed and graffiti were ubiquitous. The sky was a sullen grey. Ominous clouds bulged. The streets were still. Except for those on our tour and an occasional peddler, signs of life were hard to find. Emerging from the Church of the Nativity, I was approached by a man selling postcards. The price was right—forty for a dollar—so I paused to look, incurring the harsh glare of the Israeli guide. This is when it happened.

---

[2] While Israel is customarily identified this way in tourism promotions, in actual fact, not one book of the Bible as we have received it was written in Israel. The books of the Hebrew Scriptures took their final form in Mesopotamia and those of the New Testament were in written countries on the northern shores of the Mediterranean Sea.

[3] At the time, I was oblivious of the simple fact that Jericho was not then, and never had been part of 'Israel' during the modern era.

I noticed that all of the postcards portrayed bright sunshine, dazzling blue skies and glistening monuments. Shepherds were captured in serene attitudes, tending their flocks in traditional costumes underneath the setting sun. Young women were shown in wonderful displays of traditional Palestinian wedding costumes, their eyes beaming, and faces exuding sheer joy. I looked up, hoping to see such happiness in a person, rather than on a post card. Instead, I saw a patrol of Israeli soldiers dressed in full combat gear: helmets, M-16s, tear gas launchers ready to fire. The tour brochures had not conveyed such images. Something was obviously wrong here, badly wrong. Bethlehem was no inner-city ghetto such as the ones I was used to. This was a city under military siege. Israelis and Palestinians were not simply uneasy neighbours. They were bitter enemies.

Most startling to me upon my arrival in the Middle East and in the ensuing years has been the broad gulf between what I expected and what I found. As Mark Twain discovered when he travelled through the countries of the Mediterranean Sea on his way to the Holy Land in 1867, image and reality are two different things. One of the most important things I learned was this: never judge a country by its postcards.

I learned a lot on my first day in the Holy Land. What did the biblical faith have to say about military occupation? In what way, if any, were the social conditions in Bethlehem at the time of Jesus' birth mirrored in what I found at the Church of the Nativity on my first visit there? Does the Bible speak to contemporary contexts? I realized then that my journey to the Holy Land would take a different course than the one I had planned. I learned that my understanding of the biblical faith would not allow me to ignore the unpleasant realities around me and treat the Holy Land like Disneyland. I wondered how either pilgrimage or biblical studies which avoided specific contexts could be harmonious with a faith based on a God who takes flesh, becomes incarnate in a specific setting and submits to the conditions of temporal existence.

Over the past ten years, I have worked with many thousands of pilgrims to the Holy Land. Most travel on tours similar to the highly scripted one I first experienced. To break out of the dominant paradigm of pilgrimage is to become vulnerable to the powerful emotions experienced by peoples who live with moral challenges of life-and-death proportions. This results in our re-examining cherished notions of right and wrong, good and evil. This, of course, is not always pleasant and is never easy, but to avoid doing so would be like a parish minister who visits a hospital, stops by the gift shop and the coffee shop, but never the bedsides of those who need pastoral care.

Since childhood, I have been trained, like many others, to believe that every argument has two sides. The old adage, 'It takes two to tango', expresses this popular, reductionist sentiment. When it comes to the Israeli-Palestinian conflict, at least, such thinking is not only naïve and simplistic, it is dead wrong.

It is symptomatic of conflict-bound thinking, i.e., the thinking of those who, themselves, are enmeshed in conflict, that states of affairs become neatly separated into two distinct compartments: good guys and bad guys, us and them, right versus wrong. However, the Israeli-Palestinian conflict is not simply one between peoples, it is one within people as well.

In winter 1993, a story appeared in an East Jerusalem newspaper, *Al-Fajr,* about a patrol of Israeli soldiers who had been sent into the Balata refugee camp in Nablus. The presence of Israeli soldiers, representing military occupation, in a refugee camp is always provocative, and on that day, a confrontation led to a hail of rocks being thrown at the soldiers. The soldiers responded with tear gas and live ammunition from their M-16s. In the melee which followed, one of the soldiers was separated from the rest of his patrol. The patrol hastened to withdraw, leaving the separated soldier behind. The lone soldier wandered through the maze of streets deep inside the refugee camp for over an hour, unable to find his way out. One can imagine what it must have been like for this young Israeli soldier surrounded by hostile Palestinians. Soldiers have been killed in such circumstances. This time, however, a small Palestinian boy approached the soldier, took him by the hand and led him out of the camp. The rest of the patrol had been waiting for help before starting a search of the camp for their lost comrade. When the soldiers saw their comrade led out of the camp by the boy, they looked at one another shaking their heads. The soldier who had been lost looked at his friends and said, 'We are crazy.'

Was this little Palestinian boy the soldier's enemy or his deliverer? Was the soldier divided against the Palestinian boy or divided within himself, torn between loyalty to duty and loyalty to humanity? While it is all too easy for those enmeshed in conflict to identify the enemy, I can imagine that that soldier did not go to sleep that night without wondering who the *real* enemy was. The line between enemy and ally is not always so easy to discern.

Everyone who has taken the time to meet with people on their trips to the Holy Land knows that the struggle called the Israeli-Palestinian conflict is more than one side against the other. It is also a private struggle within individuals. Many Palestinians display relics from their ancestral homes in their new homes. It might be a large iron key to a home in Jaffa, lost in 1948. It might be a sack of soil from the family garden in Jerusalem. Once I had the opportunity to visit the Falastine refugee camp in Damascus. I was hosted by a family displaced before the 'outbreak' of the Arab-Israeli War in 1948.[4] My Arabic is good enough to have a conversation with a five year old, and I asked a little girl where she was from. She said, 'I am from Haifa'. The answer was telling, because it is unlikely that even the girl's parents had ever seen Haifa. But for Palestinians, in contradistinction to Americans, 'where you are from' is not about where you live or have lived. It is about who you are.

The conflict known as the Israeli-Palestinian conflict is not just *between* Israelis and Palestinians. It is *within* them. Much has been made of the so-called 'final status' negotiations and the 'most

---

[4] Western historiography almost uniformly dates the outbreak of what Israel calls 'The War of Independence' to 15 May 1948. A more careful and even examination of the facts shows that by that date, more than 200,000 Palestinians had been removed from their homes and villages, several notorious instances of war crimes had occurred, and Zionist fighters had advanced way beyond the boundaries delineated in the UN Partition Plan of 1947.

difficult' issues of borders, refugees, settlements and the future of Jerusalem. In fact, the most difficult issues have nothing to do with any of these. The most difficult issue is restoring the dignity and honour of injured people. The most difficult issue has to do with healing emotional and psychological wounds which have been left festering for fifty years.

There is a story told of a man who found himself trapped on the second floor of his burning house. In order to escape incineration, the man leaped from the second floor window. In the process, he landed on his neighbour, causing severe injury. The neighbour complained, 'Look what you've done to me!' The man could only reply, 'But look at my home!' Israelis and Palestinians are like the figures in the story. Both people have experienced monumental suffering. Neither finds it easy to acknowledge the suffering of the other. It is difficult for many travellers to the Holy Land to fathom that the experience of suffering has not engendered identity with other peoples' suffering. I often hear students express this sentiment: 'How can the Jews, who suffered so much in Europe in this century, cause so much suffering themselves?' But human suffering is a peculiar phenomenon. As universal as suffering is, it is also a self-centred phenomenon. When we suffer, it feels unique, like there is no suffering to match our own. The experience of suffering prevents those who suffer from identifying on a fundamental level with others who suffer. Inner healing within individuals is a necessary prerequisite for healing between people. Irrespective of what ultimately is resolved regarding settlements, refugees, borders and the future of Jerusalem, even more difficult issues loom. Long after the final status negotiations are ended, the struggle for dignity, honour and healing will continue.

How does the biblical faith help us understand these dimensions of contemporary reality in the Holy Land or any other real life context? This is the question which is raised by contextual biblical study and authentic pilgrimage.

Looking back over the past twelve years, it is evident that my education in biblical studies only vaguely prepared me for my experiences in the Holy Land—the land of the Bible. Notwithstanding a respectable academic pedigree, including studies at Union Theological Seminary (New York City), Harvard Divinity School, and Boston University School of Theology, upon arriving in the Holy Land for the first time I became aware that my academic training had ignored what I now take to be crucial elements of study. My years of work in the Holy Land since my first journey there in 1988 has reinforced this conviction.

Biblical studies today is dominated by an academic elite obsessed with literature. Texts, rather than context is the interest of most biblical scholars. I take it as a rather sad commentary on the state of the art of modern biblical scholarship that I study under the tutelage of scholars who themselves have never been to the eastern Mediterranean. The historical-critical method is still the dominant model for biblical study today. The components of the historical-critical method—redaction criticism, form criticism, source criticism and text criticism—are exclusively oriented toward the analysis of literature. Even the more recent developments in the evolution of the historical-critical method, e.g., literary analysis and rhetorical analysis, display the dominant preoccupation with texts to the exclusion of geographical context. Not even the development of sociological analysis, i.e., the process of assessing the cultural backgrounds of biblical texts, corrects the situation, because literature still makes up the primary source material.

Moreover, the assumptions which dominate the academic establishment about how one learns about the Bible are uncritically accepted, yet by no means self-evident. Biblical scholars presume that insight, wisdom and knowledge are derived by breaking down the texts into their component parts. Texts are dissected, and the subatomic parts are analyzed. But I wonder: would I understand a car by breaking it down into an engine, transmission, chassis, and body, and then by breaking these down into further sub-parts? Just because I know what a spark plug is, what a carburettor is, what a fly-wheel is, what a piston is does not mean I know what a motor is. Biblical scholars make presumptions about knowledge which merit examination and should not be adopted uncritically.

Due to the impulse to atomise the study of the Bible, the field of biblical scholarship is characterized by increasingly extreme specialization. Sadly, as specialization has increased discourse across special interest areas has decreased. The consequence is that advances in one field which should aid another are not communicated.

Perhaps the most telling defect in biblical scholarship is the simple, yet surprising reality that moral questions about the Bible are, by and large, ignored. For example in the fall of 1997, I took a course in Old Testament narratology. The graduate seminar examined passages which featured rape, incest, murder, genocide and, among other things, cannibalism, but not once did the professor or any student ask, 'What do these stories tell us about the value systems which they presume?' Michael Prior's two most recent books, *The Bible and Colonialism. A Moral Critique* (1997a) and *Zionism and the State of Israel. A Moral Inquiry* (1999a), as their sub-titles indicate, thoroughly examine the tragic consequences of the embarrassing failure of Western scholarship to explore the moral impact of land traditions in the Old Testament on modern peoples. The process of Western colonialism with its obviously disastrous effects on indigenous populations around the world was legitimated by appeal to the land traditions of the Old Testament. Western scholarship has failed to prevent the use of the Bible as a blunt instrument against indigenous peoples. This strikes me as an obvious and catastrophic shortcoming in scholarship. How can such scholarship, geared toward an ivory tower academic elite, prepare anyone for the challenging realities of the Holy Land, not to mention the rest of the world, or human life in general?

I have come to learn, through my experience in the Holy Land, that biblical scholarship needs to be reformed. What use are our Bibles if our reading of them is not rooted in some specific setting? Biblical scholarship needs to be made accessible, relevant and useful in contemporary contexts.

Contextual biblical study differs from the academic study of the Bible in several distinct ways. Rather than standing *outside* the Bible and examining its atomic parts as a scientist might examine a specimen under glass, contextual study of the Bible would have us stand in the midst of the Bible itself, and look out at the world, or at least a particular situation in the world, through it. The presumption of modern biblical scholarship that we learn about the Bible by analysing its component parts is faulty. We learn more about the Bible by leaving it whole, and applying its moral imperatives to the challenges implied in particular contexts.

After twelve years of visiting the Holy Land as a pilgrim, living there as a missionary, and working there in my current capacity as a teacher, I have seen, experienced and learned enough to fill several volumes. Yet, I could summarize all I have learned in four simple sentences:

1.   Never judge a country by its postcards.

2.   The worn-out bromide that there are two sides to every argument is simplistic and dead wrong when it comes to the Israeli-Palestinian conflict.

3.   The idea of pilgrimage needs to be redeemed and restored.

4.   The prevailing paradigm for biblical scholarship in the late 20th century requires radical revision.

The idea of pilgrimage needs to be redeemed and restored. Travel to the Holy Land which ignores the realities which challenge Palestinians and Israelis, Christians, Muslims and Jews is not pilgrimage at all. Like biblical scholarship which ignores moral issues, pilgrimage which ignores moral issues is not redemptive.

THE WILL AND THE DREAM
Kenneth Cragg

I

Few alert students of Zion and Zionism could fail to kindle to the fervour of Theodor Herzl's cry in *Der Judenstaat*: 'If we will it, it is not a dream!' Something of my own private retrospect over sixty years of discovery of Israel and Islam might be captured by an interchange of his words: 'As we dream it, what of the will?' What of it?, many would reply. Has Zionism not been proven to the full? Are not its resilience, its opportunism, its verve, its staying power, its solid achievement, not plain for all to see? Has it not supplied all the personnel it needed, right souls in right places, ever since Herzl himself, and even before him Pinsker and Moses Hess, dreaming—from Italian unification via Mazzini's Rome to Ben Gurion's Jerusalem? Was will ever lacking in Chaim Weizmann's astute diplomacy, drawing the Balfour Declaration, against the fears of British Jewry, from a half-reluctant British War Cabinet? Was not Abba Eban the precise mouthpiece when the United Nations pondered partition and his persuasive powers prevailed? The Golda Meirs, the Moshe Dayans, the Menachem Begins have all availed at critical points to 'will the dream' through all the flux of its translation into massive fact, into irreversible reality.

Yet the retrospect, the present prospect, together hold for every thoughtful lover of Jerusalem the sense of a great irony. In what things has the dream entailed the will? Has it vindicated or compromised the Judaism that gave it birth? What did the dream forfeit, of its warrant and its conscience, in the shape its realisation required the will to take? The psalmist in Psalm 122 pictured a Jerusalem 'compact', at peace with itself and inwardly quieted. He invited all its lovers to yearn in their private souls to see and love it indeed as the sum of their own 'prosperity', thanks to 'the thrones of judgement' sited there.

Strange prelude these lines, perhaps seemingly pretentious, in any personal 'Gentile' reflection on experience of the story. One might enlist Robert Browning's Karshish the physician, with his strange 'Epistle' to his superior, replete with medical allusions and reporting:

> 'I reach Jerusalem at morn,
> There set in order my experience
> Gather what most deserves and give thee all.'

Karshish had come from Jericho, and so must have crested the Mount of Olives, and seen, as thousands more, the city spread before him like a tapestry of time and destiny. Of this, his mind preoccupied with herbs and remedies, he tells nothing. Rather he tells his Abib, his fellow connoisseur of pharmacy, that he will 'void the stuffing of (his) travel scrip and share ... whatever Jewry yields.'

His scrip was doubtless a satchel to take care of scraps of notes, a bag suited to a pilgrim, or a receptacle for alms as to a beggar. All these are capacities in which I came to Jerusalem—by taxi from Beirut and Haifa, and in my case over the northern hill close to the edges of Jeremiah's Anathoth where, in 1939 though now no longer, the holy city was still a panorama unconcealed by high rise bastions planted on a flattened hill. The domes of Temple Mount, the church-tower beside the Holy Sepulchre were plain to see attended by the domed roofs of hidden market *suqs* and alleys, soon to be explored—as they only can—on foot.

So began a deepening acquaintance—perhaps not yet ended—reaching into 1996. Its incidence was mostly in the fifties, sixties and seventies, more intermittent otherwise. My being there had to do with things part ecclesiastical and part academic, one hopes a salutary combination. It certainly entailed a long, sometimes soul-vexing, effort to understand, to penetrate, and to communicate. To be sure, I was more directly involved in Christian-Muslim study but 'what Jewry yields' could never be far from central to all else.

II

What, then, did it yield and how have my perceptions changed? When the evolving history was discerned, even tentatively, was it to be supremely admired, uneasily suspected, perhaps a mixture of both? There was always the built-in dilemma attending all assessments of Zionism, namely that antisemitism and, later the *Shoah*, had given it an abiding warrant to resist all query round it, as *ipso facto*, stemming from those evil sources, or conspiring darkly with them. It was necessary to fall back on the conviction that it was the very love for Israel that required the disallowance of perpetual exoneration, if extenuating things ever needed to be noted, in the context of issues prone to harsh controversy. Histories, not least where 'holiness' adheres, become themselves partisan and so need the more urgent vigilance.

Thus the issue for me, over long reflection, has always reverted to 'the dream and the will'. For all its monumental success and finality, might the very success of Zionism in its political shape be seen as also a tragic aberration? 'Can we be blamed for winning?' was often asked after 1967, the more credibly given the folly and ineptitude on 'the other side.' Yet had Jewry and Zionism betaken themselves into a dream and its success in terms which, in any way, might evoke thoughts like those, according to Josephus, of Eleazar and his comrades on Masada about 'conjecturing the purpose of God much sooner?' What might *this* Zionism be doing to Zion?

In those dire moments, their logic about an inviolate land was given a final veto. They had retreated to the last limit of a territorial inviolability and were in an impregnable fortress. But Roman counter-will, and engineering, had cancelled both. In heroic nobility of mind Eleazar pondered how, earlier, they might have enquired what Yahweh intended for them and, perhaps, perceived the different wisdom of Yavneh-style survival through surrender rather than the impatient gesture of their corporate suicide.

There is nothing comparable in that tragic heroism and the supremely achieving prowess of Zionism, from Herzl to Barak, via all the heroes of its crowded narrative, except that haunting caveat about 'the purpose of God'. For, exploring how it might be read can be the surest condition of right decision by those 'thrones of judgement' in things where they now are. The reasons run far back and deserve some patient review—a review which must ponder the entire irony in Zion.

That irony might be told as a dream about, and a will to, a vacancy that was not there. It had a logic of separatism for which no morally feasible separateness availed. Being inherently confrontational, it could not innocently succeed. Yet the logic that made it necessarily invasive in its chosen geography was imperatively reached by the experience through which Jewry had passed over long centuries and, more immediately, in the 19th when it had ventured into trust in the Enlightenment and visualised a viable diaspora as even its ultimate vocation.

Thus the form which political Zionism believed it must take, i.e., land for statehood, and statehood for power, was precisely the form that ensured—and indeed argued—its local unwantedness and the rejectionism that opposed its strategy. All was a tragic irony in which what could not be other than it was in concept could not be otherwise than it became in event, namely mutual strife and enmity and impasse.

How well I remember during that first journey from Ras al-Naqura the sad futility of those Teggart fortresses of the Palestine Police, concrete bunker-like structures telling so clearly the odds they faced from conflicting partisans and frequent ambushings. The hapless Mandatory was caught in more than a 'policing' situation thanks to the guilty ambiguity of its Balfour Declaration to which the League of Nations had tied it. Symbolising so much costly frustration, those buildings were eloquent of intractable realities.

It is well to realise how, from its side, political Zionism made it so, given the inevitable counter-action from what that Declaration had oddly dubbed 'the existing non-Jewish population.' The case that Herzl and others had made insisted that 'host nation' status for Jewry in a world that others governed was hopelessly inimical to a true Jewishness. That world was incorrigibly hostile, irreversibly so, and could no longer be trusted to concede an authentic Jewishness in its midst. Jews themselves must solve the 'problem' by extricating themselves. A 'Gentile' jury was all the while inhibiting Jewish self-expression in the Sabbath, in dietary laws, in Yiddish culture. There was always the menace of assimilation, or otherwise of persecution. Neither was longer to be undergone. It was a virtual vote of no confidence in 'common humanity' and tragically, decades later, Hitler justified it to the hilt, at least in Germany and the Nazi fields of conquest.

It follows that political Zionism was not seeking 'host nation' tolerance in an Arab context, instead of a European. It was proposing an end of 'host nation' existence for good and all. Thus *ab initio*—in logic if not explicitly as yet—statehood was always 'in the frame.' The fact that it was not expressly so, made for an ambivalence that only served towards frustration, though it was politic and opportunist.

Thus there was little suspicion in the early twenties, even a moment of affability between Faisal and Weizmann, while the Wafd in Egypt only had queries about where the boundary of the Mandate would be, with Sinai excluded. It was also congenially represented at the inauguration of the Hebrew University in Jerusalem.

Given the traditional hospitality of the Arab soul, it is conceivable that a simple agricultural Zionism, some Hibbet Zion of soil-lovers, would have been entirely welcome. Some such were long commemorated by the Montefiore windmill across from the Jaffa Gate. But by Herzl's criteria such a toothless and vulnerable presence in Palestine would be no answer to the plight of Jewry as history confirmed it to him. Likewise, those starry-eyed 'bi-federalists' like Judah Magnes and Norman Bentwich, who stood for some form of political co-existence. It might be good to have their idealism in the public view, for ambivalence had its role to play, but though sincerely proposed their welcome notions lacked all political and secular realism.

They also ran counter to the orthodox sense, perpetuated later in the two equilateral triangles of the Israeli flag, of the inter-necessity of land and people, both under Yahweh. The land had a destiny which its one people shared. Only there—the Talmud taught—

245

could the Torah be obeyed. Only there could the prophets be heard. The land had a sanctity that, beyond, all need for Jewish *Lebensraum* required to be duly inhabited, just as Jewry found itself authentic only in the destined territory.

It was this strange unison of a secular politics and an orthodox Judaica which—at long range—decisively precluded any possibility of a unitary state in Palestine. To have thought it feasible would have betrayed both the mind Ben Gurion so robustly exemplified *and* the temper of Gush Emunim and Baruch Goldstein. Yet, integral to these strands of Zionism as the politicisation was, it is odd now to remember how uncongenial it was in Herzl's day to the Jewish world at large. Political Zionism was so far a minority voice. Hence the necessary challenge and fervour of the 'dream' language. Hence the puzzled, if not pained, surprise that *Der Judenstaat* aroused. It denied the vocation of diaspora as validly a Jewish thing. So doing, it further undermined the will of masses of Jews across Europe to prove themselves worthy citizens of their several states. It implied a dubiety about their honest allegiance in proposing a destiny elsewhere. It could even fuel antisemitism as, indeed, in some measure, did the Zionists themselves when they sought to galvanise an incredulous audience into action by invoking the usual antisemitic picture of craven, ghettoised, hapless Jews, immured in counting-houses, victims of their own frailty. That Zionism constituted such a radical interrogation of the soul of Jewry itself is exactly a measure of how radical its thesis was.

Yet, as is well known from the first aberration of the Basle Congress of 1897 about any location chance and choice might afford, only in Palestine could fulfilment consistently be had. And Palestine was not untenanted. Moreover, the Mandate, which might facilitate (must facilitate—said the Jewish Agency) the creation of 'the dream' of statehood, was also in fee to the 'rights' of 'the existing population'. Palestinianism, though it would only become aggressively articulate reciprocally to Zionism, had already been steeled in the fire of revolt against a long 'Ottomanism', and saw itself destined for autonomy, the postponement of which only made the goal of it the more ardent.

It became no small part of the inclusive irony that Palestinianism could and did recruit precisely the logic, in its own idiom, that Zionism pleaded. Only in our land can we be who we are. Land without statehood, being defenceless, is ever in potential forfeit. The case was there in the Jerusalem Talmud (Kilayyim 7.5): 'Though soil cannot be stolen, a man can forfeit his right to this soil by giving up hope of ever regaining it.' So political Zionism had argued. The land had never been spiritually vacated. 'Next year in Jerusalem' had been said—and meant—at every Passover. Zionism was now, at long last, giving it occasion.

Likewise, the rubric of those who held themselves to be in legitimate and historic possession, since original Canaan, with 'Zion' itself a Jebusite name, they too, registering what would stay 'stolen' if allowed to happen, 'would not forfeit their right ... by giving up hope of for ever regaining it.' And when by their own ineptitude, the sorry deeds of their neighbours and the weight of international disfavour, they experienced its forfeiture, should they not *a fortiori* refuse to abandon hope, but rather invoke the very Zionist resolve that said: 'We are only defeated when we think we are.' Such was, such remains, the alternative 'dream'.

III

As a raw recruit in 1939, I could not have known all this or ever found words in which to give it shape. But in all the retrospect, it is articulate enough now, and plain for all to see. It argues powerfully the onus for compatibility in the territory, on the ground, in political form and with spiritual warrant and human seal—a seal some at least would want to be divine too. 'How can these things be?' Surely Jewry, alike in Israel and diaspora, discovers that acceptance can only come by being mutual. Political Zionism did something to Judaism by making Judaism an intensifying problem to itself.

The quest for statehood interrogated what the religion is: the pursuit of it has accentuated the puzzle. Given the long sustained burden from the wrongs and tribulations inflicted by antisemitism, no one should question the right of Jewry *not* to be condemned to statelessness for ever—the right, positively, to land and nation and the power these presuppose. Yet not all Jews—as Ben Gurion demanded—can go to populate the State of Israel. Diaspora remains indispensable to the very viability of the land that rebukes it. Indeed, it is only from diaspora—and 'Gentile' sinews—that Israel endures. That paradox need cause no disquiet.

Beyond it, the fact remains that the State of Israel has provoked a sustained political unwantedness and thus on its own premise of people-*qua*-politics a human unwantedness. It did so by the very terms in which it came. Yet those were the only terms which it came to think the world, and history, allowed. Zionism was a search for acceptance frustrated of its hope by its own very means. So far has the dream failed. The task now is for a revision of the will that dreamed it. It can found itself on what has been decisively achieved. The compromises of that achievement can be retrieved by a magnanimity now conceding their guilt and their reproach and then overtaking these in the will to the mutualities of peace.

When Menahem Begin reportedly said: 'If this *is* Palestine, then we *are* invaders.' But it is not, so we are not. Thus for many in Israel the logic has been 'A land was without a people waiting for a people without a land.' Neither part of the proposition was true but the will to the myth of innocence persisted in long credible, but illusory self-perception. There were those who truly believed that all could be serene and harmonious *if only* Palestinians had accepted—as they well might, had a stateless agriculture been in mind. But, on any Zionist principles, how could they have said: 'By all means, *ahlan wa sahlan* ... —'welcome, gentles all,' as Shakespeare might have phrased it?

Inevitably invasive it had all to be. Sincere as the myth of innocence was, there were those who knew from the outset that sinister things would be involved. The Crane-King Commission of 1919 reported at the outset, from their soundings

Zionists look forward to a practically complete
dispossession of the present non-Jewish population(in
Kirk 1948: 152).

Vladimir Jabotinsky was quite forthright:

'It is impossible to dream of a voluntary agreement
between us and the Arabs of Eretz Israel ... Every nation
(sic) civilised or primitive, sees its land as a national
home, where it wants to stay as the sole landlord for
ever ... Every nation fights the settlers ... as long as
there is a glimmer of hope in their hearts that they can
prevent the changing of Palestine into Israel (trans. from
On the Iron Wall in Silver 1984: 12).

Thus, inevitably in the vicissitudes of human passion and
calculation through which the sequences transpired, violent it had
to be, whether in the controlled prowess of Haganah and Israeli
Defence Forces (as, not 'Army', they were always styled), or in the
more 'terrorist' guise of the Irgun or the Stern Gang.

In sum, the long and strong Zionist vision of its separatist
acceptance in ancestral land failed of what it coveted and was rewarded
only with another version of hostility—a version which the forceful
shape of Zionism had done most to legitimate. Yet, sadly, it could be
read though falsely—as yet another brand of antisemitism. Had political
Zionism, then, mistaken what Judaism truly was? Ought it to have
'conjectured the purpose of God' differently—and much sooner?
Could it still morally legitimate the future of its 'dream' by some
discernible revision of its will?

It was bewildering to pass one's years as an outsider, a
'Gentile', in the unremitting episodes of this unfolding 'Greek tragedy'
of Israeli/Palestinian politics. There was so much partisanship into
which one might unwittingly, or passionately, be drawn, like many in
the same milieu. How was one to find an honesty to measure the
thwarting, by its own politics, of Jewish vision, or to undertake the

trauma in the Palestinian soul—too often among Jews a thing suppressed—as the suffering by which Israel existed, the price its success had exacted in the gaining of its prize?

There was that outpouring of Palestinian pathos in its contemporary poesy. I had two of its poets in our hostel, named after Justin, a Palestinian Christian martyr of the 2nd century, namely Tawfiq Sayigh and Kamal Nasir, both of whom died tragically early, the latter the victim of Israeli gunmen (later decorated for valour) coming cunningly ashore on Deadman's Beach, Beirut, to assassinate men who held themselves, like their attackers did, 'fighters for the right'. Tawfiq Sayigh translated T S Eliot (a figure much revered among his Arab generation) and *The Wasteland*, finding its register of human futility so apt a portrayal of the 'thievish stealth of time'. Was this the search of Jewry to be legitimately at home in the world, to belong inter-humanly where Jewry most ardently willed to be?

The outsider anyway, feel as he might, was somehow excluded from the equation, a non-participant—if he would not become a partisan. And all this, this direness, this morass of bitterness, was in the name of 'the holy land', and had to do with 'the peace of Jerusalem', where—the psalmist thought—were 'the thrones of Judgement' (Psalm 122.5) What right, anyway, much Jewish thinking had it, did the Christian Church, or the Christian soul, have to think what Israel should do or be? 'Christian Zionists', for their part, demanded an Israel exonerated from all assessment save unlimited approval. After the Holocaust, antisemitism would be the only motive in anything less. Israel had entire will to be what she would and the option need not include the sense of being suffered for by others. That possibility had to be remote from minds so long accustomed to the world's ill-usage. Perhaps one should relapse into an easy cynicism and cry with one of William Faulkner's 'fallen' characters, himself a failed cleric: 'Poor humans, poor humanity!'

IV

Rescue, it came to seem to me—rescue for partisans and participants alike—could be found in the great tradition of Hebrew prophethood. What the excessive pietism of Jerusalem, whether Judaic, Christian or Muslim, needed was all there in the courageous 'Temple Sermon' of Jeremiah (7.1-16). It needed his cleansing brand of moral realism. And how apposite also was an earlier prophet about creeping settlements in a deliberate policy that might preclude their later reversal, and so obviate any threat to the *fait accompli*, while negotiations stayed wilfully protracted.

> Woe to them who join house to house and field to field,
> till there be no room, that they may be left alone in the
> midst of the earth (Isaiah 5.8),

with connecting roads linking their privacies in a separate commonweal, jeopardising the economic viability of what they by-passed and scarring the landscape with the resulting screes. In such situation, blame is never unilateral, save where power and initiatives are.

But that ethicism of the great prophets of former Israel clearly argues a will to inter-human community. The search for acceptance via statehood that Zionism made and, thus far necessarily failed to find on its chosen ground, has now to turn itself to that pre-eminently local task. Its international status is accomplished, but not its vital, intimately territorial, task. Palestine, not America, was always its most urgent realm of duty, its surest soul-quarry.

The time seems ripe. Palestinianism in its virtual lack of power in leverage seems ready, in a readiness which may even seem to Israelis as ripe for disregard. That verdict would be a moral suicide. If only the comparable perceptions of Palestinians with their Palestine, however truncated—namely the 'who' of us, in the 'where' of us, at the 'whence' of us, as the 'how' of us (the only legitimate 'how')— are recognised as what Zionists must allow, then its realisation is the immediate agenda and imperative.

251

It is, of course, precisely here that Jerusalem becomes the pleaded symbol of an obduracy that will not think this way. The 'internationalisation' of the Holy City, which was part of the original UN Resolution by which, juridically, Israel exists, has long receded from debate. Jerusalem is seen as 'the eternal and unshared capital of the Jewish people', the only authentic keystone of Eretz Yisrael. That it should be monopolised thus brings deep sorrow of heart to its lovers round the world.

And there is irony as well as sadness. For physical Jerusalem contains two surely inalienable shrines for ever commanding loyalties Israeli sovereignty can never detach from them. To be sure, Christians must say, we do not need to govern in order to revere and cherish. That was the error of the Crusades. Since 'the road to Jerusalem is in the heart' the need to go there, for any Christian diaspora, is both kindled and transcended. But given the indigenous Christian presence, however attenuated by measures of exclusion, the Church of the Resurrection and the Garden of Gethsemane have an Arab allegiance that deserves political expression.

The same is truer still concerning Temple Mount, the first *qiblah* of Islam and the third *qutb*, or axis, of Islamic piety. The brief tenure of the Crusaders apart, those shrines—like the land at large—have been in Muslim régimes from 640 to 1918. What length may not now warrant, sanity and magnanimity might now acknowledge in the vexed determining of the City's possession. The cry may seek to bind Jerusalem *de jure* into a resolute exclusivism: it can never do so *de facto*. There is more invested in Jerusalem than can ever be monopolised as one spiritual property. What has been diplomatically seen as the last hurdle of negotiation becomes the primary test of wisdom and integrity, and these the very crux of the dream.

It has been, no doubt, pretentious to respond to request for thoughts in long retrospect as the present book has done. How has your faith related to what it underwent? Or the question Haggai once asked his hearers: 'How do you see it now? (2.3) Can it ever matter how I see it? —only if I can be among those the Psalmist called 'companions'. They were somehow distinguished from 'brethren' (an ethnic term). Can mere 'companions' care if they can contrive to be such and be acknowledged so?

In Psalm 35.27, there is a kind of *Magnificat* saluting what it calls 'the prosperity *(shalom)* of His servant.' What is this 'prosperity'? In what may it consist? How—with that 'prosperity' theme recurring in Psalm 122—is it to have Jerusalem for home and symbol, those 'who pray for it' included? Only by the inter-humanness that Jerusalem enshrines.

Thought has come round full circle to 'the will and the dream'. It was reported that, as Theodor Herzl lay dying in 1904— so prematurely in the reckoning of time and task—he said enigmatically to those who stood around: 'Make no mistake when I am gone.' There can only be conjecture about what he had in mind—no alternative location, no misreading of the text, no shrinking from the task and perhaps, as clue to all, no final arrogance.

For the arrogance of exclusivism, with Jerusalem above all else its sign and walls, would be the supreme *superbia* of a political Zionism betraying Zion itself. For then, the reality of the long achievement, a 20th-century epic, would have failed to turn these, at long last, into a comprehending peace. Jerusalem, like all shrines and legendary cities, can only iconise what its custodians hold it to be. 'An inalienable, eternal, exclusified, Israeli Jerusalem' would betray the fullness of Jerusalem. How Herzl the pioneer might have read the present scene who shall say? 'The Name we might take in vain' is the Lord's alone.

JEWS, CHRISTIANS, AND MUSLIMS
IN THE HOLY LAND
David B Burrell, C.S.C.

M y first acquaintance with the land came in a privileged way in 1975, in a gathering of mostly younger people—Jews, Christians, Muslims—arranged by Sister Marie Goldstein, RSHM, whose family origins had predisposed her to work towards Jewish-Christian understanding, yet whose instinct moved her to embrace Muslims in the local dialogue in Jerusalem. We convened for six weeks at the Ecumenical Institute of Tantur, standing between Jerusalem and Bethlehem, where we learned from one another and from others about our respective religious faiths, and made small steps towards praying with one another. I was engaged at the same time with my colleagues at Notre Dame—notably Joseph Blenkinsopp, Stanley Hauerwas, Robert Wilken, and John Howard Yoder—in revamping our graduate theology programme to accommodate a Judaica position which had been given to us. We wanted the incumbent to be an integral part of our theology faculty, and so configured our traditional sectors of Old Testament, New Testament, and Patristics, into a module entitled 'Judaism and Christianity in Antiquity'. As chair of the department during the seventies, I came to appreciate the theological potential of Judaism as a stimulus to doing Christian theology—a strategy confirmed at the end of the seventies by Karl Rahner's celebrated 'world-church' lecture which focused on the symbolic dates of 70 and 1970 as bracketing nineteen centuries of 'western European Christianity' (*Theological Studies* 1979). It was my growing acquaintance with the 'parting of the ways' (in 70 AD) which set me up to understand the import of 1970, as Rahner saw it, for setting Christianity *vis-à-vis* other religions of the world in a way quite beyond colonial power, with the promise of dialogue and mutual illumination.

Moreover, the fact that the summer among persons of the three Abrahamic faiths was followed by an initial teaching stint in Bangladesh—a 92 percent Muslim country—doubtless contributed to my decision to begin a study of Islam when I ceased to serve as department chair in 1980. That decision represented my response to Rahner's thesis, and was facilitated by a year's service as Rector of Tantur, followed by a second year in Jerusalem in the Isaias House community of Marcel Dubois, O.P. Our daily prayers in Hebrew prepared me to pursue Arabic studies at Hebrew University, as well as teach a seminar comparing Moses Maimonides with Thomas Aquinas. The initial year of Arabic study was followed by others, of course, as my pursuit of Islamic philosophical theology took me to Cairo in subsequent summers to live with the French Dominican community and work with Georges Anawati, O.P. The fruit of those summers appeared in my first comparative study of Maimonides, Aquinas, and Avicenna: *Knowing the Unknowable God* (1986). It was the two years in Jerusalem, however, from 1980 to 1982, which effected my bonding with the land—a process begun in the 1975 seminar and continued ever since. The most immediate testimony to that is the book jointly edited with Yehezkel Landau, who was among our participants in that initial summer and has remained a close friend since: *Voices from Jerusalem* (1990).

Being just fifteen years old in 1948, I had had little awareness of the situation in Palestine as it had been between the wars, and no conscious awareness of Zionism. We were all soon weaned, however, on the exploits of Jews seeking a homecoming after the horrors of the camps, fed by Leon Uris' *Exodus* and Lapierre and Collins' *O Jerusalem*. The next moment of awareness came in a symposium at Notre Dame in the late sixties, where I had just begun teaching philosophy and was deeply involved with students facing being drafted to fight the war in Vietnam. In an environment championed by the slogan 'God, County, Notre Dame', we had had to work hard simply to activate the classical 'just war' teaching as a way of discerning our involvement in that conflict as Americans. (I have subsequently become aware that what young people today regard as the 'craziness' of the sixties was required to break the codicil which had regularly kept any just war teaching inoperative: 'the presumption lies with authority.' For that presumption is one we all need, so dislodging it would demand aggressiveness quite out of proportion to the issues at hand.)

The symposium in question represented an early response to the Vatican document *Nostra Aetate*, which sought to correct the standing view among Christians that the New Testament had replaced the Old. In the wake of the 1967 war, a rabbi present hailed the Israeli victory as a sign of God's hand reaching out to favour his people—after the divine silence surrounding Auschwitz. I shall never forget the *frisson* of terror which invaded me at that moment: fresh from dissuading Americans that God must be 'on our side' in Vietnam, here was a rabbi invoking the 'Old Testament' version which had massacred the Amalekites—men, women, children, and all the animals! That could certainly not be the God I worshipped; and even though I could not repudiate the Hebrew Scriptures, I had to resist so literal an application of them. That remark and the attitude it represented— that the State of Israel was sanctioned by divine right—came into direct conflict with the way in which the war in Vietnam was relativising the state, precisely to activate a classical Christian teaching regarding war and the legitimacy of participating in it. Here was another example of a xenophobic attitude claiming divine sanction, and doing so directly from the scriptures themselves.

It was at this point that my direct encounter with Israel/ Palestine began, as I have described our 1975 summer exchanges at Tantur in Jerusalem. I was privileged to be in conversation with Muslims as well as with Jews, all intent on finding a way in which they could live together. So I was quite insulated from a chauvinistic Israeli attitude or from vitriolic Arab rhetoric. Indeed, as history shows, the Palestinian movement was yet to gain momentum, in the wake of the disaster (*Nakba*) of '67. Israeli occupation was deemed 'benign', and the young Palestinians with whom we were speaking were trying to find ways to live with it. The *Intifada*, after all, was not to begin until 1987, twenty years after the '67 war. My return in

1980 would be in the second half of that period of occupation, during the first hegemony of the Likud party under Menachem Begin, yet after the 1973 war and closely following Anwar Sadat's historic visit to Jerusalem in 1979. So there were contrary winds criss-crossing Israel and Palestine, with few markers to get one's bearings. My first year was spent at Tantur, in constant contact with Palestinians, Christian and Muslim, and my second in West Jerusalem in the midst of Jews and of Christians dedicated to healing centuries of 'teaching of contempt'. While respecting that mission, I was nonetheless chagrined that the attitudes of these intelligent educated westerners towards the people with whom I had lived the year previous proved so stereotyped and unsympathetic. I had, after all, only moved a few miles but found myself in another world! That is Jerusalem, I would quickly learn.

What had I learned at Tantur, largely from the people working there, which I found so unappreciated a few miles away? I had met people of grace and dignity, some educated, many barely so, but all literate and intelligent. I had come to taste the hospitality of their homes, and see how a good education was seldom rewarded with commensurate employment, since Israel dominated that market, yet those who were objectively 'underemployed' soldiered on, conscious of their responsibility to rear and educate a family. Education was universally valued, despite its meagre rewards, and conversation was invariably rich and welcoming. Moreover, these attitudes perdured in the face of frequent, if not daily hassles and intimidation at checkpoints, or randomly along the street, by young Israelis serving their military service between high school and university, as an occupying force. Occupation is always a messy business, of course, but the image of its being 'benign' was wearing quite thin in the face of one report after another of their lands being expropriated and their dignity assaulted. Yet on the other side of the line, in West Jerusalem, my Jewish and Christian friends could only regard these stories as propaganda. What I soon realised, of course, is that they had to so regard them, or their carefully constructed image would crumble, and they would be faced with the same kind of self-assessment that we had undergone as Americans in the face of Vietnam. Indeed, could one even expect that of a nation so young and still beleaguered as Israel?

It was at this point, in the midst of beginning a study of Arabic and teaching a seminar in Maimonides and Aquinas at Hebrew University, that I began a careful re-assessment of Israel's claim to 'the land'. For despite my profound objection to the rabbi's invocation of the Hebrew Scriptures in assessing the 1967 victory of Israeli forces, I had also signed on to *Nostra Aetate*'s citation of Paul, insisting that 'God does not take back his gifts or renounce his promises.' What if God did indeed promise the land to his chosen people? I could not expect Palestinians or international jurists to accept that argument, but I might have to. Despite the fact that a group of 'crazies' (fuelled by a 'dispensational theology' spawned in Dallas) had appropriated the term, could I not accept the denomination of 'Christian Zionist'? Indeed, did not my faith require that I do so? Closer scrutiny of those scriptural promises, however, convinced me that they were never unconditional; in fact, they were expressly conditional on Israel's observing the Torah, including respect for the strangers in their midst. So I was clearly absolved from having to accept the Zionist return as fulfilling a divine promise, given the way in which current Israelis were carrying out their occupation of that part of the land gained in an aggressive war.

The one who really helped me in that regard, however, was an imposing man who was closely associated with our community at Isaias House: Yeshayahu Leibowitz. Physicist and philosopher, general editor of the *Israeli Encyclopaedia*, Professor Leibowitz had been an uncompromising opponent of the views of Judah Magnes and Martin Buber, who were party to the intense Zionist discussions held between the wars. They had sought ways to accommodate Arabs in a democratic state, whereas Leibowitz's argument was that Jews needed a state to develop their considerable cultural capital, and that state needed to be Jewish in order to realise its specificity and to survive. (In retrospect, one can see how firmly this intellectual had his pulse on pervasive Jewish attitudes in the *diaspora*; certainly nothing short of a 'Jewish state' would have galvanised the support that was in fact forthcoming.) To liberal democrats like myself, such attitudes were hardly palatable, though one could appreciate them, especially when defended by a person of such stature. What really commended him to me, however, was his transformation in the wake of 1967 from intellectual to prophet. In the euphoria following the 'six-day war', he insisted publicly and forthrightly: 'give it back!' Like prophets of old, his voice was taken to be traitorous, but his argument crystal clear: having campaigned consistently for a Jewish state, he insisted on a normative sense of 'Jewish' which could not allow Israel to continue to be *Jewish* while ruling over a people who resent and resist its rule. (One can find a similar argument, somewhat recast, in Arthur Hertzberg's recent *The Jews* (1999).

Unpalatable as it was in the event, one could say that his argument has in time prevailed. In the spirit of Socrates, Leibowitz was reminding his people that injustice does more harm to the perpetrator than it does to the victim. Hardly a popular position for the dominating power to hear, it inevitably takes time to be verified, but verified it will be. If one thinks of slave-owners in the American south, or tyrannical powers anywhere, the truth of Socrates' dictum will win out, it seems, and especially so among Jews who have themselves known persecution and whose scriptures teach an uncompromising ethos of justice. So despite the pseudo-religious voices invoking divine right or sanctioning ethnic cleansing of Palestinians, more and more Israelis are today speaking of 'Israel/ Palestine', and hoping for the day when they can drive to Damascus and buy a rug! And some are even working for that day by mounting programmes promoting mutual respect among young Palestinians and Israelis, or working together to rebuild homes destroyed by state enforcement of unjust statutes.

There is a long way to go, of course, especially in inculcating in Israelis respect for a law higher than that of the state. Legal positivism runs rampant in theory and in practice; 'conscientious objection' has yet to gain legal recognition. And cheap Palestinian labour hardly breeds respect; an American is constantly reminded of the situation of blacks before civil rights statutes. But Palestinians were not imported into an alien land as slaves; they wear their dignity on their face, however financially trammelled they may be for the present. That they have retained that dignity in the face of continuing humiliation, and subject to an apparently unyielding Israeli arrogance, bodes well for a future in which Israelis individually and *en bloc* can come to appreciate how much they have to learn from their ancient neighbours. Ironies abound in human history, of course, but nowhere more than in the Middle East, and especially in the 'holy land'. Three dismal years of Likud hegemony, under a prime minister whose moves were so transparently Machiavellian that they made Machiavelli look noble, had the overall effect of diverting much previously uncritical support for Israel, and opening up pathways for peace hitherto unimaginable in America. Moreover, the behaviour of political leaders on both sides has shifted public opinion towards supporting those groups operating in civil society whose political impact can be anticipated to outrun that of the elected officials.

What is required now, of course, is continued vigilance. Groups are operating, and continue to operate, who try to cajole Israeli public opinion into supporting their 'Jewish' agenda, while the proverbial silent majority stands by, not to be distracted from looking after its own interests. Valiant individuals and movements will have to continue to mobilise 'people of good will' from all sectors of both societies, lest inertia simply hand the victory to moneyed interests. Legal initiatives, like the Society of Saint Yves, in Bethlehem, as well as a plethora of NGOs, like Catholic Relief Services, will continue to be indispensable, alerting the wider world to the systematic ways in which the laws and services of the current form of 'Jewish state' function in a decidedly undemocratic fashion, overtly prejudicial against those who are not themselves Jewish. The real test will be Jerusalem: can the dominant society, the State of Israel, make the arrangements necessary to accommodate those sectors of the extended city which are and have been Arab, in such a way that the entire city can serve as capital of two countries? The evidence is that Jerusalem itself has enough consistency, in its multicultural history, to serve in that capacity. But is the political will available to allow it to do so?

Interminable political analyses will attempt to take the pulse of this volatile region, while its inhabitants will continue to seek what people do everywhere: enough tranquillity to raise and educate a family. Two contrary sets of ingrained attitudes are constantly rubbing each other raw: a Jewish sensitivity to criticism, fruit of centuries of antisemitism, especially in the Christian West, as well as Arab (and especially Palestinian) resentment at the way in which Jews have been able to monopolise the status of victim, turning it into one of victor, while at the same time reinforcing the Arab-Muslim stereotype of *terrorist*. A pervasive inheritance of fear on the one side and of resentment on the other certainly blocks straightforward communication. Yet the affinities between the peoples keep emerging in prolonged negotiation sessions, and the growing desire of recent generations of Israelis to live within the region makes it imperative to search for ways to make peace. History remains present in the region, however, and in the hearts of Jewish people everywhere, so trust will be a long time in coming. Yet efforts to build it, beginning with young people, and exploiting the resources of the standing religious communities for reconciliation, heads the agenda of a new millennium.

Many Jews, Christians, and Muslims are coming to realise that people of faith share a constructive agenda in an age and climate in which 'the market' tends to dictate all facets of human life so as to nullify humane values. There is a 'globalisation from below' in which communities of faith have been learning to make common cause with those of other faiths, with friendships developing which point to new forms of 'sharing in difference'. And there is increasing evidence that such patterns of sharing will become increasingly attractive to people as they sense the inhumanity of 'market' domination. It is my conviction that Islam may well point the way towards a sense of family and of community in constructive opposition to those corrosive elements of 'the market' which liberal society seems so powerless to resist. All this will be taking place on a scale much larger than the pressure-cooker of the 'holy land', but progressive initiatives in one region of the globe quickly redound to others in this age of instant communication. So the world-wide diaspora of Islam may well supply Muslims in the 'holy land' with lessons not unlike those which Judaism learned during the many centuries of absence from their land. A new era of living together with 'others' whom we have come to realise we need, in order to be ourselves, is clearly what the new millennium calls for. Whether we can overcome our ingrained habits of exclusive nationalism, however, remains the decisive question. Religious persons have no better imperative than this, however, to direct constructively the widespread disillusion with the emptiness of secular politics and society. The challenge of the Balkans is precisely that: to see to it that nationalist politicians can no longer play the 'religious card'. And that challenge can only be met by an interfaith response. While the 'holy land' is indeed a crucible, that may also be the laboratory needed to test the resources of religious faiths to be faithful to their essential teachings of peace and reconciliation.

BIBLIOGRAPHY

Only those works referred to in the text are included here

Al Haq, 1988. *Punishing a Nation: Human Rights Violations during the Palestinian Uprising December 1988-December 1989*. Ramallah: Al Haq

Angelou, Maya. 1994. *On the Pulse of Morning, Contained in the Complete Collection of Poems*. London: Virago

Ateek, Naim Stifan. 1989. *Justice and Only Justice. A Palestinian Theology of Liberation*. Maryknoll, NY: Orbis

Ateek, Naim, Cedar Duaybis and Marla Schrader (eds). 1997. *Jerusalem, What Makes for Peace? A Palestinian Christian Contribution to Peacemaking*. London: Melisende

Ateek, Naim and Michael Prior (eds). 1999. *Holy Land—Hollow Jubilee: God, Justice and the Palestinians*. London: Melisende

Barlow, Elizabeth. 1994 (third edition). *Evaluation of Secondary-Level Textbooks for Coverage of the Middle East and North Africa*. Ann Arbor, MI: Center for Middle Eastern and North African Studies

Barraclough, Ray. 1992. *Reflections from the Holy Land—Place of Conflict, Place of Hope*. Sydney: Australian Board of Missions

Barraclough, Ray. 1999. *Equal and More—Equality and Authority amongst Christian Disciples with John's Gospel as the Resource Text*. Brisbane: Ray Barraclough

Baum, Gregory. 1975. *Religion and Alienation—A Theological Reading of Sociology*. New York: Paulist

Beit-Hallahmi, Benjamin. 1992. *Original Sins*. London: Pluto Press

Brueggemann, Walter. 1977. *The Land. Place as Gift, Promise, and Challenge in Biblical Faith*. Philadelphia: Fortress

Burge, Gary. 1993. *Who are God's People in the Middle East?* Grand Rapids: Zondervan

Burrell, David B. 1986. *Knowing the Unknowable God: Ibn -Sina, Maimonides, Aquinas*. Notre Dame, IN: University of Notre Dame Press

Burrell, David B. 1993. *Freedom and Creation in Three Traditions*. Notre Dame, IN: University of Notre Dame Press

Burrell, David B. 1993. *Al-Ghazali on the Ninety-Nine Beautiful Names of God*. Cambridge: Islamic Texts Society

Burrell, David B. 2000. *Al-Ghazali on Faith in Divine Unity and Trust in Divine Providence* (= Book 35 of Al-Ghazali's *Ihya Ulum ad-Din*). Louisville: Fons Vitae

Burrell, David B. and Elena Malits. 1998. *Original Peace*. New York: Paulist

Chacour, Elias. 1985. *Blood Brothers. A Palestinian's Struggle for Reconciliation in the Middle East*. Eastbourne: Kingsway Publications

Chacour, Elias. 1990. *We Belong to the Land*. New York: Harper Collins

Chapman, Colin. 1983. *Whose Promised Land?* Oxford: Lion

Churches Together in Britain and Ireland. 1999. *Planning a Pilgrimage to the Holy Land?* London: CTBI/Christian Aid

Cragg, Kenneth. 1982. *This Year in Jerusalem*. London: Darton, Longman and Todd

Cragg, Kenneth. 1992. *The Arab Christian. A History of the Middle East*. London: Mowbray

Cragg, Kenneth. 1997. *Palestine. The Prize and Price of Zion*. London and Washington: Cassell

Davies, W D. 1974. *The Gospel and the Land. Early Christianity and Jewish Territorial Doctrine*. Berkeley: University of California Press

Davies, W D. 1982. *The Territorial Dimensions of Judaism*. Berkeley: University of California Press

Davies, W D. 1991. *The Territorial Dimensions of Judaism. With a Symposium and Further Reflections*. Minneapolis: Fortress

Davis, Uri. 1987. *Israel An Apartheid State*. London: Zed

Deist, F E. 1994. 'The Dangers of Deuteronomy: A Page from the Reception History of the Book', in Martínez, F. García, A. Hilhorst, J T A G M van Ruiten, and A S van der Woud (eds), *Studies in Deuteronomy. In Honour of C J Labuschagne on the Occasion of his 65th Birthday*. Leiden/New York/Köln: Brill, 13-29

Ellis, Marc H. 1987. *Toward a Jewish Theology of Liberation*. Maryknoll, NY: Orbis

Ellis, Marc H. 1999. *O, Jerusalem! The Contested Future of the Jewish Covenant*. Minneapolis: Fortress Press

Elon, Amos. 1991. *Jerusalem—City of Mirrors*. Glasgow: Fontana

Findley, Paul. 1985. *They Dare to Speak Out: People and Institutions Confront Israel's Lobby*. Chicago: Lawrence Hill Books

Fromkin, David. 1989. *The Peace To End All Peace—Creating the Modern Middle East 1914-1922*. London: Penguin

Gordon, Graham. 1999. 'Tearfund Principles for Christian Development Applied to Tourism', Discussion Paper. October 1999

Hewitt, Garth. 1986. *Nero's Watching Video*. London: Hodder

Hewitt, Garth. 1996. *Pilgrims and Peacemaker. A Journey through Lent towards Jerusalem*. Oxford: The Bible Reading Fellowship

Hewitt, Garth. 1999. *A Candle of Hope. A Journey through Advent, Christmas and the New Year to Bethlehem*. Oxford: The Bible Reading Fellowship

Hummel, Thomas, Kevork Hintlian, and Ulf Carmesund (eds). 1999. *Patterns of the Past, Prospects for the Future. The Christian Heritage in the Holy Land*. London: Melisende

Hummel, Ruth and Thomas Hummel. 1995. *Patterns of the Sacred. English Protestant and Russian Orthodox Pilgrims of the Nineteenth Century*. London: Scorpion Cavendish

Kirk, George E. 1948. *A Short History of the Middle East. From the Rise of Islam to Modern Times*. London: Methuen

Lamadrid, A G. 1981. 'Canaán y América. La Biblia y la Teologia medieval ante la Conquista de la Tierra', in *Escritos de Biblia y Oriente. Bibliotheca Salmanticensis Estudios* 38. Salamanca-Jerusalén: Universidad Pontificia, 329-46

Lindsey, Hal. 1970. *The Late Great Planet Earth*. London: Lakeland

Lindsey, Hal. 1983. *There's a New World Coming*. London: Coverdale

Lohfink, Norbert. 1996. 'The Laws of Deuteronomy. Project for a World without any Poor', *Scripture Bulletin* 26: 2-19

March, W Eugene, 1994. *Israel and the Politics of Land. A Theological Case Study*. Louisville: Westminster/John Knox Press

Middle East Council of Churches. 1988. *What is Western Fundamentalist Christian Zionism?* Limassol, Cyprus: MECC

O'Neill, Dan and Don Wagner. 1993. *Peace or Armageddon?* Grand Rapids: Zondervan

O'Mahony, Anthony, with G Gunner and K Hintlian. 1995. *The Christian Heritage in the Holy Land*. London: Scorpion Cavendish

Prior, Michael. 1984. 'Israel: Library, Land and Peoples', *Scripture Bulletin* 15: 6-11

Prior, Michael. 1989. 'Living Stones: A Retreat with Palestinian Christians', *New Blackfriars* 70: 119-23

Prior, Michael. 1990. 'A Christian Perspective on the Intifada', *The Month* 23: 478-85

Prior, Michael. 1992. 'Living Stones: Christians in the Holy Land', *Doctrine and Life* 42: 128-34

Prior, Michael. 1993a. 'Palestinian Christians and the Liberation of Theology', *The Month* 26: 482-90

Prior, Michael. 1993b. 'Christian Presence in the Occupied Territories', *Living Stones Magazine* no. 9: 3-4

Prior, Michael. 1993c. 'Living or Dead Stones? The Future of Christians in the Holy Land', *Living Stones Magazine* no. 9: 4-6

Prior, Michael. 1994. 'The Vatican-Israel Fundamental Agreement', *Living Stones Magazine* no. 10: 2-4

Prior, Michael. 1995a. *Jesus the Liberator. Nazareth Liberation Theology (Luke 4.16-30)*. Sheffield: Sheffield Academic Press

Prior, Michael. 1995b. 'The Bible as Instrument of Oppression', *Scripture Bulletin* 25: 2-14

Prior, Michael. 1995c. 'If the Torah is from Heaven ...', *Living Stones Magazine* no. 12: 8-12

Prior, Michael. 1997a. *The Bible and Colonialism. A Moral Critique*. Sheffield: Sheffield Academic Press

Prior, Michael. 1997b. *A Land flowing with Milk, Honey, and People*. Cambridge: Von Hügel Institute, and *Scripture Bulletin* 28(1998): 2-17

Prior, Michael (ed.). 1998. *Western Scholarship and the History of Palestine*. London: Melisende

Prior, Michael. 1999a. *Zionism and the State of Israel: A Moral Inquiry*. London and New York: Routledge

Prior, Michael. 1999b. 'The Bible and the Redeeming Idea of Colonialism', in Althaus-Reid, Marcella and Jack Thompson (eds). *Postcolonialism and Religion. Studies in World Christianity*, Vol. 5 (2). Edinburgh: Edinburgh University Press and Maryknoll, NY: Orbis: 129-55

Prior, Michael. 2000. 'Zionist Ethnic Cleansing: the Fulfilment of Biblical Prophecy?', *Epworth Review* 27 (2): 49-60

Prior, Michael and William Taylor. 1994. *Christians in the Holy Land*. London: World of Islam Festival Trust

Rad, Gerhard von. 1966. 'The Promised Land and Yahweh's Land in the Hexateuch', in *The Problem of the Hexateuch and Other Essays* (repr. 1984). London: SCM, and Philadelphia: Fortress

Rantisi, Audeh. 1990. *Blessed are the Peacemakers*. Guildford: Eagle

Reynolds, Henry. 1992. *The Law of the Land*. Maryborough: Penguin

Robinson, Edward E. 1842. *Biblical Researches in Palestine, Mount Sinai and Arabian Petraea. A Journal of Travels in the Year 1838*. Boston: Crocker and Brewster

Rubenstein, Richard L and John K Roth. 1987. *Approaches to Auschwitz— The Legacy of the Shoah*. London: SCM

Said, Edward W. 1994. *Culture and Imperialism*. New York: Knopf

Said, Edward W. 1992 (second ed.). *The Question of Palestine*. London: Vintage

Said, Edward W. 1994. *The Politics of Dispossession. The Struggle for Palestinian Self-Determination, 1969-1994*. New York: Pantheon Books

Said, Edward W. 1996. *Peace and its Discontents. Gaza-Jericho 1993-1995*. London: Vintage

Sakakini, Hala. 1990. *Jerusalem and I: A Personal Record*. Amman: Economic Press Company

Sharif, Regina. 1983. *Non-Jewish Zionism. Its Roots in Western History*. London: Zed Press

Shehadeh, Raja. 1982. *The Third Way. A Journal of Life in the West Bank*. London: Quartet Books

Silberman, Neal A. 1982. *Digging for God and Country*. New York: Knopf

Silberman, Neal A. 1997. 'Structuring the Past: Israelis, Palestinians, and the Symbolic Authority of Archaeological Monuments', in Silberman, Neil Asher and David Small *The Archaeology of Israel. Constructing the Past, Interpreting the Present*. Sheffield: Sheffield Academic Press, 62-81

Silver, Eric. 1984. *Begin: A Biography*. London: Weidenfeld and Nicolson

Sizer, Stephen. 1994. *Pilgrimages to the Holy Land*. Unpublished Masters Thesis, Oxford University

Sizer, Stephen. 1996. 'Where to find Christ in the Promised Land', *Evangelicals Now*, October: 16

Sizer, Stephen. 1997a. 'The Mountain of the Wall, The Battle for Jerusalem', *Evangelicals Now*, May: 9

Sizer, Stephen. 1997b. 'Pilgrimages and Politics, A Survey of British Holy Land Tour Operators', *Living Stones Magazine*, Spring: 14-17

Sizer, Stephen. 1997c. 'The Hidden Face of Holy Land Pilgrimage Tourism', *International Journal of Contemporary Hospitality Management* 9: 34-35

Sizer, Stephen. 1997d. *Responsible Tourism: The Ethical Challenges of Managing Pilgrimages to the Holy Land*. Unpublished D.Phil Thesis, International Management Centres, Buckingham

Sizer, Stephen. 1998a. ' "Render to Caesar". The Politics of Pilgrimage Tourism to the Holy Land', *International Journal of Contemporary Hospitality Management* 10: 39-41

Sizer, Stephen. 1998b. 'Building Site Shatters Peace: Stephen Sizer explains the Background to Robin Cook's visit to the Disputed Fields of Har Homa', *Church Times*, 20 March: 7

Sizer, Stephen. 1998c. *The Panorama of the Holy Land*. Guildford: Eagle

Sizer, Stephen. 1998d. 'Christian Zionism: True Friends of Israel?', *Living Stones Magazine*, Autumn: 18-24

Sizer, Stephen. 1999a. 'Christian Zionism: A British Perspective', in Ateek and Prior (eds) 1999: 189-98

Sizer, Stephen (ed.). 1999b. 'Ethics in Tourism', *International Journal of Contemporary Hospitality Management*. MCB University Press 11: 2-3

Sizer, Stephen. 1999c. 'The Ethical Challenges of Managing Pilgrimages to the Holy Land', in Sizer (ed.) 1999b: 85-90

Sizer, Stephen. 1999d. 'Barak and the Bulldozers', *Evangelicals Now*, August: 10

Sizer, Stephen. 1999e. 'An Alternative Theology of the Holy Land: A Critique of Christian Zionism', *Churchman* 113(2):125-146

Tawil, Raymonda. 1983. *My Home, My Prison.* London: Zed Books

Vester, Bertha Spafford. 1988. *Our Jerusalem—An American Family in the Holy City 1881-1949.* Jerusalem: Ariel

Volf, Miroslav. 1996. *Exclusion and Embrace.* Nashville: Abingdon Press

Wagner, Donald. 1995. *Anxious for Armageddon.* Scottdale: Herald

Walker, Peter W L. 1996. *Jesus and the Holy City. New Testament Perspectives on Jerusalem.* Grand Rapids, MI and Cambridge, UK: Eerdmans

White, Patrick. 1989. *Children of Bethlehem: Innocents in the Storm.* Leominster: Gracewings

Whitelam, Keith. 1996. *The Invention of Ancient Israel. The Silencing of Palestinian History.* London and New York: Routledge

Whitelam, Keith. 1998. 'Western Scholarship and the Silencing of Palestinian History', in Prior, Michael (ed.), *Western Scholarship and the History of Palestine.* London: Melisende, 9-21

Wills, David. 1997. *Living Stones by God Appointed, The Experience of the Christian Church in Israel Today.* Liverpool: Mossley Hill Parish Church.

Other related titles

PATTERNS OF THE PAST, PROSPECTS FOR THE FUTURE
THE CHRISTIAN HERITAGE IN THE HOLY LAND
eds.Thomas Hummel, Kevork Hintlian and Ulf Carmesund £15.00 ppr,
330 pages, 1999

PATTERNS OF THE SACRED, ENGLISH PROTESTANT AND RUSSIAN
ORTHODOX PILGRIMS OF THE NINETEENTH CENTURY
Thomas and Ruth Hummel £10.00 ppr, 96 pages, 1995

THE CHRISTIAN HERITAGE IN THE HOLY LAND
eds. A O'Mahony with G Gunner and K Hintlian £15.95 ppr, 320 pages, 1995

THE NOBLE HERITAGE, A PORTRAIT OF THE CHURCH OF THE
RESURRECTION
Alistair Duncan £15.00 hbk, 80 pages, 1986

MAMLUK JERUSALEM: AN ARCHITECTURAL STUDY
Michael Burgoyne £125.00 hbk, 622 pages, 1987
(World of Islam Festival Trust)

LIFE AT THE CROSSROADS. A HISTORY OF GAZA
Gerald Butt £16.95 hbk, 208 pages, 1995
(Rimal)

JERUSALEM:WHAT MAKES FOR PEACE!
A PALESTINIAN CHRISTIAN CONTRIBUTION TO PEACEMAKING
eds. Naim Ateek, Cedar Duaybis and Marla Schrader £12.50 ppr, 372 pages,
1997

WESTERN SCHOLARSHIP AND THE HISTORY OF PALESTINE
ed. Michael Prior CM £8.50 ppr, 128 pages, 1998

CHRISTIANS IN THE HOLY LAND
eds. Michael Prior and William Taylor £12.50 ppr, 254 pages, 1995
(World of Islam Festival Trust)

HOLY LAND–HOLLOW JUBILEE: GOD, JUSTICE AND THE
PALESTINIANS
eds. Naim Ateek and Michael Prior. £12.50 ppr, 334 pages, 1999

PALESTINIAN CHRISTIANS: RELIGION, POLITICS AND SOCIETY IN
THE HOLY LAND
A. O'Mahony £12.50 ppr, 224 pages, 1999

FORTHCOMING

OTTOMAN JERUSALEM: THE LIVING CITY 1517-1917
eds. Sylvia Auld and Robert Hillenbrand
architectural survey by Yusuf Natsheh £145.00 hbk 2000
(Altajir World of Islam Trust)

A THIRD MILLENNIUM GUIDE TO PILGRIMAGE TO
THE HOLY LAND
ed. Duncan Macpherson £9.95 ppr, 2000

DYING IN THE LAND OF PROMISE
Donald E Wagner £12.50 ppr, 2000

*All available
from*

Melisende
39 Chelmsford Road
London E18 2PW England
tel. +44 (0)20 8 498 9768
fax +44 (0)20 8 504 2558
e-mail: melisende@cwcom.net
www.melisende.cwc.net